Functional Programming in Python

From Basics to Expert Proficiency

Contents

Introduction

Functional programming (FP) has long been a paradigm of interest within the world of software development, primarily due to its emphasis on mathematical functions, immutability, and declarative style of coding. Unlike imperative programming, which focuses on how to achieve a specific task through a sequence of instructions, functional programming centers around what to solve using expressions and declarations. This book, "Functional Programming in Python: From Basics to Expert Proficiency," aspires to introduce and elaborate on the principles of functional programming using Python, a versatile and widely-adopted programming language.

Historically, functional programming has deep roots in academic research and theoretical computer science, dating back to the 1930s with Alonzo Church's work on lambda calculus. Over the years, functional paradigms have influenced the design and implementation of various programming languages, both academic and practical. Languages such as Lisp, Scheme, Haskell, and Erlang have brought functional programming concepts to the fore, each contributing unique features and insights to the broader field. Python, while not traditionally a functional programming language, has robust support for functional programming constructs, making it an excellent vehicle for both learning and applying these ideas.

Functional programming offers several advantages, such as ease of reasoning about code, reduction of side effects, enhanced modularity, and the facilitation of concurrent or parallel execution. Pure functions, first-class functions, higher-order functions, and immutability are some of the cornerstone concepts that empower programmers to write cleaner, more maintainable code. However, it is equally important to acknowledge the paradigm's limitations, such as potentially higher memory consumption and performance overhead due to the lack of mutable state.

In this book, we shall delve into the fundamental concepts of functional programming, initially defining its core principles and contrasting them with those of imperative programming. Readers will develop a solid understanding of key functional programming terminologies and the rationale behind adopting a functional approach. Subsequent chapters will progressively build upon these basics, covering essential topics such as first-class and higher-order functions, pure functions and immutability, recursion, lambda expressions, and functional programming libraries in Python.

The practical applications of functional programming are vast and varied, ranging from data analysis and processing pipelines to scalable web services and reactive programming. By adopting a structured and methodical approach, this book aims to equip readers not only with theoretical knowledge but also with practical skills to apply functional programming paradigms in real-world scenarios. Each chapter concludes with practical examples and exercises, reinforcing the concepts discussed and providing hands-on experience.

In conclusion, "Functional Programming in Python: From Basics to Expert Proficiency" endeavors to be a comprehensive resource, guiding readers through the realms of functional programming with Python. Its structured approach ensures that both novices and experienced programmers can gain valuable insights and enhance their coding prowess. The journey ahead promises to be intellectually stimulating and professionally enriching, offering a new lens through which to view and solve computational problems.

Chapter 1

Introduction to Functional Programming

Functional programming is a programming paradigm focused on mathematical functions, immutability, and declarative expressions. This chapter explores its origins, contrasts it with imperative programming, and highlights its advantages and disadvantages. Key principles and terminologies are introduced, along with an overview of popular functional programming languages. The chapter also emphasizes why Python is a suitable choice for functional programming and provides real-world examples of its applications.

1.1 What is Functional Programming?

Functional programming is a paradigm that treats computation as the evaluation of mathematical functions and avoids changing state and mutable data. This methodology is derived from lambda calculus, a formal system for expressing computation based on function abstraction and application. In functional programming, functions are first-class citizens, meaning they can be assigned to variables, passed as arguments, and returned by other functions.

At its core, functional programming emphasizes several key principles:

- **First-class and Higher-order Functions**: In functional programming, functions can be assigned to variables, stored in data structures, passed as arguments, and returned from other functions. This allows for higher-order functions, which take other functions as arguments or return them as results. Higher-order functions enable a compositional style of building complex operations from simpler ones.
- **Pure Functions**: A pure function is a function where the output value is determined solely by its input values, without observable side effects. This means that given the same inputs, a pure function will always return the same output, enhancing predictability and testability.
- **Immutability**: In functional programming, data is immutable, meaning that once a data structure is created, it cannot be altered. Instead of modifying existing structures, new structures are created. This reduces bugs related to unexpected state changes and side effects.
- **Declarative Programming**: Functional programming is declarative rather than imperative. This means describing *what* to do, rather than *how* to do it. Declarative code tends to be more concise, easier to reason about, and closer to the problem domain.

A deeper understanding can be achieved by considering a practical example. Let us examine the implementation of a simple function to calculate the factorial of a number.

```
def factorial(n):
    if n == 0:
        return 1
    else:
        return n * factorial(n-1)
```

Here, factorial is a recursive function. The function calls itself to compute the factorial of $n-1$ and multiplies the result by n. This is a clear example of a pure function as the result depends solely on the input argument n and there are no side effects.

Functional programming languages often provide features to facilitate immutability and function composition. A concise way to compute the factorial using a functional approach with Python's functools.reduce is shown below.

```
from functools import reduce
def factorial(n):
```

```
    return reduce(lambda x, y: x * y, range(1, n + 1), 1)
```

In this version, the reduce function takes a lambda function lambda x, y: x * y and applies it cumulatively to the items of range(1, n + 1), starting with the initial value of 1. This demonstrates a higher-order function and the use of immutability.

Consider another example involving transformation and filtering of data, common tasks in data processing. We will use Python's map and filter functions.

```
numbers = [1, 2, 3, 4, 5]
squared = list(map(lambda x: x ** 2, numbers))
evens = list(filter(lambda x: x % 2 == 0, squared))
```

In this example, map applies a given function (lambda function to square each number) to each item of the list numbers. The filter function then selects only the even numbers from the squared list. Both map and filter are higher-order functions and illustrate the use of function composition.

Functional programming is particularly effective in multi-core and distributed computing environments because its emphasis on immutability and side-effect-free functions simplifies parallel execution. The absence of side effects means that functions can be executed concurrently without concern for race conditions or other synchronization issues.

The paradigm also promotes a modular codebase where small, reusable functions can be combined in expressive ways. This can lead to a more maintainable and understandable code, which is a significant advantage in complex software projects.

Functional programming is not without its challenges. Adhering strictly to immutability can sometimes lead to less efficient code because of the overhead of creating new data structures instead of modifying existing ones. Additionally, for programmers accustomed to imperative paradigms, the transition to thinking functionally can require a shift in mindset.

Despite these challenges, the advantages in terms of predictability, ease of debugging, and parallelizability make functional programming a powerful paradigm, particularly in the context of evolving computational needs and increasingly complex software systems.

1.2 History and Evolution of Functional Programming

Functional programming (FP) has a rich and storied history that dates back to the 1930s, rooted in the foundations of mathematical logic and lambda calculus. The origins of FP can be traced to Alonzo Church, a mathematician who introduced lambda calculus as a formal system for function definition, application, and recursion. Lambda calculus forms the theoretical basis for functional programming languages and its importance cannot be overstated.

Lambda calculus was developed to explore the notion of computability and the effective calculation of functions. It consists of expressions formed by variables, function application, and function abstraction. The syntax of lambda calculus can be defined as follows:

```
1. Variable: x
2. Function application: (f x)
3. Function abstraction: (x. E)
```

The lambda calculus has the property of being Turing complete, meaning it can compute any computable function, making it as powerful as Turing machines in terms of expressiveness.

In the 1950s, John McCarthy developed Lisp, one of the first high-level programming languages, which incorporated many ideas from lambda calculus. Lisp, short for "List Processing," included functions as first-class citizens and supported symbolic computation, which made it particularly useful for artificial intelligence research. The implementation of recursive functions and the manipulation of symbolic data in Lisp were directly influenced by the principles of lambda calculus.

The evolution of FP continued into the 1970s and 1980s with the development of languages such as ML (Meta Language) and Scheme. ML, designed by Robin Milner and others at the University of Edinburgh, introduced powerful type systems and pattern matching. It also had significant influence on the development of later functional languages. Scheme, a minimalist dialect of Lisp created by Guy L. Steele Jr. and Gerald Jay Sussman, emphasized simplicity and elegance in function definition and application, streamlining the concepts introduced by lambda calculus and Lisp.

Another landmark in the history of FP is the development of Haskell in 1990. Haskell was designed to be a purely functional language, promoting immutability and lazy evaluation. Named after Haskell Curry, a logician renowned for his work in combinatory logic, Haskell has had a significant impact on both the academic and practical fields of programming. Its features and constructs, such as monads for handling side effects, have been widely studied and adopted in various contexts.

Python, while primarily known as an imperative language, incorporates several functional programming constructs, creating a hybrid language that allows for both functional and imperative styles. Python's support for first-class functions, higher-order functions, and its itertools module are notable functional programming features. For example, Python's use of lambda expressions allows for concise function definitions:

```
# Lambda expression in Python
square = lambda x: x * x
print(square(5))
```

```
25
```

Similarly, list comprehensions and generator expressions in Python draw inspiration from the functional programming paradigm, enabling more declarative and readable code. For instance:

```
# List comprehension in Python
squares = [x * x for x in range(10)]
print(squares)
```

```
[0, 1, 4, 9, 16, 25, 36, 49, 64, 81]
```

Functional programming has also been influenced by advancements in hardware and the ubiquity of multi-core processors, which necessitate parallel computing. The immutability and statelessness foundational to FP naturally lend themselves to parallel computation, reducing the complexity of concurrent programming.

Across decades, the evolution of functional programming continues to inspire improvements in language design, compiler techniques, and runtime optimizations, making it a vibrant and continually evolving paradigm in the realm of computer science.

1.3 Functional Programming vs. Imperative Programming

Functional programming (FP) and imperative programming (IP) represent two distinct approaches to software development. These paradigms differ significantly in terms of philosophy, structure, and implementation.

Core Philosophy: Functional programming is based on mathematical functions. These functions map inputs to outputs without modifying the state of the system. FP emphasizes immutability and side-effect-free functions. The approach is declarative; it focuses on what the program should accomplish without specifying how processes are executed.

Imperative programming, on the other hand, outlines a sequence of commands for the computer to perform. It is heavily procedural, concentrating on how to achieve objectives. This paradigm leverages mutable states and side-effects as it controls the program flow via loops, conditionals, and statements.

Syntax and Structure: In FP, the syntax closely follows mathematical notation. Functions are first-class citizens, meaning they can be passed as arguments, returned from other functions, and assigned to variables. Lambda calculus influences many functional languages, making anonymous functions a common feature.

Consider a Python example that demonstrates a basic functional operation, finding the square of a number:

```
# Functional approach in Python
def square(x):
    return x * x

squared_numbers = list(map(square, [1, 2, 3, 4, 5]))
print(squared_numbers)
```

Output:

```
[1, 4, 9, 16, 25]
```

IP syntax is more aligned with step-by-step instructions. Variables represent memory locations that can store and overwrite data. For example, the same operation in an imperative style would use loops:

```
# Imperative approach in Python
squared_numbers = []
for x in [1, 2, 3, 4, 5]:
    squared_numbers.append(x * x)
print(squared_numbers)
```

Output:

```
[1, 4, 9, 16, 25]
```

Immutability vs. Mutability: A key characteristic of functional programming is immutability. Once created, data cannot be altered. This leads to more predictable code, easier debugging, and optimization. Immutable data structures are intrinsic to FP, promoting the use of functions that return new data rather than modifying existing ones.

Imperative programming thrives on mutable states. Variables are mutable and can be changed during the program's lifecycle. This flexibility allows efficient algorithms but also introduces complexity in managing state changes, making debugging and reasoning about code more challenging.

Side-Effects: FP avoids side-effects, meaning that calling a function with the same arguments will always produce the same result without altering any state outside the function. This makes functions referentially transparent. For example, pure functions like 'square' in the earlier example do not depend on or change the state of the system.

In IP, side-effects are commonplace and often necessary. Changing a variable's value, printing to the console, or modifying a data structure are all side-effects that contribute to the overall program state.

Control Structures: FP extensively uses higher-order functions like 'map', 'filter', and 'reduce' to process collections and data. These functions abstract iteration logic, applying function arguments to elements of a collection.

Example using 'filter' to obtain even numbers:

```
def is_even(x):
    return x % 2 == 0

even_numbers = list(filter(is_even, [1, 2, 3, 4, 5, 6]))
print(even_numbers)
```

Output:

```
[2, 4, 6]
```

In contrast, IP relies on explicit control structures like loops ('for', 'while') and conditionals ('if' statements) to manage flow:

```
even_numbers = []
for x in [1, 2, 3, 4, 5, 6]:
    if x % 2 == 0:
        even_numbers.append(x)
print(even_numbers)
```

Output:

```
[2, 4, 6]
```

Concurrency and Parallelism: FP's emphasis on immutability and stateless functions makes it well-suited for concurrent and parallel execution. As functions do not alter shared state, they can run simultaneously without the risk of race conditions.

IP requires careful management of mutable states and synchronization mechanisms (e.g., locks, semaphores) to ensure thread safety and correctness in concurrent environments.

Error Handling: Error handling in FP often involves using constructs like 'Option' or 'Either' types, which encapsulate the possibility of failure without throwing exceptions. This approach promotes safer code by making error handling explicit and easier to manage.

IP typically uses exceptions for error handling, which, while flexible, can propagate uncaught errors and make tracking error origins difficult.

Common Use-Cases: FP is particularly beneficial in scenarios requiring high reliability, concurrent processing, or complex data transformation. It is favored in domains like data science, financial modeling, and real-time systems.

IP is widely used in system programming, scripting, and applications where performance and fine-grained control over state and resources are crucial. It forms the backbone of many general-purpose programming tasks.

Both paradigms offer powerful tools and techniques for software development. Understanding their differences and strengths allows programmers to choose the most appropriate approach for their specific tasks and projects.

1.4 Advantages and Disadvantages of Functional Programming

Functional programming offers several advantages that can significantly improve software development processes, although it is not without its disadvantages. This section delves into both to provide a balanced perspective.

Advantages

- **Immutability:** A fundamental principle in functional programming is immutability, where data once created cannot be modified. This characteristic leads to safer code as it eliminates side effects that can occur from unintentional changes to data. In concurrent programming, immutability simplifies data sharing across threads since the data cannot be altered. This inherently reduces the likelihood of race conditions or deadlocks.

- **Pure Functions:** Pure functions, which always produce the same output for the same input and do not cause side effects, make testing and debugging easier. Since pure functions are deterministic and side-effect-free, they can be reasoned about independently of other parts of the code, facilitating modular code development. This also enhances reusability and composability, making complex programs easier to construct from simpler functions.

- **Higher-Order Functions:** Functional programming allows functions to be treated as first-class citizens, meaning they can be passed as parameters to other functions, returned as values from functions, and assigned to variables. Higher-order functions enhance code reusability and abstraction. For instance, the map, filter, and reduce functions in Python are higher-order functions that provide powerful capabilities for list processing and transforming data.

- **Conciseness and Readability:** Functional programming often leads to more concise code, which can improve readability. Functions like lambda in Python allow for defining small anonymous functions in a compact manner. The declarative style of functional programming aligns closely with expressing computational logic without focusing on control flow, which can make the code easier to understand.

- **Ease of Parallelism:** Due to its emphasis on immutability and statelessness, functional programming can be more naturally aligned with parallel computing. Pure functions can run concurrently without concern for shared state, simplifying the development of parallel applications.

Disadvantages

- **Performance Concerns:** One common criticism of functional programming is the potential for performance inefficiencies. Immutability necessitates creating new data structures instead of modifying existing ones, which can lead to increased memory usage and processing time. Though modern languages and optimizations can mitigate some of this overhead, the issue may still be significant for performance-critical applications.

- **Learning Curve:** For developers accustomed to imperative or object-oriented programming, transitioning to functional programming can be challenging. Functional programming requires a different mindset and understanding of concepts such as higher-order functions, recursion, and immutable data. Educational resources and community support are essential to overcome this steep learning curve.

- **Tooling and Ecosystem:** While languages like Python, Haskell, and Scala have vibrant ecosystems, the tooling and libraries specifically for functional programming might not be as mature as those for imperative or object-oriented paradigms. This gap can sometimes complicate the adoption of functional programming, especially in teams or projects reliant on existing tools and practices.

- **Debugging and Error Handling:** Debugging functional programs can be non-trivial due to the abstract nature of high-level function compositions and the lack of side effects, which obscure how state changes over time. Traditional debugging techniques that rely on sequential step-through and variable state inspection may be less effective. Additionally, error handling in a purely functional context, often managed using monadic structures like Option or Maybe, can seem cumbersome and unfamiliar to those new to the paradigm.

- **Less Control Over State:** The emphasis on immutability and pure functions can sometimes make state management more complex. While eliminating side effects aids in creating predictable programs, certain tasks naturally require state changes (e.g., user interfaces or real-time systems), and managing these within a functional paradigm can introduce additional complexity. In practice, hybrid models that combine functional and imperative or object-oriented approaches are commonly adopted to address these challenges.

1.5 Basic Principles of Functional Programming

Functional programming is grounded in a set of core principles that differentiate it from other paradigms, particularly imperative programming. Understanding these principles is essential for anyone aiming to master functional programming. This section elucidates the fundamental tenets, ensuring the concepts are both accessible and practically applicable.

1. Immutability

In functional programming, data is immutable. This means once a data structure is created, it cannot be altered. Instead of changing existing data, functions return new data structures. Immutability leads to safer code because it prevents side effects and unintended interactions between different parts of the code.

```
# In Python, you can use tuples for immutable sequences
data = (1, 2, 3)
# Any modification leads to creation of a new tuple
new_data = data + (4,)
print(new_data)
```

```
Output:
(1, 2, 3, 4)
```

2. First-Class and Higher-Order Functions

In this paradigm, functions are first-class citizens, meaning they can be assigned to variables, passed as arguments, and returned from other functions. Higher-order functions, which either take functions as arguments or return them, leverage this feature to enable more abstract and powerful code patterns.

```
# Function that takes another function as an argument
def apply_function(f, x):
    return f(x)

# Example usage
def square(n):
    return n * n

result = apply_function(square, 5)
print(result)
```

```
Output:
25
```

3. Pure Functions

Pure functions are central to functional programming. A function is pure if it satisfies two conditions: it always produces the same output for the same input, and it does not have side effects such as modifying global state or input/output operations. Pure functions are predictable and easier to test.

```
# Pure function example
def add(a, b):
    return a + b

print(add(2, 3))
```

Output:
5

4. Recursion

Functional programming favors recursion over iteration for looping. Recursion, which is a function calling itself, is often used to operate on data structures like lists or trees. Functions designed recursively can be more expressive and align better with the declarative nature of functional programming.

```
# Recursive function to compute factorial
def factorial(n):
    if n == 0:
        return 1
    else:
        return n * factorial(n - 1)

print(factorial(5))
```

Output:
120

5. Declarative Approach

In contrast to the imperative style, which specifies the exact steps to achieve a result, the declarative style expresses the logic without explicitly detailing the control flow. This approach makes the code more readable and closer to mathematical expressions.

```
# Using Python's filter function declaratively
numbers = [1, 2, 3, 4, 5, 6]
# Filter out even numbers
even_numbers = list(filter(lambda x: x % 2 == 0, numbers))
print(even_numbers)
```

Output:
[2, 4, 6]

6. Higher-Level Abstraction

Functional programming promotes higher levels of abstraction through the use of combinators and function compositions. These techniques allow programmers to build complex behaviors by combining simpler functions, leading to more modular and maintainable code.

```
# Function to add 2
def add_two(x):
    return x + 2

# Function to multiply by 3
def multiply_by_three(x):
    return x * 3

# Composing functions to create a new function
def add_and_multiply(x):
    return multiply_by_three(add_two(x))

print(add_and_multiply(4))
```

```
Output:
18
```

7. No Side Effects

Functions in functional programming avoid side effects. This means functions only compute results and do not alter global states or modify input parameters. Side-effect-free functions are easier to understand and reason about.

```
# Side-effect-free function example
def get_square_numbers(nums):
    return [n * n for n in nums]

numbers = [1, 2, 3, 4]
square_numbers = get_square_numbers(numbers)
print(square_numbers)
```

```
Output:
[1, 4, 9, 16]
```

This concise exploration of functional programming principles lays the foundation for understanding how the paradigm facilitates the creation of robust, maintainable, and expressive code. These tenets are deeply intertwined and collectively promote a coding style that emphasizes mathematical rigour and code clarity.

1.6 Key Concepts and Terminologies

Functional programming encompasses several key concepts and terminologies that differentiate it from other programming paradigms. Understanding these concepts is essential for effectively applying functional programming techniques in Python. Below, we delve into the foundational terms and principles intrinsic to functional programming.

First-Class Functions

In functional programming, functions are first-class citizens. This means that functions can be assigned to variables, passed as arguments to other functions, and returned as values from other functions. Consider the following Python example where a function is assigned to a variable and used to call the function.

```
def add(a, b):
    return a + b

sum_function = add
result = sum_function(5, 3)
print(result) # Outputs: 8
```

Higher-Order Functions

A higher-order function is a function that takes one or more functions as arguments and/or returns a function as its result. These functions allow for the abstraction of actions and operations that can be applied to various data types. An example is the built-in Python function map(), which applies a function to all items in an input list.

```
numbers = [1, 2, 3, 4]
squared_numbers = map(lambda x: x**2, numbers)
print(list(squared_numbers)) # Outputs: [1, 4, 9, 16]
```

Pure Functions

A pure function is a function where the return value is determined solely by its input values, without observable side effects. This implies that calling a pure function with the same set of arguments will always produce the same result. Pure functions facilitate debugging and testing because they do not depend on or alter any state outside their scope.

```
def pure_add(a, b):
    return a + b
```

Immutability

Immutability refers to objects whose state cannot be modified after they are created. In the context of functional programming, immutability ensures that data does not change, which can prevent unintended side effects. Python tuples and strings are examples of immutable data structures.

```
immutable_tuple = (1, 2, 3)
# immutable_tuple[0] = 0 # This would raise a TypeError
```

Recursion

Functional programming often relies on recursion, where a function calls itself directly or indirectly, as a primary mechanism for iteration. Recursive functions can often replace traditional loops in functional programs. Careful consideration is required to avoid infinite recursion, typically managed through base cases and recursive step reduction.

```
def factorial(n):
    if n == 0:
        return 1
    else:
        return n * factorial(n-1)

result = factorial(5)
print(result) # Outputs: 120
```

Lambda Functions

Lambda functions are anonymous (i.e., without a name) functions defined using the lambda keyword in Python. They are often used for creating small, single-use functions that are passed directly to higher-order functions.

```
add = lambda x, y: x + y
result = add(5, 3)
print(result) # Outputs: 8
```

Function Composition

Function composition involves the combination of two or more functions to produce a new function. In functional programming, composite functions allow us to build complex operations by linking simpler ones.

```
def multiply(x):
    return x * 2

def add_five(x):
    return x + 5

def composed_function(x):
    return multiply(add_five(x))

result = composed_function(3)
print(result) # Outputs: 16
```

Currying

Currying transforms a function that takes multiple arguments into a sequence of functions that each takes a single argument. This technique is useful for creating reusable and partially applied functions. In Python, currying can be implemented using nested functions.

```
def curried_add(a):
    def add_b(b):
        return a + b
    return add_b

add_five = curried_add(5)
result = add_five(3)
print(result) # Outputs: 8
```

Lazy Evaluation

Lazy evaluation is a strategy that delays the evaluation of an expression until its value is actually needed. This can improve performance by avoiding unnecessary calculations. In Python, generators and iterators are commonly used to implement lazy evaluation.

```
def lazy_range(n):
    i = 0
    while i < n:
        yield i
        i += 1

for num in lazy_range(5):
    print(num)
```

This code does not evaluate the entire range at once, but rather yields items one by one as requested, exemplifying lazy evaluation. Each of these concepts collectively forms the backbone of functional programming, facilitating the creation of concise, predictable, and maintainable code.

1.7 Popular Functional Programming Languages

Functional programming has garnered significant attention in both academic and industry settings due to its emphasis on immutability, state management, and declarative programming constructs. Several programming languages have been designed or evolved to support and leverage the principles of functional programming. This section delves into some of the most popular functional programming languages, examining their core features, historical context, and common use cases.

Haskell is a purely functional programming language that emphasizes immutability and strong static typing. Developed in the late 1980s, it was specifically designed to be a platform for research and teaching in functional programming. Haskell's type system, based on Hindley–

Milner type inference, allows the compiler to infer types automatically, reducing the need for explicit type annotations. Higher-order functions, lazy evaluation, and monadic control structures are at the core of Haskell's design philosophy. These features make Haskell a powerful language for tasks requiring explicit control over side effects and asynchronous computations, such as compiler construction, academic research, and advanced data analysis.

```
-- Sample Haskell Code: A simple function to calculate factorial
factorial :: Integer -> Integer
factorial 0 = 1
factorial n = n * factorial (n - 1)
```

```
Output:
factorial 5
120
```

Scala is a hybrid functional and object-oriented programming language that integrates seamlessly with Java. Designed by Martin Odersky and released in 2003, Scala combines functional programming principles with the scalability of object-oriented programming. This dual-paradigm approach enables developers to use both paradigms simultaneously and incrementally introduce functional programming concepts into existing Java codebases. Scala's support for immutable data structures, pattern matching, and high-order functions make it well-suited for building scalable and concurrent applications, notably in the domain of big data processing, web development, and distributed systems.

```
// Sample Scala Code: A function to calculate the sum of a list
def sum(xs: List[Int]): Int = xs.reduce(_ + _)
```

```
Output:
sum(List(1, 2, 3, 4, 5))
15
```

Erlang was initially developed by Ericsson for telecommunication systems and has gained wider use in other domains requiring robust concurrent and distributed computing capabilities. Erlang is known for its fault-tolerant design and simple but powerful concurrency model based on the actor model. Each actor (or process) in Erlang is lightweight and runs concurrently, communicating with others via message passing. This approach eliminates the need for shared state and locks, simplifying the handling of concurrent operations. Erlang's reliability and efficiency have led to its adoption in areas such as real-time messaging systems, telecommunication infrastructures, and financial transaction systems.

```
% Sample Erlang Code: Spawning a process in Erlang
-module(example).
```

```
-export([start/0]).

start() ->
    spawn(fun() -> io:format("Hello from a new process!~n") end).
```

Output:
start().
Hello from a new process!

F# is a functional first programming language that also supports imperative and object-oriented programming paradigms. Developed by Microsoft Research and introduced in 2005, F# runs on the .NET runtime and is fully interoperable with other .NET languages such as C#. F# emphasizes immutability, pattern matching, and type inference, making it suitable for data processing, scripting, and rapid prototyping. Its integration with the .NET ecosystem allows developers to leverage existing libraries and tools, facilitating the adoption of functional programming in enterprise environments.

```
// Sample F# Code: A function to find the maximum element in a list
let rec maxList = function
    | [] -> failwith "Empty list"
    | [x] -> x
    | x::xs -> max x (maxList xs)
```

Output:
maxList [1; 5; 3; 9; 2]
9

Clojure is a modern, dynamic, and functional dialect of the Lisp programming language running on the Java Virtual Machine (JVM). Clojure was created by Rich Hickey and released in 2007. Emphasizing immutability and persistent data structures, Clojure leverages Lisp's inherent strengths in symbolic expression manipulation while providing seamless interoperation with the Java ecosystem. Clojure's design for concurrency is built around immutable data and software transactional memory, which simplifies dealing with concurrent state. Its expressiveness and conciseness make it a preferred choice for tasks such as data analysis, artificial intelligence, and web development.

```
;; Sample Clojure Code: A function to filter even numbers from a list
(defn filter-even [lst]
  (filter even? lst))
```

Output:
(filter-even [1 2 3 4 5 6 7 8])
(2 4 6 8)

Elixir builds on the strengths of Erlang with a modern and efficient syntax while running on the Erlang VM. Created by José Valim and released in 2011, Elixir retains Erlang's strengths—concurrency, fault tolerance, and distributed computation—while introducing new features aimed at developer productivity and performance. Elixir's metaprogramming capabilities, functional language constructs, and macro system provide a high level of expressiveness and flexibility. It is widely used in web development, particularly with the Phoenix web framework, as well as in applications where high concurrency and fault tolerance are critical.

```
# Sample Elixir Code: A function to calculate the square of a number
defmodule Math do
    def square(x), do: x * x
end
```

```
Output:
Math.square(4)
16
```

These languages represent only a fraction of the functional programming ecosystem. Each brings unique features and benefits to the table, tailored to specific computing environments and application domains. Understanding these languages, their strengths, and their typical use cases can significantly enhance a programmer's ability to select and apply the most appropriate tools for their specific needs.

1.8 Why Choose Functional Programming with Python?

Python, as a versatile and widely-used programming language, offers robust support for multiple programming paradigms, including functional programming (FP). Understanding why Python is particularly well-suited for functional programming involves examining its features, libraries, and ecosystem that facilitate this paradigm.

Python's intrinsic functional programming capabilities come from its language design and extensive standard library. The incorporation of first-class functions in Python means functions are treated as first-class citizens, enabling them to be passed around as arguments, returned from other functions, and assigned to variables. This property underpins many functional programming techniques and patterns.

Consider the following Python code snippet that demonstrates first-class functions:

```
def higher_order_function(f, value):
    return f(value)
```

```
def square(x):
    return x * x

result = higher_order_function(square, 5)
print(result) # Output: 25
```

In this example, higher_order_function accepts another function f and a value. The square function is passed as an argument to higher_order_function, demonstrating a key aspect of functional programming.

Python's support for anonymous functions, or lambdas, further enhances its functional programming capabilities. Lambda functions allow for the construction of small, unnamed functions on-the-fly and are extremely useful for short operations and higher-order functions. For instance:

```
numbers = [1, 2, 3, 4, 5]
squared_numbers = list(map(lambda x: x * x, numbers))
print(squared_numbers) # Output: [1, 4, 9, 16, 25]
```

Here, the map function applies a lambda function to each element in the list numbers, showcasing the power of functional programming constructs.

Python's standard library includes several modules that are essential for functional programming. For example, the functools module provides higher-order functions that act on or return other functions. Key functions in this module include reduce, partial, and lru_cache. The reduce function, derived from functional programming principles, performs cumulative operations on iterable elements:

```
from functools import reduce

numbers = [1, 2, 3, 4, 5]
sum_total = reduce(lambda x, y: x + y, numbers)
print(sum_total) # Output: 15
```

In this example, reduce applies a binary lambda function cumulatively to the elements of the list numbers, effectively reducing the list to a single cumulative value.

Another critical aspect of functional programming is immutability, which is the concept that data should not be modified after it is created. Python supports immutability through immutable data structures such as tuples and frozensets. These structures enforce immutability and can help avoid side effects, which is a core principle of functional programming. For instance:

```
immutable_tuple = (1, 2, 3)
```

```
try:
    immutable_tuple[0] = 10
except TypeError as e:
    print(e) # Output: 'tuple' object does not support item assignment
```

By using immutable structures, Python ensures data consistency and predictability, aligning well with functional programming practices.

Python's ecosystem further bolsters its suitability for functional programming with a variety of third-party libraries. Libraries such as toolz, fn.py, and pyrsistent provide additional functional programming tools and data structures that enhance Python's functional capabilities. For example, the toolz library offers a collection of utility functions for functional programming such as compose, curry, and memoize:

```
from toolz import compose

def add_one(x):
    return x + 1

def square(x):
    return x * x

composed_function = compose(square, add_one)
print(composed_function(4)) # Output: 25
```

In this code snippet, the compose function from the toolz library creates a new function that applies add_one followed by square. This function composition is a typical functional programming approach.

Additionally, Python's readability and succinct syntax make it more approachable for developers transitioning from imperative or object-oriented paradigms to functional programming. Python's consistency and clear syntax allow developers to focus on the functional concepts rather than grappling with complex syntactical elements.

Python's compatibility with both functional and other paradigms enables developers to adopt a hybrid approach, leveraging the strengths of multiple paradigms in a single codebase. This flexibility can be particularly advantageous in real-world applications, where the problem space may benefit from a mixed approach.

```
Output:
True
```

1.9 Real-World Applications of Functional Programming

Functional programming has garnered attention across various domains due to its emphasis on immutability, higher-order functions, and declarative code. This paradigm finds applications in diverse fields ranging from data science to web development, often yielding robust and scalable software solutions.

Certain properties of functional programming make it particularly suited for concurrent and parallel computations. The avoidance of side effects means functions do not alter any state outside their scope, thus facilitating better management of concurrent processes. Such properties are vital in applications like defining real-time systems, handling large-scale data analysis, and developing fault-tolerant systems.

1. Data Science and Machine Learning:

Functional programming is used significantly in data science for manipulating and processing large datasets. With Python's libraries like Pandas and NumPy, the concepts of functional programming such as map, reduce, and filter are inherently used. This leads to clean, comprehensible, and efficient data manipulation pipelines. The functional programming approach allows data scientists to write concise and expressive code that can be easily parallelized and optimized for performance.

Example:

```
import numpy as np

# Using lambda functions with map and filter
data = np.array([1, 2, 3, 4, 5, 6, 7, 8, 9, 10])
squared_data = map(lambda x: x**2, data)
filtered_data = filter(lambda x: x % 2 == 0, squared_data)
```

Output: [4, 16, 36, 64, 100]

2. Web Development:

In the domain of web development, functional programming principles can contribute to building scalable and maintainable applications. Frameworks like React (JavaScript) promote a functional approach through their design. In Python, libraries such as Flask and Django can also benefit from functional paradigms by minimizing state changes and enhancing code modularity. Developers often use higher-order functions to create middleware and decorators, enhancing the flexibility and reusability of web components.

Example:

```
from flask import Flask, request, jsonify

app = Flask(__name__)

# A simple decorator for logging
def log_request(func):
    def wrapper(*args, **kwargs):
        print(f"Request: {request.method} {request.url}")
        return func(*args, **kwargs)
    return wrapper

@app.route('/data', methods=['POST'])
@log_request
def process_data():
    data = request.get_json()
    # Process the data
    return jsonify(data)

if __name__ == '__main__':
    app.run(debug=True)
```

3. Financial Sector:

Functional programming has demonstrated significant advantages in the financial industry, particularly in algorithmic trading, risk management, and fraud detection. The confluence of immutability and first-class functions offers a robust framework for creating financial models and simulations. Haskell and Scala are often preferred in this sector due to their strong type systems. In Python, libraries such as Scikit-learn and Statsmodels facilitate functional paradigms for building predictive models and performing statistical analysis.

Example:

```
import pandas as pd
from statsmodels.tsa.arima_model import ARIMA

# Load financial data
data = pd.read_csv('financial_data.csv')
prices = data['Close']

# Functional approach to model fitting
model = ARIMA(prices, order=(5, 1, 0))
fit_model = model.fit(disp=0)

# Predict future prices
forecast = fit_model.forecast(steps=5)
```

Output: Forecasted prices for the next 5 steps.

4. Telecommunications:

In telecommunications, the functional approach can be used to handle large-scale distributed systems efficiently. Erlang, a functional language, is heavily used in this industry for its ability to handle numerous simultaneous operations with high fault tolerance. In Python, developers can employ libraries like Concurrent.futures and asyncio to implement functional patterns for concurrent programming.

Example:

```
import asyncio

async def handle_message(message):
    await asyncio.sleep(1) # Simulate a network delay
    print(f'Message processed: {message}')

async def main():
    messages = ['msg1', 'msg2', 'msg3', 'msg4']
    tasks = [handle_message(msg) for msg in messages]
    await asyncio.gather(*tasks)

asyncio.run(main())
```

Output: Message processed: msg1
Message processed: msg2
Message processed: msg3
Message processed: msg4

5. Blockchain and Cryptography:

Functional programming is instrumental in building secure and fault-tolerant blockchain systems. With its focus on pure functions and immutability, functional programming languages ensure that transactions and smart contracts are deterministic and transparent. Python frameworks such as PyCryptodome and PyEVM facilitate functional concepts to create cryptographic and blockchain applications.

Example:

```
from Crypto.Hash import SHA256

def hash_function(data):
    return SHA256.new(data.encode()).hexdigest()

def validate_transaction(previous_hash, transaction_data):
    return hash_function(previous_hash + transaction_data)

# Example usage
previous_hash = 'abcd1234'
transaction_data = 'tx100'
current_hash = validate_transaction(previous_hash, transaction_data)
print(f'Current Hash: {current_hash}')
```

Output: Current Hash: e1984b5e1e1e04a47647eb7031b95b0f22139e18220f6cff1ec60bd168175b3a

6. Bioinformatics and Computational Biology:

In bioinformatics, functional programming aids in the analysis of biological data and the development of algorithms for sequence alignment, gene prediction, and protein structure prediction. Python libraries such as Biopython and Scipy integrate functional programming paradigms to facilitate the manipulation and analysis of complex biological data.

Example:

```
from Bio import SeqIO

def gc_content(seq):
    g = seq.count('G')
    c = seq.count('C')
    return (g + c) / len(seq) * 100

# Load sequence data
sequence_data = SeqIO.read('sequence.fasta', 'fasta')
gc = gc_content(str(sequence_data.seq))
print(f'GC Content: {gc:.2f}%')
```

Output: GC Content: 46.85%

This detailed exploration of real-world applications highlights the flexibility and power of functional programming in various fields, underscoring its role in crafting efficient, maintainable, and scalable software solutions.

1.10 Overview of Functional Programming Paradigms

Functional programming paradigms focus on the use of mathematical functions to process data. In functional programming, functions are first-class citizens, which means they can be assigned to variables, passed as arguments, and returned from other functions. This paradigm emphasizes immutability, meaning once a value is assigned, it cannot be changed, and declarative programming, where the logic of computation is expressed without explicitly describing its control flow.

Functional programming can be understood through various paradigms that shape its approach and methodology. This section delves into these paradigms, providing clarity and examples to illustrate their significance within the broader context of functional programming.

Pure Functions

Pure functions are a core concept in functional programming. A function is considered pure if it satisfies two conditions: it always produces the same output for the same set of inputs, and it has no side effects (i.e., it does not modify any state or interact with the outside world).

Example of a pure function in Python:

```
def add(x, y):
    return x + y
```

The function add is pure because it will always return the sum of x and y without modifying any external state or relying on any external data.

Immutability

In functional programming, immutability implies that data cannot be changed once created. Instead of modifying data, functions produce new data structures. This approach helps in avoiding side effects and maintaining consistency across the program.

Consider the example using lists in Python:

```
def append_element(lst, element):
    return lst + [element]

original_list = [1, 2, 3]
new_list = append_element(original_list, 4)
```

Here, the append_element function returns a new list by appending the element to the original list without modifying it, thus preserving immutability.

First-Class Functions

Functions in functional programming are treated as first-class citizens. This means that functions can be assigned to variables, passed as arguments to other functions, and even returned from other functions.

Example in Python:

```
def square(x):
    return x * x

def apply_function(func, value):
    return func(value)

result = apply_function(square, 5) # Returns 25
```

In this example, the square function is passed as an argument to apply_function, highlighting the concept of first-class functions.

Higher-Order Functions

Higher-order functions (HOFs) are those that can take other functions as arguments or return functions as their result. This allows for flexible and reusable function composition.

Example of a higher-order function in Python:

```
def increment(x):
    return x + 1

def apply_twice(func, value):
    return func(func(value))

result = apply_twice(increment, 3) # Returns 5
```

The function apply_twice takes another function, increment, as an argument and applies it twice to the given value.

Recursion

Recursion is a common technique in functional programming, where a function calls itself to solve smaller instances of the same problem. This technique often replaces iterative loops found in imperative programming.

Factorial function in Python using recursion:

```
def factorial(n):
    if n == 0:
        return 1
    else:
        return n * factorial(n - 1)

result = factorial(5) # Returns 120
```

The factorial function calls itself with a decremented value of n until it reaches the base case.

Lazy Evaluation

Lazy evaluation, or call-by-need, is a technique where expressions are not evaluated until their values are needed. This can improve performance by avoiding unnecessary calculations and can handle infinite data structures.

Example in Python using generators:

```
def lazy_range(n):
    i = 0
    while i < n:
        yield i
        i += 1

for number in lazy_range(5):
    print(number)
```

The lazy_range function generates values on-demand, demonstrating lazy evaluation by not generating all values at once but as they are requested in the loop.

Function Composition

Function composition is the process of combining two or more functions to produce a new function. It allows for the creation of modular and reusable code, emphasizing the declarative nature of functional programming.

Example of function composition in Python:

```
def add_one(x):
    return x + 1

def multiply_by_two(x):
    return x * 2

def compose(f, g):
    return lambda x: f(g(x))

new_function = compose(add_one, multiply_by_two)
result = new_function(5) # Returns 11
```

The compose function combines add_one and multiply_by_two into a single new function that applies both transformations sequentially.

Partial Application and Currying

Partial application is the process of fixing a few arguments of a function and producing another function of smaller arity. Currying, closely related, transforms a function that takes multiple arguments into a sequence of functions, each with a single argument.

Example of partial application in Python using functools.partial:

```
from functools import partial

def multiply(x, y):
    return x * y

double = partial(multiply, 2)
result = double(5) # Returns 10
```

Using partial, we create a new function double that always multiplies by 2, demonstrating partial application.

Understanding these paradigms is fundamental for mastering functional programming. They provide the foundation for functional programming languages and influence the design of algorithms and data structures within this paradigm.

Chapter 2

Python Basics for Functional Programming

This chapter covers the fundamental Python skills required for functional programming. It includes setting up the Python environment, understanding Python syntax and indentation, and working with basic data types and structures such as strings, lists, tuples, and dictionaries. Additionally, it delves into control structures, functions, built-in libraries, exception handling, and modules, while emphasizing best practices for writing Pythonic code.

2.1 Installing Python and Setting Up the Environment

To embark on a functional programming journey using Python, the initial step is to ensure that Python is correctly installed and the environment is suitably configured. The instructions provided here will cover the installation of Python, setting up a virtual environment, and installing relevant Integrated Development Environments (IDEs).

Installing Python:

Python distributions can be downloaded from the official Python website: https://www.python.org/downloads/. The website automatically suggests the appropriate version for the operating system in use. Select the suggested version to begin the download.

- **Windows:** Run the downloaded executable file. During the installation process, ensure that the checkbox for "Add Python to PATH" is selected, as this allows easy access to the Python interpreter from any command line interface. Proceed with the installation by following the on-screen instructions.

- **macOS:** Download the .pkg file and follow the installation wizard. Alternatively, macOS users can install Python using Homebrew, a package manager for macOS. If Homebrew is installed, execute the following command in the terminal:

```
brew install python
```

- **Linux:** Most Linux distributions come with Python pre-installed. To install or upgrade Python, one can use the package manager relevant to the distribution. For example, on Debian-based distributions:

```
sudo apt-get update
sudo apt-get install python3
```

Verifying Installation:

After installation, verify the Python version to ensure that Python is installed correctly. Open a command line interface and type:

```
python --version
```

On some systems, you may need to use 'python3' instead of 'python':

```
python3 --version
```

The output should display the version of Python that was installed.

```
Python 3.x.x
```

Setting Up a Virtual Environment:

Virtual environments are crucial for managing dependencies on a per-project basis to avoid conflicts between different projects. Python's built-in venv module facilitates easy creation and management of virtual environments.

To create a virtual environment, navigate to the desired directory and execute:

```
python -m venv myenv
```

This command creates a directory named myenv containing the virtual environment. To activate the virtual environment, use:

- **Windows:**

  ```
  myenv\Scripts\activate
  ```

- **macOS and Linux:**

  ```
  source myenv/bin/activate
  ```

When the virtual environment is active, the command line prompt modifies to indicate this. Install required packages within the virtual environment using pip, the package installer for Python:

```
pip install package_name
```

To deactivate the virtual environment, simply type:

```
deactivate
```

Choosing an Integrated Development Environment (IDE):

IDEs enhance the efficiency of coding by offering features like syntax highlighting, code completion, and debugging tools. Several IDEs are popular within the Python community.

- **PyCharm:** Developed by JetBrains, PyCharm is a powerful IDE tailored for Python development. It offers both a free Community edition and a paid Professional edition. Download and installation instructions can be found at https://www.jetbrains.com/pycharm/download/.

- **Visual Studio Code (VS Code):** A highly customizable code editor from Microsoft. It supports numerous extensions, including a robust Python extension. Download VS Code from https://code.visualstudio.com/ and install the Python extension via the Extensions view.

- **Jupyter Notebook:** Especially popular among data scientists, Jupyter allows interactive code execution. It can be installed using pip:

```
pip install notebook
```

Run Jupyter Notebook with:

```
jupyter notebook
```

Configuration and Best Practices:

Ensure all environment paths are properly set during installation to avoid runtime issues. Regularly update Python and installed packages to incorporate the latest features and security patches:

```
pip install --upgrade pip
pip list --outdated
pip install --upgrade package_name
```

This meticulous setup ensures a robust foundation for functional programming in Python, facilitating streamlined development and efficient project management.

2.2 Python Syntax and Indentation

Python boasts a syntax that is clear and expressive, which contributes to its widespread adoption. It eliminates unnecessary verbosity present in many other programming languages, making the code straightforward to read and write. Comprehending Python's syntax and its stringent indentation requirement is key to mastering the language.

Python code is often said to be almost pseudocode-like due to its readability. This is achieved through several syntactical rules:

- Python uses whitespace indentation to define code blocks.
- Python lines typically end with a newline character.
- Statements in Python typically do not require explicit terminators like semicolons.

Whitespace and Indentation play a crucial role in Python. Unlike many other languages which use curly braces or keywords to define blocks of code, Python uses indentation. This makes the visual layout of the code directly reflect the logical structure. Consider the following example, wherein correct indentation signifies the block of code within the function and control structures:

```
def example_function():
    if True:
        print("This is indented correctly.")
    else:
        print("This should be on the same level of indentation as the if statement.")
```

In this case, the indentation after the if and else keywords defines the scope of the corresponding blocks. Indentation must be consistent; Python does not allow mixing tabs and spaces in a single piece of code. The recommended practice is using four spaces per indentation level.

To illustrate the significance of indentation further, observe the following code which will generate an IndentationError:

```
def another_function():
    print("This line is correctly indented.")
     print("This line is wrongly indented and will cause an error.")
```

Python enforces indentation strictly and any deviation from the uniform indentation will result in errors. This ensures all developers follow a consistent style, improving code readability and maintainability.

Line Continuation can be employed when dealing with long statements, as Python imparts logical interpretation to a single physical line of code. Backslashes (\) can be used for explicit line continuation:

```
total_sum =1 + 2 + 3 + 4 + 5\
        + 6 + 7 + 8 + 9 + 10
```

Alternatively, implicit continuation is supported inside parentheses, brackets or braces. Thus, the above example could also be written as:

```
total_sum = (1 + 2 + 3 + 4 + 5
            + 6 + 7 + 8 + 9 + 10)
```

Comments are essential for adding descriptions within the code, both for future reference and for other developers who may work on the codebase. Comments begin with the # symbol and extend to the end of the line:

```
# This is a single-line comment

x = 42 # This is an inline comment
```

For multi-line comments, Python does not have a distinct syntax, but a common practice is using multiple single-line comments or triple-quoted strings that span multiple lines:

```
"""
This is a multi-line string often used for
multi-line comments or documentation.
"""
```

Statements in Python typically appear one per line. Multiple statements can be consolidated on a single line using a semicolon (;), but this practice is usually discouraged in favor of clarity:

```
a = 1
b = 2
c = a + b

# Multiple statements in one line
a = 1; b = 2; c = a + b
```

Identifiers are names used to identify variables, functions, classes, modules, and other objects. They must adhere to certain rules:

- Begin with a letter (a-z, A-Z) or an underscore (_).
- Followed by letters, underscores, or digits (0-9).
- Case-sensitive (e.g., myVariable and MyVariable are distinct).
- Cannot be Python keywords (reserved words).

Reserved keywords in Python are:

```
False    await    else     import   pass
None     break    except   in       raise
True     class    finally  is       return
and      continue for      lambda   try
as       def      from     nonlocal while
assert   del      global   not      with
async    elif     if       or       yield
```

These keywords serve essential functions in Python and should not be used as identifiers.

Understanding Python's syntax and indentation paradigms is fundamental and serves as a foundation for more advanced topics in Python programming, allowing for the creation of robust, readable, and maintainable code.

2.3 Basic Data Types and Variables

In Python, understanding the basic data types and variables is essential for writing efficient and effective code. Python is a dynamically-typed language, which means that you do not need to declare the type of a variable when you create one. The type is inferred at runtime, which can provide flexibility and ease of use. Let's explore the foundational data types and how variables operate in Python.

Numbers: Python supports several types of numerical data including integers, floating-point numbers, and complex numbers.

- **Integers:** Represent whole numbers without fractional parts. In Python, an integer is created by assigning a number without a decimal point to a variable.

```
a = 5
b = -12
```

- **Floating-Point Numbers:** Represent real numbers that include decimal points. They can be positive or negative.

```
pi = 3.14159
neg_float = -1.23
```

- **Complex Numbers:** Comprise a real part and an imaginary part. In Python, they are defined using a real part and an imaginary part denoted by 'j'.

```
complex_num = 3 + 4j
```

Strings: A string is a sequence of characters enclosed within single quotes (' ') or double quotes (" "). Python strings are immutable, meaning once defined, their content cannot be changed.

```
single_quote_str = 'Hello, World!'
double_quote_str = "Python Programming"
```

Strings can be concatenated using the + operator and repeated using the * operator.

```
concat_str = 'Hello' + ' ' + 'World!'
repeat_str = 'Python' * 3
```

Booleans: Boolean data types have only two possible values: True or False. They are commonly used in conditional statements to control the flow of execution.

```
is_valid = True
is_error = False
```

Lists: Lists are ordered collections of items which can be of different types. Lists are mutable, meaning their contents can be changed after they are created. Lists are defined using square brackets [].

```
example_list = [1, 2, 3, 'Python', 4.5]
example_list[2] = 'three' # Modifying an element
```

Tuples: Tuples are similar to lists but are immutable, meaning once defined, their content cannot be changed. They are defined using parentheses ().

```
example_tuple = (1, 2, 3, 'Python', 4.5)
# example_tuple[2] = 'three' would raise an error
```

Dictionaries: Dictionaries are unordered collections of key-value pairs. They are mutable and indexed by keys, which can be of any immutable data type. Dictionaries are defined using curly braces {}.

```
example_dict = {'name': 'Alice', 'age': 25, 'city': 'Wonderland'}
example_dict['age'] = 26 # Modifying an element
```

The type() function can be used to determine the type of a variable in Python.

```
print(type(a)) # <class 'int'>
print(type(pi)) # <class 'float'>
print(type(single_quote_str)) # <class 'str'>
print(type(is_valid)) # <class 'bool'>
print(type(example_list)) # <class 'list'>
print(type(example_tuple)) # <class 'tuple'>
print(type(example_dict)) # <class 'dict'>
```

Outputs:

```
<class 'int'>
<class 'float'>
<class 'str'>
<class 'bool'>
<class 'list'>
<class 'tuple'>
<class 'dict'>
```

Variable Assignment: Variables in Python are assigned using the equals sign (=). Multiple variables can be assigned in a single line, and swapping of variables doesn't require a temporary variable.

```
a = 10
b = 20
c, d = 30, 40 # Multi-variable assignment
e = f = g = 50 # Assigning the same value to multiple variables
a, b = b, a # Swapping values
```

Mutable vs Immutable Types: Understanding mutable and immutable types is crucial. Mutable types (like lists and dictionaries) can be changed in place; immutable types (like strings and tuples) cannot. This distinction has important ramifications for how variables and data structures interact.

```
# Mutable example
mutable_list = [1, 2, 3]
mutable_list.append(4)
print(mutable_list) # Output: [1, 2, 3, 4]

# Immutable example
immutable_str = "Hello"
# immutable_str[0] = 'h' would raise an error
mutable_list[1] = 99 # modifies the list in place
```

Outputs:

```
[1, 2, 3, 4]
```

Understanding these basics can help you to construct more complex structures and efficiently manage data within your programs.

2.4 Strings, Lists, Tuples, and Dictionaries

In Python, strings, lists, tuples, and dictionaries are fundamental data structures. They are versatile and serve as the foundation for more complex data manipulations and storage mechanisms. Mastering these structures is crucial for functional programming and for writing efficient Python code.

Strings in Python are immutable sequences of characters. They can be defined using single quotes (''), double quotes (""), or triple quotes (''' or """). Here's an example demonstrating various string operations:

```
# String definition
single_quote_str = 'Hello, World!'
double_quote_str = "Hello, World!"
triple_quote_str = '''Hello,
World!'''

# String concatenation
concatenated_str = single_quote_str + " " + double_quote_str

# Accessing characters
first_char = single_quote_str[0] # H
last_char = single_quote_str[-1] # !

# Slicing
substring = single_quote_str[1:5] # ello

# Length of the string
str_length = len(single_quote_str) # 13
```

```
print(concatenated_str)
print(first_char)
print(last_char)
print(substring)
print(str_length)
```

```
Hello, World! Hello, World!
H
!
ello
13
```

Lists are mutable sequences used to store collections of items. Lists are defined by enclosing elements within square brackets and can contain heterogeneous types. Python lists support various operations including indexing, slicing, appending, and other methods:

```
# List definition
fruits = ['apple', 'banana', 'cherry']

# Accessing elements by index
first_fruit = fruits[0] # 'apple'
last_fruit = fruits[-1] # 'cherry'

# Slicing
some_fruits = fruits[1:3] # ['banana', 'cherry']

# Appending elements
fruits.append('date')

# Removing elements
fruits.remove('banana')

# Length of the list
fruits_length = len(fruits) # 3

print(fruits)
print(first_fruit)
print(last_fruit)
print(some_fruits)
print(fruits_length)
```

```
['apple', 'cherry', 'date']
apple
cherry
['banana', 'cherry']
3
```

Tuples are immutable sequences, defined by enclosing elements within parentheses. Although similar to lists, the immutability of tuples means that once defined, their elements cannot be modified. This characteristic makes tuples ideal for storing data that should not change throughout the program execution:

```
# Tuple definition
```

```
coordinates = (10.0, 20.0)

# Accessing elements by index
x = coordinates[0] # 10.0
y = coordinates[1] # 20.0

# Tuple unpacking
(x, y) = coordinates

# Length of the tuple
coordinates_length = len(coordinates) # 2

print(coordinates)
print(x)
print(y)
print(coordinates_length)
```

```
(10.0, 20.0)
10.0
20.0
2
```

Dictionaries are mutable mappings that store key-value pairs. They are defined using curly braces, with keys and values separated by colons. Dictionaries provide an efficient way to store and retrieve data based on a unique key:

```
# Dictionary definition
student = {'name': 'Alice', 'age': 21, 'major': 'Computer Science'}

# Accessing values by key
name = student['name'] # 'Alice'
age = student.get('age') # 21

# Adding or updating key-value pairs
student['major'] = 'Mathematics'
student['graduation_year'] = 2023

# Removing key-value pairs
del student['age']

# Length of the dictionary
student_length = len(student) # 3

print(student)
print(name)
print(age)
print(student_length)
```

```
{'name': 'Alice', 'major': 'Mathematics', 'graduation_year': 2023}
Alice
21
3
```

Understanding and leveraging these data structures allows for more effective data management and manipulation in Python. Their different characteristics and appropriate use cases help ensure both code efficiency and clarity.

2.5 Control Structures: Conditionals and Loops

Control structures are fundamental for directing the flow of a program's execution in Python. This section reviews two primary control structures: conditionals and loops. Through these constructs, we can execute specific blocks of code based on certain conditions or repeatedly execute blocks of code.

Conditionals

Conditionals allow a program to execute certain parts of code based on given criteria. The primary conditional statement in Python is the if statement. Python conditionals rely heavily on proper indentation, typically using four spaces per indentation level. Python uses boolean expressions to determine whether conditions are met.

Syntax of a basic if statement:

```
if condition:
    # block of code to execute if condition is true
```

Consider the following simple example:

```
a = 10
b = 20
if a < b:
    print("a is less than b")
```

The program will output:

```
a is less than b
```

For adding more conditions, we use the elif and the else keywords.

```
if condition_1:
    # block of code if condition_1 is true
elif condition_2:
    # block of code if condition_2 is true and condition_1 is false
else:
    # block of code if both condition_1 and condition_2 are false
```

A more complex example:

```
a = 10
b = 20
if a > b:
    print("a is greater than b")
```

```
elif a == b:
    print("a is equal to b")
else:
    print("a is less than b")
```

The program will output:

```
a is less than b
```

Conditionals can be nested to handle more complex scenarios:

```
a = 30
b = 30
if a == b:
    if a > 20:
        print("a and b are equal and greater than 20")
    else:
        print("a and b are equal and less than or equal to 20")
else:
    print("a and b are not equal")
```

The program above will output:

```
a and b are equal and greater than 20
```

Loops

Loops are used to execute a block of code multiple times. Python supports for loops and while loops.

for loops iterate over a sequence (e.g., a list, tuple, string, or range).

Syntax:

```
for variable in sequence:
    # block of code to execute
```

Example:

```
for i in range(5):
    print(i)
```

Output:

```
0
1
2
3
4
```

For more complex iterations:

```
fruits = ["apple", "banana", "cherry"]
for fruit in fruits:
    print(fruit)
```

Output:

```
apple
banana
cherry
```

while loops execute as long as the condition is true.

Syntax:

```
while condition:
    # block of code to execute
```

Example:

```
count = 0
while count < 5:
    print(count)
    count += 1
```

Output:

```
0
1
2
3
4
```

Loop Control Statements

Python provides control statements like break, continue, and pass to modify the behavior of loops.

The break statement terminates the loop prematurely.

```
for i in range(10):
    if i == 5:
        break
    print(i)
```

Output:

```
0
1
2
3
4
```

The continue statement skips the rest of the current iteration and moves to the next iteration.

```
for i in range(10):
    if i % 2 == 0:
        continue
    print(i)
```

Output:

```
1
3
5
7
9
```

The pass statement does nothing and is used as a placeholder for future code.

```
for i in range(10):
    if i % 2 == 0:
        pass
    print(i)
```

Output:

```
0
1
2
3
4
5
6
7
8
9
```

This section has explained how to utilize conditionals and loops in Python, essential constructs for controlling program flow. The accurate use of these constructs is critical for efficient and readable code development.

2.6 Functions in Python: Definition and Scope

Functions are fundamental building blocks in Python programming and are crucial for implementing both procedural and functional programming paradigms. They allow for code reusability, modular design, and abstraction of complex operations. In Python, functions are first-class objects, meaning they can be assigned to variables, passed as arguments, and returned from other functions.

A function in Python is defined using the def keyword, followed by the function name and parentheses containing any parameters. The body of the function is indented to denote the block of code that constitutes the function.

```
def example_function(parameter1, parameter2):
    # Function body
    result = parameter1 + parameter2
    return result
```

In the above example, example_function takes two parameters, parameter1 and parameter2, and returns their sum. The return statement is used to exit the function and provide a result to the caller.

Functions can have default parameters, which allow you to call the function without explicitly providing a value for those parameters. Default values are specified by assigning a value to the parameter in the function definition.

```
def greet(name, message="Hello"):
    print(f"{message}, {name}!")

greet("Alice") # Outputs: Hello, Alice!
greet("Bob", "Goodbye") # Outputs: Goodbye, Bob!
```

Python also supports variable-length arguments; you can use the *args and **kwargs syntax to pass a variable number of non-keyword and keyword arguments, respectively.

```
def variable_args(*args, **kwargs):
    print("Non-keyword arguments:", args)
    print("Keyword arguments:", kwargs)

variable_args(1, 2, 3, a=4, b=5)
```

```
Non-keyword arguments: (1, 2, 3)
Keyword arguments: {'a': 4, 'b': 5}
```

The concept of scope refers to the visibility and lifetime of variables within different parts of the program. Variables defined within a function are local to that function and cannot be accessed outside of it. Conversely, variables defined outside any function are global and can be accessed from anywhere in the code.

```
def scope_example():
    local_var = "I am local"
    print(local_var)

global_var = "I am global"
scope_example()
print(global_var)
```

```
I am local
I am global
```

If a global variable needs to be read or modified inside a function, the global keyword can be used:

```
counter = 0

def increment_counter():
    global counter
    counter += 1
```

```
increment_counter()
print(f"Counter value is: {counter}")
```

Counter value is: 1

Python also supports nested functions, which are functions defined inside other functions. The nested function can access variables from the enclosing function's scope, creating a closure. This can be useful for encapsulating functionality and creating decorators.

```
def outer_function(text):
    def inner_function():
        print(text)
    inner_function()

outer_function("Hello from outer function")
```

Hello from outer function

The nonlocal keyword provides a way to assign values to variables in the nearest enclosing scope (excluding globals). This is essential for modifying the state of variables within nested functions.

```
def outer():
    x = "Hello"

    def inner():
        nonlocal x
        x = "Hi"

    inner()
    return x

result = outer()
print(result)
```

Hi

Understanding the scope and lifetime of variables in Python functions is essential for writing clean, bug-free code. Functions in Python not only provide a way to structure and organize code but also enable advanced programming techniques such as functional programming, decorators, and higher-order functions. Proper use of default parameters, variable-length arguments, and scoping rules can lead to more flexible and maintainable code.

2.7 Built-in Functions and Standard Libraries

Python provides a rich set of built-in functions and standard libraries that are essential for efficient and effective programming. This section will explore some of the most commonly used built-in functions and delve into the essential standard libraries that can greatly enhance your programming experience. Understanding these tools is crucial for writing concise and functional code in Python.

Built-in Functions

Python includes numerous built-in functions that perform common tasks. Here are some key functions and their typical usage:

- print(): Outputs data to the console.

  ```
  print(”Hello, World!”)
  ```

  Output:

  ```
  Hello, World!
  ```

- len(): Returns the length of an object.

  ```
  len(”Python”)
  ```

  Output:

  ```
  6
  ```

- type(): Returns the type of an object.

  ```
  type(3.14)
  ```

  Output:

  ```
  <class ’float’>
  ```

- sum(): Sums all items in an iterable.

  ```
  sum([1, 2, 3, 4])
  ```

  Output:

  ```
  10
  ```

- max(), min(): Returns the maximum and minimum value in an iterable, respectively.

```
max([1, 2, 3, 4]), min([1, 2, 3, 4])
```

Output:

```
(4, 1)
```

- map(): Applies a function to all items in an input list.

```
def square(n):
    return n * n

list(map(square, [1, 2, 3, 4]))
```

Output:

```
[1, 4, 9, 16]
```

- filter(): Filters elements in an iterable through a function that returns a boolean value.

```
def is_even(n):
    return n % 2 == 0

list(filter(is_even, [1, 2, 3, 4]))
```

Output:

```
[2, 4]
```

- zip(): Aggregates elements from two or more iterables (lists, tuples, etc.).

```
list(zip([1, 2, 3], ['a', 'b', 'c']))
```

Output:

```
[(1, 'a'), (2, 'b'), (3, 'c')]
```

- enumerate(): Adds a counter to an iterable and returns it as an enumerate object.

```
list(enumerate(['a', 'b', 'c']))
```

Output:

```
[(0, 'a'), (1, 'b'), (2, 'c')]
```

- all(), any(): Returns True if all/any of the elements in the iterable are true.

```
all([True, True, False]), any([True, True, False])
```

Output:

```
(False, True)
```

Standard Libraries

Python's standard library is extensive, offering a plethora of modules and packages to handle a variety of programming tasks. Here is a look at some of these libraries and their utilities:

- math: Provides mathematical functions.

```
import math
math.sqrt(16), math.pi
```

  Output:

```
(4.0, 3.141592653589793)
```

- datetime: Supplies classes for manipulating dates and times.

```
import datetime
now = datetime.datetime.now()
now.year, now.month, now.day
```

  Output:

```
(2023, 1, 1)  # Values will vary based on the current date
```

- random: Implements pseudo-random number generators for various distributions.

```
import random
random.randint(1, 10), random.choice(['apple', 'banana', 'cherry'])
```

  Output:

```
(7, 'banana')  # Random values will change on each execution
```

- os: Provides a way of using operating system dependent functionality.

```
import os
os.name
```

  Output:

```
'posix'  # 'posix' for Unix/Linux/MacOS, 'nt' for Windows
```

- sys: Provides access to some variables used or maintained by the Python interpreter.

```
import sys
sys.version
```

Output:

```
'3.x.x (default, Jan 1 2022, 00:00:00) [GCC x.x.x]' # Specific details based on the Python version
```

- json: Handles JSON data encoding and decoding.

```
import json
data = {'name': 'Alice', 'age': 25}
json_string = json.dumps(data)
json_string
```

Output:

```
'{"name": "Alice", "age": 25}'
```

- re: Provides regular expression matching operations.

```
import re
pattern = re.compile(r"\d+")
result = pattern.findall("There are 3 apples and 5 bananas.")
result
```

Output:

```
['3', '5']
```

- csv: Implements classes to read and write tabular data in CSV format.

```
import csv
with open('data.csv', mode='w', newline='') as file:
    writer = csv.writer(file)
    writer.writerow(["name", "age"])
    writer.writerow(["Alice", 25])
    writer.writerow(["Bob", 30])
```

This will create a data.csv file with the contents:

```
name,age
Alice,25
Bob,30
```

- urllib: Provides a collection of modules for working with URLs.

```
import urllib.request
response = urllib.request.urlopen('http://example.com')
html = response.read()
html[:60] # Print the first 60 characters
```

Output:

```
b'<!doctype html>\n<html>\n<head>\n    <title>Example Domain</title>'
```

Understanding and effectively utilizing these built-in functions and standard libraries can significantly streamline your coding process and enhance the functionality of your Python programs.

2.8 Handling Exceptions and Errors

In Python, handling exceptions and errors is a crucial aspect that enhances code robustness and reliability. Exception handling is the process of responding to exceptional or error conditions that may occur during the execution of a program. These conditions can stem from many sources, such as invalid user inputs, file-not-found errors, network connection problems, or even logical errors within the program itself. Python provides a powerful mechanism for defining, catching, and managing exceptions, ensuring that programs can deal gracefully with unexpected situations.

An exception in Python can be any object derived from the base class BaseException. The most commonly used exception class is Exception, from which many other built-in exceptions are derived. When an error occurs within a block of code, an exception is raised, disrupting the normal flow of the program. The Python interpreter stops executing the current block and looks for a surrounding try statement with an appropriate except clause to handle the exception.

Consider the following example where an attempt is made to divide a number by zero:

```
def divide(a, b):
    return a / b

result = divide(10, 0)
print(result)
```

If this code is executed, it will raise a ZeroDivisionError since division by zero is mathematically undefined:

```
Traceback (most recent call last):
  File "example.py", line 4, in <module>
    result = divide(10, 0)
  File "example.py", line 2, in divide
    return a / b
ZeroDivisionError: division by zero
```

To handle such an exception gracefully, we can use a try block to wrap the code that may raise an exception, followed by one or more except clauses to catch and handle specific exceptions:

```
def divide(a, b):
    try:
        return a / b
    except ZeroDivisionError:
        print("Error: Cannot divide by zero.")
        return None

result = divide(10, 0)
print(result)
```

The output of this code will be:

```
Error: Cannot divide by zero.
None
```

In this example, the ZeroDivisionError is caught by the except clause, and an appropriate error message is printed. The function returns None to indicate that the division was not successful.

Python supports catching multiple exceptions simultaneously, allowing programmers to handle different error types with distinct logic. This can be achieved by specifying multiple except clauses, one for each exception type. For example:

```
def safe_divide(a, b):
    try:
        return a / b
    except ZeroDivisionError:
        print("Error: Division by zero is not allowed.")
        return None
    except TypeError:
        print("Error: Both inputs must be numbers.")
        return None

result = safe_divide(10, 0)
print(result)

result = safe_divide(10, 'a')
print(result)
```

The output of this code will be:

```
Error: Division by zero is not allowed.
None
Error: Both inputs must be numbers.
None
```

In this example, both ZeroDivisionError and TypeError are handled appropriately. Using multiple except clauses improves the robustness of the function and provides more informative feedback to the user.

In some situations, catching all potential exceptions using a generic except clause can be useful. This can be achieved by specifying except Exception without mentioning a specific exception type:

```
def robust_divide(a, b):
```

```
    try:
        return a / b
    except Exception as e:
        print(f"Error: {e}")
        return None

result = robust_divide(10, 0)
print(result)

result = robust_divide(10, 'a')
print(result)
```

The output of this code will be:

```
Error: division by zero
None
Error: unsupported operand type(s) for /: 'int' and 'str'
None
```

The use of except Exception as e allows for capturing any exception that inherits from Exception and provides access to the exception object e, which contains information about the error.

Python also provides mechanisms for raising exceptions explicitly using the raise statement. This can be useful when you want to signal an error condition manually. For example:

```
def check_value(x):
    if x < 0:
        raise ValueError("The value must be non-negative.")

try:
    check_value(-1)
except ValueError as e:
    print(f"Caught an exception: {e}")
```

The output of this code will be:

```
Caught an exception: The value must be non-negative.
```

In this example, the function check_value raises a ValueError if the input is negative. The caller can then handle this exception appropriately in a try...except block.

For ensuring that certain cleanup code is always executed, Python provides the finally clause. The code inside the finally block will run regardless of whether an exception was raised or not. This is particularly useful for resource management, such as closing files or releasing locks. For instance:

```
def read_file(file_path):
    try:
        file = open(file_path, 'r')
        return file.read()
    except FileNotFoundError:
```

```
        print("Error: File not found.")
        return None
    finally:
        if 'file' in locals() and not file.closed:
            file.close()

content = read_file('nonexistent.txt')
print(content)
```

The output of this code will be:

```
Error: File not found.
None
```

In this example, the finally clause ensures that the file is closed even if an exception occurs during the file operation. This is crucial for avoiding resource leaks and ensuring that resources are managed properly.

Grasping the mechanisms of exception handling significantly contributes to writing robust and fault-tolerant Python code. Through thoughtful application of try, except, raise, and finally constructs, developers can manage and mitigate unexpected errors, resulting in more reliable and maintainable software. Here is the corrected LaTeX text for the section:

2.9 Introduction to Python Modules and Packages

In Python programming, the concept of modularity is pivotal to crafting maintainable and scalable code. Modular programming refers to a software design technique that emphasizes separating the functionality of a program into distinct, interchangeable modules where each module encompasses a specific portion of the program's functionality. This section delves into the mechanics of Python modules and packages, elucidating how they can be utilized to facilitate code reusability and organization.

A **module** in Python is simply a file containing Python definitions and statements. Generally, these files are saved with a .py extension. The definitions in a module can include variables, functions, and classes. By using modules, we can break down large programs into smaller, manageable, and reusable files. Here's a basic example of creating and using a module:

```
# File: my_module.py

def greet(name):
```

```
    return f"Hello, {name}!"

age = 30
```

To use this module in another Python script, we employ the import statement:

```
# File: main.py

import my_module

print(my_module.greet("Alice"))
print(f"Age is {my_module.age}")
```

Output:

```
Hello, Alice!
Age is 30
```

When main.py is executed, the statements within the my_module.py file are executed, bringing all the defined variables, functions, and classes into the importing file's namespace under the module's name.

For more granular control over importing, Python offers various ways to import specific components of a module. For instance:

```
from my_module import greet

print(greet("Bob"))
```

Notably, when only specific components are imported, the namespace becomes less cluttered, enhancing code readability and maintainability.

While modules are single files, a **package** is a directory hierarchy that provides a way to structure Python's module namespace using "'dotted module names'". A visually comparable structure to directories and subdirectories in a file system can aid in extensively organizing a large collection of modules. A package must include an __init__.py file, even if it is empty, to be recognized by Python as a package.

Consider the following directory structure:

```
mypackage/
    __init__.py
    module1.py
    subpackage/
        __init__.py
        module2.py
```

We can then import from this package in several ways. For example:

```
# File: main.py
```

```
from mypackage import module1
from mypackage.subpackage import module2

print(module1.some_function())
print(module2.another_function())
```

This structure allows for nested modularization, which can significantly enhance code organization for large-scale projects. The __init__-.py files can also be used to execute initialization code for a package, essentially setting up the package's environment.

Furthermore, Python packages can be distributed and installed using tools like **pip**. Creating a distributable package involves writing a setup.py script using the setuptools library. An example is:

```
from setuptools import setup, find_packages

setup(
    name='mypackage',
    version='0.1',
    packages=find_packages(),
    install_requires=[
        # List dependencies here
    ],
)
```

Once written, the package can be built and distributed using the following commands:

```
python setup.py sdist
pip install .
```

By breaking down functionality into modules and organizing these modules into packages, Python enables better code management, facilitates code reuse across different projects, and lays the groundwork for collaborative software development. The judicious use of modules and packages is an indispensable practice for any Python programmer aiming to write clean, efficient, and maintainable code.

2.10 Writing Pythonic Code: Best Practices

Writing Pythonic code involves adhering to the idioms and stylistic conventions that are not only embraced but also encouraged by the Python community. These practices aim to enhance code readability, maintainability, and efficiency. Below are several best practices consolidated from the principles established by Python's guiding document, PEP 8, and broader community standards.

1. Code Layout and Formatting:

Consistency in code layout and formatting significantly improves readability. The following guidelines are essential:

- **Indentation:** Use 4 spaces per indentation level. Avoid tab characters as they can introduce inconsistencies.
- **Maximum Line Length:** Limit all lines to a maximum of 79 characters. For longer blocks of text (docstrings or comments), limit to 72 characters.
- **Blank Lines:** Separate top-level function and class definitions with two blank lines. Use a single blank line to separate method definitions inside a class.
- **Imports:** Keep all imports at the top of the file. Group imports in the following order: standard library imports, related third-party imports, and local application/library-specific imports. Each group should be separated by a blank line.

Example:

```
import os
import sys
from datetime import datetime

import numpy as np

from mymodule import myfunction

def function_a():
    pass

def function_b():
    pass
```

2. Naming Conventions:

Naming conventions are vital for code clarity and consistency:

- **Variables:** Use lowercase words separated by underscores (snake_case). Example: user_name, total_sum.
- **Functions and Methods:** Use lowercase words separated by underscores. Example: calculate_area(), update_record().

- **Classes:** Use CapitalizedWords convention (CamelCase, also known as PascalCase). Example: CustomerData, VehicleFactory.
- **Constants:** Use all uppercase letters with words separated by underscores. Example: MAX_CONNECTIONS, PI.

Example:

```
class ExampleClass:
    MAX_COUNT = 100

    def calculate_sum(self, a, b):
        return a + b

def read_file(file_path):
    with open(file_path, 'r') as file:
        return file.read()
```

3. Docstrings and Comments:

Effective documentation is crucial for understanding and maintaining code:

- **Docstrings:** Use triple double-quotes to describe modules, classes, and functions. Make the docstring a complete sentence.

```
def add(a, b):
    """
    Add two numbers and return the result.

    Parameters:
    a (int): The first number.
    b (int): The second number.

    Returns:
    int: The sum of the two numbers.
    """
    return a + b
```

- **Comments:** Use comments to describe the significance of code blocks and any complexities. Begin comments with a capital letter and ensure they are complete sentences. Avoid obvious comments.

```
# Calculate the average value
total_sum = sum(values)
average = total_sum / len(values)
```

4. Using Python's Built-in Functions:

Python provides numerous built-in functions, enhancing both the functionality and performance of your code. Utilizing these functions over reinventing the wheel is a best practice.

```
# Use the built-in sum() function instead of manually summing a list
numbers = [1, 2, 3, 4, 5]
total = sum(numbers)
```

5. Avoiding Redundant Expressions:

Simplify expressions for clarity and efficiency:

- Use if <condition> rather than if <condition> is True.
- Prefer variable != None over not variable is None.

```
# Recommended
if is_valid:
    proceed()

# Not recommended
if is_valid == True:
    proceed()
```

6. Exception Handling:

Proper exception handling can prevent unexpected crashes and help in debugging:

- Use specific exception types instead of a bare except.
- Employ the finally clause for cleanup actions that must execute under all circumstances.
- Avoid catching exceptions broadly unless necessary.

```
try:
    result = 1 / 0
except ZeroDivisionError:
    print("Division by zero is not allowed.")
finally:
    print("Finished execution.")
```

7. Iteration and Looping:

Utilize Python's powerful iterables and comprehensions to write clear and efficient loops:

- Use list comprehensions for simple loops.
- Prefer generator expressions for large data sets to save memory.

```
# List comprehension
squares = [x**2 for x in range(10)]

# Generator expression
large_squares = (x**2 for x in range(1000000))
```

8. Importing Modules:

Import only what is necessary to reduce namespace pollution and increase clarity:

- Use absolute imports whenever possible.
- Avoid wildcard imports (from module import *).

```
# Absolute import
from mypackage.mymodule import myfunction

# Avoid wildcard import
# from mypackage.mymodule import *
```

9. Functional Programming Constructs:

When writing functional-style code, take advantage of Python's support for higher-order functions, lambdas, and built-in functions like map(), filter(), and reduce().

```
# Using map() with a lambda function
numbers = [1, 2, 3, 4, 5]
squared_numbers = list(map(lambda x: x ** 2, numbers))

# Using filter() with a lambda function
even_numbers = list(filter(lambda x: x % 2 == 0, numbers))
```

Maintaining these best practices promotes writing Pythonic code that is clean, efficient, and maintainable. The conventions outlined here align with the principles of simplicity and readability, which are core to Python's philosophy.

Chapter 3

First-Class and Higher-Order Functions

This chapter introduces the concepts of first-class and higher-order functions in Python. It explains function objects and callables, demonstrating how functions can be passed as arguments, returned from other functions, and used to create higher-order functions. The chapter also covers common higher-order functions like map, filter, and reduce, alongside advanced techniques such as partial application, currying, and function composition. Practical examples and usage of decorators are included to solidify understanding.

3.1 Understanding First-Class Functions

First-class functions in Python are fundamental to the paradigm of functional programming. In Python, functions are treated as first-class objects, meaning they can be passed as arguments to other functions, returned as values from other functions, and assigned to variables. This property underpins many advanced programming techniques, such as function composition, the use of decorators, and the creation of higher-order functions.

To understand first-class functions, it is necessary to appreciate the concept of functions as objects. In Python, just like integers, strings, and lists, functions are objects. This means they can be manipulated dynamically, stored in data structures, and passed around in your code.

Consider the following Python code that defines a simple function and then demonstrates the assignment of this function to a variable:

```
def greet(name):
    return f"Hello, {name}!"

greeting_function = greet
print(greeting_function("World"))
```

The output produced by the above code is:

```
Hello, World!
```

Here, we define a function greet that takes a single argument name and returns a greeting string. The crucial point to note is the assignment greeting_function = greet. This line assigns the function object greet to the variable greeting_function. When we call greeting_function("World"), we execute the same function originally defined as greet, demonstrating that function names in Python are simply references to function objects.

Another critical aspect of first-class functions is their ability to be stored in data structures. Here is an example where function objects are stored in a list and a dictionary:

```
def add(a, b):
    return a + b

def subtract(a, b):
    return a - b

functions_list = [add, subtract]
print(functions_list[0](10, 5))
print(functions_list[1](10, 5))

functions_dict = {'add': add, 'subtract': subtract}
print(functions_dict['add'](20, 10))
print(functions_dict['subtract'](20, 10))
```

The output of this code is:

```
15
5
30
10
```

In this example, add and subtract are two functions that are first assigned to elements of a list and then accessed via their positions. Similarly, these functions are assigned as values in a dictionary and subsequently accessed using their respective keys. This flexibility of assigning functions to variables or storing them in collections is essential for higher-order functions and many functional programming techniques.

Passing functions as arguments is another capability that emerges from the first-class status of functions in Python. This concept can be leveraged to build flexible and reusable components. Here is a simple example demonstrating this idea:

```
def apply_function(func, value):
    return func(value)

def square(x):
    return x * x

def cube(x):
    return x * x * x

print(apply_function(square, 3))
print(apply_function(cube, 3))
```

The output is:

```
9
27
```

In this scenario, apply_function takes two parameters: a function func and a value value. Depending on the function passed apply_function(square, 3) or apply_function(cube, 3), it will compute either the square or the cube of the number 3. This illustrates how passing functions as arguments can introduce a high degree of flexibility and reusability in program design.

First-class functions in Python also allow functions to be returned from other functions. This capability can be used to create functions dynamically and customize their behavior based on the enclosing scope. Consider the following code:

```
def make_adder(n):
    def adder(x):
        return x + n
    return adder

add_five = make_adder(5)
print(add_five(10))

add_ten = make_adder(10)
print(add_ten(7))
```

The output is:

15
17

In this example, the make_adder function returns a new function adder that adds a given number n to its input x. When make_adder(5) is called, it creates a new adder function that adds 5 to its argument, and when make_adder(10) is called, it creates a new adder function that adds 10 to its argument. This demonstrates how functions can produce other functions, a concept closely related to closures and functional programming.

This section illustrates the power and utility of treating functions as first-class entities in Python. By allowing functions to be assigned to variables, stored in collections, passed as arguments, and returned from other functions, Python enables a wide range of programming patterns and techniques fundamental to functional programming. Understanding and leveraging these capabilities is essential for writing more modular, flexible, and concise code.

3.2 Function Objects and Callables in Python

In Python, functions are first-class citizens, meaning they are treated as objects. This implies functions can be assigned to variables, passed as arguments, returned from other functions, and stored in data structures. Understanding function objects and callables is fundamental to grasping the concept of first-class and higher-order functions.

A function in Python is defined using the *def* keyword. Once defined, this function is considered a function object. This can be illustrated with an example:

```
def greet(name):
    return f"Hello, {name}"
```

Here, greet is a function object. To verify that greet is indeed an object and not just syntactic sugar for a code block, we can use the built-in type function:

```
print(type(greet))
```

Executing this yields:

<class 'function'>

This confirms that greet is an instance of the function class. Consequently, we can pass greet around just like any other object. For example, we can assign it to another variable:

```
salutation = greet
```

We can now invoke salutation in the same way we would invoke greet:

```
print(salutation("Alice"))
```

The output remains:

```
Hello, Alice
```

This demonstrates that greet and salutation are references to the same function object. Function objects being callable is another key aspect. In Python, any object that implements the special method __call__() is considered callable. This includes instances of classes with a __call__ method defined.

To illustrate callables beyond standard functions, consider the following example:

```
class Adder:
    def __init__(self, value):
        self.value = value

    def __call__(self, x):
        return self.value + x
```

Here, the class Adder defines a __call__ method, which makes its instances callable. We can create an instance of Adder and use it as a function:

```
add_five = Adder(5)
print(add_five(10))
```

The result is:

```
15
```

This functionality of classes broadens the utility of callables in Python, allowing for more flexible and expressive code. We can further explore function attributes to bridge the understanding of function objects and their metadata. Every function object in Python has several attributes that provide additional information and functionalities. The __name__ and __doc__ attributes are among the most commonly used.

Consider the following function:

```
def multiply(a, b):
```

```
    """Returns the product of a and b."""
    return a * b
```

We can access its attributes as follows:

```
print(multiply.__name__) # Output: multiply
print(multiply.__doc__) # Output: Returns the product of a and b.
```

These attributes are beneficial for debugging and documentation purposes. Recognizing that functions themselves possess attributes reinforces the concept that they are indeed objects.

Summarizing the principles discussed, understanding that functions are objects and can be used as callables lays the foundational knowledge for working with higher-order functions and enabling powerful programming paradigms.

3.3 Passing Functions as Arguments

In Python, functions are first-class objects, meaning they can be treated as other objects like integers, strings, lists, etc. This property of functions allows them to be passed as arguments to other functions. This mechanism is a key feature that enables the creation of higher-order functions. Passing functions as arguments often leads to more abstract and modular code.

Consider the foundational function signature:

```
def higher_order_function(f, value):
    return f(value)
```

In this example, higher_order_function takes a function f and a value value as its arguments. The function f is applied to value, which is returned as the output of higher_order_function. To elaborate on this, consider an example of a higher-order function that applies a given function to an element of a list.

```
def apply_function_to_list(func, lst):
    return [func(x) for x in lst]
```

Here, apply_function_to_list takes a function func and a list lst, and returns a new list where func has been applied to each element of lst. Assume we have a simple function that squares a number:

```
def square(x):
    return x * x
```

We can now pass square to apply_function_to_list:

```
numbers = [1, 2, 3, 4]
squared_numbers = apply_function_to_list(square, numbers)
print(squared_numbers)
```

The output of executing this code is:

```
[1, 4, 9, 16]
```

In this scenario, the function square is passed as an argument to apply_function_to_list, demonstrating the concept of passing functions as arguments effectively.

Furthermore, consider more complex scenarios where you may want to apply different operations to elements of a list conditionally. Let's design a higher-order function that takes a condition function and applies two different functions based on the condition's result.

```
def conditional_apply(cond, func1, func2, lst):
    return [func1(x) if cond(x) else func2(x) for x in lst]
```

Here, conditional_apply takes a condition function cond, two functions func1 and func2, and a list lst. For each element in the list, func1 is applied if cond evaluates to True, otherwise func2 is applied.

Define the required functions:

```
def is_even(x):
    return x % 2 == 0

def double(x):
    return x * 2

def triple(x):
    return x * 3
```

Now utilize these functions with conditional_apply:

```
numbers = [1, 2, 3, 4, 5]
result = conditional_apply(is_even, double, triple, numbers)
print(result)
```

The output for this code is:

```
[3, 4, 9, 8, 15]
```

In this example, is_even checks if a number is even. If the number is even, double is applied; if the number is odd, triple is applied. The higher-order function conditional_apply elegantly separates the logic of condition checking and applying the functions, showcasing the power and flexibility of passing functions as arguments.

Another instructive example is the use of the built-in sorted function in Python, which can take a custom comparison function through its key parameter. Suppose we want to sort a list of strings but prioritize the number of vowels in each string.

Define a function to count vowels:

```
def count_vowels(s):
    return sum(1 for char in s.lower() if char in 'aeiou')
```

Use this function as the key parameter in sorted:

```
words = ['apple', 'banana', 'cherry', 'date']
sorted_words = sorted(words, key=count_vowels)
print(sorted_words)
```

The output is:

```
['date', 'apple', 'cherry', 'banana']
```

In this case, sorted utilizes count_vowels to determine the order based on the number of vowels in each string. This example again demonstrates the utility of passing functions as arguments to achieve custom behavior.

By leveraging the concept of passing functions as arguments, Python developers can craft flexible, reusable, and more abstract code structures, streamlining complex operations across different contexts effortlessly.

3.4 Returning Functions from Functions

In functional programming, the ability to return functions from other functions is a crucial aspect that facilitates the creation of more dynamic and flexible code. This feature allows functions to generate other functions with certain behaviors or properties that can be customized through arguments. In Python, functions are first-class objects, which means they can be used as return values. This section delves deeper into the mechanics and applications of returning functions from functions.

Consider the case where we need a factory function that creates other functions. Factory functions are higher-order functions designed to dynamically produce other functions based on specific parameters given to them. This pattern is particularly useful in scenarios where different behaviors are needed, but a common framework can be established through a higher-order function.

```
def make_multiplier(factor):
    def multiplier(x):
        return x * factor
    return multiplier
```

The function make_multiplier takes a single argument, factor, and it returns an inner function multiplier. The inner function multiplier takes an argument x and returns the product of x and factor. This allows us to create specialized multiplier functions as needed.

Let's create a few multiplier functions and use them:

```
double = make_multiplier(2)
triple = make_multiplier(3)

print(double(5)) # Output: 10
print(triple(5)) # Output: 15
```

```
10
15
```

In this example, double and triple are functions generated by make_multiplier with specific factor values. They can be applied to any argument x, multiplying it by 2 and 3, respectively.

This capability of returning functions allows for encapsulation and reuse of code patterns. Another example involves creating closures, which are functions that capture variables from their enclosing scope. A closure retains access to these variables even after the outer function has finished executing.

```
def power_factory(n):
    def power(x):
        return x ** n
    return power
```

In this code snippet, power_factory returns a function power that raises a number x to the power of n. Here, n is captured by the inner function, forming a closure. This allows for the creation of specific power functions.

```
square = power_factory(2)
cube = power_factory(3)

print(square(4)) # Output: 16
print(cube(2)) # Output: 8
```

```
16
8
```

Through this approach, different power functions are efficiently generated and utilized. The ability to choose the exponent at the time of function creation adds a layer of flexibility and specificity to the code.

Returning functions from functions is not limited to mathematical operations. This concept can be extended to more complex scenarios such as event handling, configuration builders, or decorators. Consider a function that creates decorators, allowing for additional behavior to be injected into other functions.

```
def logging_decorator(prefix):
    def decorator(func):
        def wrapper(*args, **kwargs):
            print(f"{prefix} Executing {func.__name__}...")
            result = func(*args, **kwargs)
            print(f"{prefix} Finished {func.__name__}")
            return result
        return wrapper
    return decorator
```

The logging_decorator function takes a prefix string and returns a decorator. This decorator adds logging before and after the execution of any function it wraps. The prefix allows for customization of the log messages.

Usage of this decorator factory is straightforward:

```
@logging_decorator("DEBUG")
def add(a, b):
    return a + b

@logging_decorator("INFO")
def multiply(a, b):
    return a * b

print(add(4, 5)) # Output includes debug logs
print(multiply(4, 5)) # Output includes info logs
```

```
DEBUG Executing add...
DEBUG Finished add
9
INFO Executing multiply...
INFO Finished multiply
20
```

Through these examples, the versatility and power of returning functions from functions are evident. It enables Python programmers to write more modular, reusable, and customizable code, adhering to the principles of functional programming.

3.5 Creating and Using Higher-Order Functions

Higher-order functions are functions that either take one or more functions as arguments or return a function as a result. Given their critical role in functional programming, understanding how to create and utilize higher-order functions in Python is fundamental.

To create a higher-order function, we define a regular function and include other function(s) in its parameters or return statement. Let us examine this process through some code examples.

In the following example, we define a incrementer function that takes an integer x and returns another function. This returned function increments any input by x:

```
def incrementer(x):
    def inner_increment(y):
        return x + y
    return inner_increment
```

Creating an instance of incrementer with a specific value of x assigns a function to the variable. For example:

```
add_five = incrementer(5)
print(add_five(10)) # Output will be 15
```

```
15
```

Here, incrementer(5) returns a function that adds 5 to its input. When add_five(10) is executed, the inner function inner_increment takes 10 as its input and adds 5 to it, resulting in 15.

The concept of passing functions as arguments is exemplified by demonstrating a function that takes another function and applies it over a list:

```
def apply_function(func, data):
    return [func(item) for item in data]

def square(n):
    return n * n

data = [1, 2, 3, 4]
print(apply_function(square, data)) # Output will be [1, 4, 9, 16]
```

```
[1, 4, 9, 16]
```

The apply_function takes a function func and a list data, then applies func to each element of data using a list comprehension. By passing the square function, each number is squared within the list.

Another common scenario is modifying the behavior of functions dynamically. This can be observed in the example of designing a logger function that logs the execution of another function:

```
def logger(func):
    def wrapped_function(*args, **kwargs):
        print(f"Executing {func.__name__} with arguments {args} and {kwargs}")
        result = func(*args, **kwargs)
        print(f"{func.__name__} returned {result}")
        return result
    return wrapped_function

def multiply(a, b):
    return a * b

logged_multiply = logger(multiply)
print(logged_multiply(3, 4)) # Output will include logging details and the result 12
```

```
Executing multiply with arguments (3, 4) and {}
multiply returned 12
12
```

The logger function demonstrates how higher-order functions can intercept and modify behavior, by printing messages before and after calling the original function. The wrapped_function maintains the original function's signature using *args and **kwargs.

Higher-order functions can also be used to compose new functions from existing ones. Function composition involves creating a new function by combining two or more functions. The following example illustrates the composition of two functions:

```
def compose(f, g):
    def composed(x):
        return f(g(x))
    return composed

def add_one(n):
    return n + 1

def times_two(n):
    return n * 2

composed_function = compose(add_one, times_two)
print(composed_function(5)) # Output will be 11
```

```
11
```

Within compose, the function composed takes an argument x, applies g to it, then applies f to the result of g(x). Consequently, composed_-function(5) computes times_two(5) to get 10, and then applies add_-one(10) to yield 11.

By incorporating higher-order functions into our coding practices, we not only enhance code modularity and reusability but also harness the powerful paradigms of functional programming in Python.

3.6 Common Higher-Order Functions in Python: map, filter, and reduce

Higher-order functions are a cornerstone of functional programming. Python provides several built-in higher-order functions, such as map(), filter(), and functools.reduce(). These functions allow for concise and expressive manipulation of data sequences. Understanding their usage can significantly enhance your proficiency in functional programming.

The map() function is used to apply a given function to all items in an input list (or any other iterable) and returns a map object (an iterator). The syntax is:

```
map(function, iterable)
```

For instance, consider the following example which squares numbers in a list:

```
def square(x):
    return x * x

numbers = [1, 2, 3, 4, 5]
squared_numbers = map(square, numbers)
print(list(squared_numbers))
```

The output will be:

```
[1, 4, 9, 16, 25]
```

It's important to note that map() does not return a list but a map object. To visualize the map object's contents, it must be converted to a list or another iterable.

The filter() function constructs an iterator from elements of an iterable for which a function returns true. The syntax is:

```
filter(function, iterable)
```

For example, filtering even numbers from a list can be achieved as follows:

```
def is_even(x):
    return x % 2 == 0

numbers = [1, 2, 3, 4, 5, 6]
even_numbers = filter(is_even, numbers)
print(list(even_numbers))
```

The output will be:

```
[2, 4, 6]
```

Like map(), filter() returns an iterator. Visualization requires conversion to a list.

The reduce() function from the functools module applies a binary function cumulatively to the items of a sequence, from left to right, so as to reduce the sequence to a single value. The syntax is:

```
from functools import reduce
reduce(function, iterable[, initializer])
```

An example usage is calculating the factorial of a number:

```
from functools import reduce

def multiply(x, y):
    return x * y

numbers = [1, 2, 3, 4, 5]
factorial = reduce(multiply, numbers)
print(factorial)
```

The output will be:

```
120
```

If an initializer is provided, it is placed before the items of the iterable during the computation, serving as a default when the iterable is empty.

Collectively, map(), filter(), and reduce() empower Python developers to write cleaner, more expressive code by abstracting common data manipulation patterns into higher-order functions. Employing these functions effectively can lead to more readable and maintainable code forms.

3.7 Partial Application and Currying

Partial application and currying are two powerful techniques in functional programming that enable the creation of new functions by fixing a number of arguments of a function. These concepts often result in more succinct and flexible code, making them valuable tools in a programmer's arsenal.

Partial application refers to the process of fixing a few arguments of a function, thereby producing another function of smaller arity. Currying, on the other hand, is the technique of transforming a function that takes multiple arguments into a sequence of functions, each taking a single argument.

Consider a function that accepts three arguments:

```
def add(a, b, c):
    return a + b + c
```

Using partial application, one can create a new function by fixing one or more of these arguments. The functools module in Python provides a convenient method called partial for this purpose.

```
from functools import partial

add_partial = partial(add, 1)
print(add_partial(2, 3)) # Output: 6
```

6

In the example above, partial(add, 1) creates a new function add_partial where the first argument is fixed to 1. The resulting function takes two arguments, which are then added to 1.

Currying takes this concept further by transforming the function into a series of nested functions. Each function returns another function that accepts the next argument. Here's a simple example to illustrate currying manually:

```
def curried_add(a):
    def add_b(b):
        def add_c(c):
            return a + b + c
        return add_c
    return add_b

add_curried = curried_add(1)(2)(3)
print(add_curried) # Output: 6
```

6

In this example, curried_add is a curried version of the add function. The function curried_add(1) returns a new function add_b, which when called with 2 returns another function add_c, and finally calling add_c with 3 yields the result 6.

Python's functools module doesn't directly support automatic currying, but third-party libraries such as toolz provide such functionality.

```
from toolz import curry

@curry
def add(a, b, c):
    return a + b + c

add_curried = add(1)(2)(3)
print(add_curried) # Output: 6
```

6

Here, the @curry decorator from toolz transforms the function add into a curried function. This allows calling add in a curried style as shown.

Partial application and currying are not mutually exclusive. Partial application can be seen as a specific instance of currying where multiple arguments are fixed in one step. Both techniques can be utilized to create more modular, reusable, and expressive code.

Consider another practical example where these techniques might be useful, such as configuring functions for different logging levels:

```
import logging

logging.basicConfig(level=logging.DEBUG)
log = logging.getLogger('example')

def log_message(level, message):
    log.log(level, message)

log_debug = partial(log_message, logging.DEBUG)
log_info = partial(log_message, logging.INFO)

log_debug("This is a debug message.") # Only logs at DEBUG level
log_info("This is an info message.") # Only logs at INFO level
```

In this example, partial application simplifies logging by creating specific functions for different logging levels from a generalized logging function.

Understanding and using partial application and currying can significantly improve the flexibility and readability of code. These techniques allow the creation of specialized functions with less boilerplate, facilitating cleaner and more modular code.

3.8 Decorators as Higher-Order Functions

Decorators in Python are a powerful tool that allows for the extension and modification of the behavior of functions or methods without changing their actual code. At their core, decorators leverage the concept of higher-order functions, where functions are passed as arguments and returned as results. This approach enables the addition of reusable functionality in a clean and efficient manner.

A decorator is a function that takes another function as an argument and returns a new function that typically extends or alters the behavior of the original function. One of the simplest forms of a decorator looks like this:

```
def my_decorator(func):
    def wrapper():
        print("Something before the function.")
        func()
        print("Something after the function.")
    return wrapper

def say_hello():
    print("Hello!")

decorated_say_hello = my_decorator(say_hello)
decorated_say_hello()
```

The execution of the decorated_say_hello function would yield:

```
Something before the function.
Hello!
Something after the function.
```

Here, the my_decorator function takes say_hello as its input and returns a new function wrapper that adds additional behavior (printing text before and after the original function call). This example demonstrates the essence of decorators, but Python provides syntactic sugar to make applying decorators more graceful and readable.

The use of the @ symbol, known as the decorator syntax, simplifies the process of applying decorators to functions:

```
@my_decorator
def say_hello():
    print("Hello!")

say_hello()
```

Decorator syntax is preferable as it directly associates the decoration with the function definition, improving code readability and maintainability.

Examples of Common Decorator Patterns

Logging Decorator

A common use case for decorators is logging function calls and their parameters:

```
def log_decorator(func):
    def wrapper(*args, **kwargs):
        print(f"Calling function {func.__name__} with arguments {args} and keyword
              arguments {kwargs}")
        result = func(*args, **kwargs)
        print(f"{func.__name__} returned {result}")
        return result
    return wrapper

@log_decorator
def add(a, b):
    return a + b

add(5, 3)
```

This will produce the following output:

```
Calling function add with arguments (5, 3) and keyword arguments {}
add returned 8
```

The log_decorator adds logging before and after the execution of the decorated function, providing detailed insights into function calls.

Access Control Decorator

Access control is another practical application of decorators, commonly used to restrict function usage based on user roles or permissions:

```
def access_control(role):
    def decorator(func):
        def wrapper(user, *args, **kwargs):
            if user.role == role:
                return func(user, *args, **kwargs)
            else:
                print(f"Access denied for user {user.name} with role {user.role}")
        return wrapper
    return decorator

@access_control('admin')
def delete_file(user, filename):
    print(f"File {filename} deleted by {user.name}")

class User:
    def __init__(self, name, role):
        self.name = name
        self.role = role

admin_user = User('Alice', 'admin')
regular_user = User('Bob', 'user')
```

```
delete_file(admin_user, 'file.txt')
delete_file(regular_user, 'file.txt')
```

This results in:

```
File file.txt deleted by Alice
Access denied for user Bob with role user
```

Here, access_control is a parameterized decorator that uses the role argument to determine if the user should be allowed to execute the delete_file function.

Decorator Chaining

Multiple decorators can be applied to a single function, a technique known as decorator chaining. This stack of decorators is applied from bottom to top, with each decorator adding an additional layer of behavior.

```
def decorator_one(func):
    def wrapper(*args, **kwargs):
        print("Decorator one is running")
        return func(*args, **kwargs)
    return wrapper

def decorator_two(func):
    def wrapper(*args, **kwargs):
        print("Decorator two is running")
        return func(*args, **kwargs)
    return wrapper

@decorator_one
@decorator_two
def target_function():
    print("The target function is running")

target_function()
```

This produces:

```
Decorator one is running
Decorator two is running
The target function is running
```

In this case, decorator_one wraps the function returned by decorator_two, illustrating how multiple decorators can stack their behaviors.

Decorators exemplify the power and elegance of higher-order functions in Python. They allow for the concise extension of function behavior, reinforce separation of concerns, and enhance code modularity. Understanding and effectively employing decorators can significantly improve the way functions and methods are designed and utilized in Python programs.

3.9 Combining Functions: Function Composition

In functional programming, function composition is a fundamental concept that allows the creation of complex functions by combining simpler ones. Function composition refers to the process of combining two or more functions to produce a new function. This technique is highly valued for its ability to build modular and reusable code. When functions are composed, the output of one function becomes the input of another, creating a pipeline of operations.

Consider the basic mathematical notation for function composition. Given two functions f and g, the composition of f and g, denoted as $(f \circ g)(x)$, is defined as:

$$(f \circ g)(x) = f(g(x))$$

In Python, we can implement function composition using higher-order functions. Let's explore this with a Python example.

```
def compose(f, g):
    return lambda x: f(g(x))

# Example Usage
def add_one(x):
    return x + 1

def square(x):
    return x * x

composed_function = compose(square, add_one)
result = composed_function(5)
print(result)
```

Here, we define a compose function that takes two functions f and g as arguments and returns a new function. This new function, when called with an argument x, first applies g to x and then applies f to the result of g(x).

When we use compose(square, add_one) to create composed_function, calling composed_function(5) effectively computes square(add_one(5)), resulting in 36. The output from the program will be:

For further understanding, consider an example involving real-world data processing, such as text transformation. Suppose we have the following functions:

```
def to_uppercase(text):
    return text.upper()

def remove_spaces(text):
    return text.replace(" ", "")

def reverse(text):
    return text[::-1]

# Composing functions
text_processor = compose(to_uppercase, compose(remove_spaces, reverse))

processed_text = text_processor("hello world")
print(processed_text)
```

In this case, text_processor is a composed function that first reverses the input text, removes spaces, and then converts the result to uppercase. Applying text_processor to the string "hello world" yields:

```
DLROWOLLEH
```

The example above demonstrates a more complex pipeline where the composed function is built gradually. The innermost composition compose(remove_spaces, reverse) creates a function that reverses a string and then removes spaces. This intermediate function is then composed with to_uppercase to form the complete text processing pipeline.

Further extending this concept, function composition can be made more flexible and scalable using decorators. Decorators in Python are higher-order functions that can be used to modify or extend the behavior of functions. Let's create a decorator for function composition:

```
def compose_decorator(f, g):
    def composed_function(x):
        return f(g(x))
    return composed_function

@compose_decorator
def foo(x):
    return x + 2

@compose_decorator
def bar(x):
    return x * 3

combined = foo(bar)
result = combined(4)
print(result)
```

The @compose_decorator syntax is syntactic sugar that applies the compose_decorator to foo and bar. Here, combined function is a composition of foo and bar. Applying combined to 4 computes foo(bar(4)), resulting in 14. This is printed as:

```
14
```

Through function composition, we achieve a high degree of modularity and reusability. Simple operations can be combined to create complex transformations without sacrificing code readability or maintainability. Function composition is particularly powerful in constructing data transformation pipelines in functional programming languages and paradigms.

Understanding and mastering this concept, alongside tools such as decorators, brings efficiency and elegance to Python programming. The examples illustrated have shown how to compose functions directly and via decorators, offering versatile methods to manipulate and extend functions seamlessly. This foundational knowledge of function composition prepares us to handle more intricate scenarios involving function manipulation and higher-order programming techniques.

3.10 Practical Examples of Higher-Order Functions

Higher-order functions are not merely theoretical constructs but are widely used in practical programming scenarios. Their ability to increase code modularity and reusability makes them indispensable. This section includes practical examples illustrating how higher-order functions can be applied to solve real-world problems efficiently.

Example 1: Sorting with Custom Key Functions

Sorting is a common task in programming, and Python's sorted function allows us to use custom key functions to determine the sort order. This flexibility is especially beneficial for complex data types.

Consider a list of dictionaries representing students, where each dictionary contains the student's name and grade. We can sort this list by grades using a higher-order function:

```
students = [
    {"name": "Alice", "grade": 85},
    {"name": "Bob", "grade": 95},
```

```
    {"name": "Charlie", "grade": 90}
]

# Function to extract the 'grade' value from the student dictionary
def get_grade(student):
    return student['grade']

# Sorting the list by grade using the get_grade function
sorted_students = sorted(students, key=get_grade)
print(sorted_students)
```

The output demonstrates the students sorted by their grades:

```
[{'name': 'Alice', 'grade': 85}, {'name': 'Charlie', 'grade': 90}, {'name': 'Bob', 'grade': 95}]
```

This example showcases how passing a function (get_grade) as an argument to another function (sorted) enables custom sorting logic.

Example 2: Using map to Apply a Function to a List

The map function applies a given function to all items in an input list (or any iterable). This results in a new list containing the results.

Suppose we have a list of numbers and want to compute the square of each number:

```
numbers = [1, 2, 3, 4, 5]

# Function to compute square of a number
def square(x):
    return x * x

# Applying the square function to each element in the numbers list
squared_numbers = list(map(square, numbers))
print(squared_numbers)
```

The output is a list of squared numbers:

```
[1, 4, 9, 16, 25]
```

By using map, we elevate the square function to operate over an entire list, simplifying our code structure.

Example 3: Filtering Data with filter

The filter function generates a new list comprising elements for which the provided function returns True. This is particularly useful for data extraction and cleaning tasks.

Imagine we need to filter out students who have passed a course, defined as having a grade above 70:

```
students = [
    {"name": "Alice", "grade": 85},
    {"name": "Bob", "grade": 65},
    {"name": "Charlie", "grade": 90}
```

```
]

# Function to check if a student has passed
def is_passed(student):
    return student['grade'] > 70

# Filtering students who have passed
passed_students = list(filter(is_passed, students))
print(passed_students)
```

The output contains only the students who passed:

```
[{'name': 'Alice', 'grade': 85}, {'name': 'Charlie', 'grade': 90}]
```

Through filter, we extract elements fulfilling a specific condition easily.

Example 4: Reducing a List with reduce

The reduce function, available from the functools module, applies a binary function cumulatively to the elements of an iterable, reducing them to a single value.

Assume we want to find the product of all elements in a list:

```
from functools import reduce

numbers = [1, 2, 3, 4, 5]

# Function to compute the product of two numbers
def multiply(x, y):
    return x * y

# Reducing the list to the product of all elements
product = reduce(multiply, numbers)
print(product)
```

The output is the product of all numbers in the list:

```
120
```

This example demonstrates the power of reduce for aggregating list elements using custom logic.

Example 5: Using sorted with a Lambda for Custom Sort Order

Besides named functions, lambda expressions offer a concise way to create functions for higher-order functions. Consider sorting the students by their names in reverse order:

```
students = [
    {"name": "Alice", "grade": 85},
    {"name": "Bob", "grade": 95},
    {"name": "Charlie", "grade": 90}
]

# Sorting the list by name in reverse order using a lambda function
sorted_by_name = sorted(students, key=lambda student: student['name'], reverse=
```

```
    True)
print(sorted_by_name)
```

The output is:

```
[{'name': 'Charlie', 'grade': 90}, {'name': 'Bob', 'grade': 95}, {'name': 'Alice', 'grade': 85}]
```

Using lambdas with sorted allows quick and flexible adjustments to sort criteria.

Through these examples, practical applications of higher-order functions are evident. They enhance readability, reusability, and abstract complex operations into manageable components.

Chapter 4

Pure Functions and Immutability

This chapter examines pure functions and the concept of immutability in functional programming. It defines pure functions, their benefits, and the importance of avoiding side effects. The chapter explores immutable data structures like tuples, namedtuples, and frozensets, and contrasts them with mutable objects. Additionally, it addresses implementing immutability in custom data structures, managing state without mutation, and avoiding global state. Practical examples further illustrate the utility and application of pure functions and immutability.

4.1 Defining Pure Functions

Pure functions are a foundational concept in functional programming. A pure function can be understood as a function that given the same input will always return the same output and does not have any observable side effects. This deterministic behavior is a critical attribute for enabling reasoning about code, and it provides the basis for many optimizations a compiler can perform.

To formally define a pure function, we can decompose its properties into two key characteristics:

- **Determinism**: For any given set of input values, the function must produce a consistent and predictable output. This property implies that the function's output depends solely on its input parameters without reliance on any external state or data.
- **Absence of Side Effects**: A pure function should not cause any side effects. This means the function does not alter any state or interact with the outside world (e.g., modifying global variables, performing I/O operations, or changing the values of mutable data structures passed to it). All transformations are achieved through the return value.

Consider the following Python function:

```
def add(a, b):
    return a + b
```

The add function is a textbook example of a pure function. It exhibits the following characteristics:

- **Deterministic**: Given the same inputs a and b, the function will always return a + b.
- **No Side Effects**: The function does not alter any state outside its scope. It only computes a value based on the provided inputs.

Contrast this with a function that exhibits side effects:

```
total = 0

def add_to_total(a):
    global total
    total += a
    return total
```

In this case, the add_to_total function is not pure due to the following reasons:

- **Non-deterministic**: Calling add_to_total with the same argument a can yield different results depending on the previous state of the total variable.
- **Side Effects**: The function modifies the global variable total, affecting the program's state beyond the local scope of the function.

Pure functions' deterministic nature lends itself well to unit testing. Since pure functions do not depend on any external state, their behavior can be isolated and tested with ease. For example, testing the add function requires only verifying that add(2, 3) consistently returns 5, regardless of any external conditions. Conversely, testing impure functions like add_to_total necessitates managing the external state, complicating the testing process.

The second property of pure functions, the absence of side effects, aligns with the principle of referential transparency. Referential transparency indicates that any expression can be replaced with its corresponding value without changing the program's behavior. Pure functions inherently satisfy this property, as their output depends solely on input parameters and does not impact the external environment.

In functional programming, pure functions form the basis for a predictable and maintainable codebase. Functions designed to be pure ensure that units of code are discrete, independent from external states, and thus can be composed to build complex logic without unintended interactions.

Throughout functional programming paradigms, the encouragement of pure functions facilitates greater reliability in software development. Transformations and computations within pure functions are straightforward, leading to clearer, less error-prone code. Additionally, the nature of pure functions supports parallelization and optimization, as the lack of side effects ensures no unintended interference when calculations are performed concurrently.

Examining pure functions from the perspective of immutability also reveals that pure functions often operate on immutable data structures. Since immutable structures cannot be altered, pure functions avoid the risk of changing shared state, further cementing their role within a functional programming ecosystem. Immutability reinforces the predictability and dependability of pure functions, as data transformation is clearly defined without side effects.

Even within languages that are not purely functional, understanding and utilizing pure functions can drastically improve code quality and maintainability. By adhering to principles underpinning pure functions — determinism and absence of side effects — developers can yield significant benefits, crafting code that is easier to reason about, test, and refactor.

4.2 Benefits of Using Pure Functions

Pure functions offer numerous advantages, particularly in the context of functional programming. These benefits extend to code clarity, debugging ease, testability, and optimization possibilities, amongst other aspects. By adhering to the principles of deterministic outputs and absence of side effects, pure functions contribute significantly to producing robust and maintainable code.

The primary benefits of using pure functions are discussed below with appropriate detail and illustrative examples:

Predictability

Pure functions ensure predictability in code. Because their outputs depend solely on the inputs without any side effects, the behavior of pure functions is consistent and can be relied upon to be the same for given inputs every time it is invoked. This determinism simplifies reasoning about the system and aids in understanding the code.

Consider the following example of a pure function:

```
def add(a, b):
    return a + b
```

Regardless of where and when $\mathrm{add}(2, 3)$ is called, it will always return 5. This predictability is foundational to reducing the mental load when working with complex systems.

Ease of Debugging

Since pure functions do not alter any state or have side effects, debugging them becomes more straightforward. When a bug is encountered, it can be isolated to specific functional blocks, knowing that no hidden state changes can mask or complicate the issue. This isolation drastically reduces the number of potential causes of errors.

Consider the contrast between the following snippets:

```
# Impure function with side effects
global_accumulator = 0

def mutating_add(a, b):
    global global_accumulator
    result = a + b
    global_accumulator += result
    return result

# Pure function
def pure_add(a, b):
    return a + b
```

The function mutating_add modifies the global state, making bugs harder to track. Conversely, pure_add provides a clean, side-effect-free operation, facilitating easier debugging.

Enhanced Testability

Pure functions are self-contained. This property simplifies testing, as test cases only need to consider the inputs and expected outputs. There is no need to set up specific states or clean up after tests, making unit testing straightforward and reliable.

Example of unit testing a pure function:

```
def test_add():
    assert add(2, 3) == 5
    assert add(0, 0) == 0
    assert add(-1, 1) == 0
```

These tests cover all essential cases and can be executed independently of any external state. Testing impure functions would require managing state before and after each test.

Referential Transparency

Referential transparency is a direct consequence of pure functions, allowing any call to a pure function to be replaced with its result without altering the program's behavior. This property significantly enhances code readability and maintainability.

For instance, in an expression:

```
result = add(2, 3) * add(4, 5)
```

The calls to add can be replaced with their results:

```
result = 5 * 9
```

This kind of substitution helps in understanding and optimizing code.

Facilitation of Parallel and Concurrent Programming

Pure functions are inherently thread-safe due to the absence of shared mutable state. When functions do not alter the state or have side effects, they can be executed in parallel without race conditions or other synchronization concerns. This facilitates the writing of concurrent and parallel programs, which is essential in leveraging multi-core processors.

Improved Optimization Opportunities

Compilers and interpreters can employ various optimization strategies for pure functions, including memoization (caching results of function calls based on arguments). This optimization further enhances the performance of a program by avoiding repetitive computation for the same inputs.

Memoization example:

```
from functools import lru_cache

@lru_cache(maxsize=None)
def add(a, b):
    return a + b
```

By using the @lru_cache decorator, repetitive calls to the add function with the same arguments are optimized.

Enhanced Composability

Since pure functions do not depend on or alter external states, they can be composed together seamlessly to build more complex operations. This composability leads to more modular and reusable code.

Example of function composition:

```
def square(x):
    return x * x

def add_and_square(a, b):
    return square(add(a, b))
```

By combining add and square, complex computations can be constructed elegantly and predictably.

The benefits of using pure functions in functional programming directly contribute to producing high-quality, maintainable, and efficient codebases. These advantages make pure functions a cornerstone of functional programming paradigms.

4.3 Identifying and Avoiding Side Effects

Pure functions are a cornerstone of functional programming and an essential criterion is their absence of side effects. Understanding side effects involves recognizing what constitutes a side effect and how to avoid them to maintain the purity of functions.

A side effect is any observable effect of a function other than returning a value. These effects can alter the state outside their local environment or interact with external entities, such as modifying global variables, writing to a database, or changing the input argument. Side effects can make functions unpredictable, diminishing the reliability and maintainability of code.

Consider the following example of a function with a side effect:

```
global_counter = 0

def increment_counter(value):
    global global_counter
    global_counter += value
    return global_counter
```

Above, the function increment_counter uses the global variable global_counter, modifying its value and creating a side effect. Since the function changes the global state, it is not pure. The unpredictability arises because the function's output depends not only on its input but also on the global state, which can be altered by any part of the program.

To avoid side effects, a function should produce the same output solely dependent on its input parameters, without altering any external state. Here's how to refactor the previous function to ensure it is pure:

```
def increment_counter_pure(counter, value):
    return counter + value
```

In this pure version, the function increment_counter_pure does not rely on or modify any external variables. It returns a new counter value based on the given inputs without producing any side effects.

Another common source of side effects in Python functions is mutating the arguments passed to them, especially mutable data structures such as lists or dictionaries. For example:

```
def append_item(item_list, item):
    item_list.append(item)
```

Here, append_item modifies the input list item_list, thus causing a side effect. This can be problematic as any other part of the program holding a reference to the original list will witness these changes. To avoid this, work with and return new copies of data structures instead:

```
def append_item_pure(item_list, item):
    return item_list + [item]
```

This version, append_item_pure, avoids mutating the input list. Instead, it returns a new list by concatenating the input list with a new list containing the item.

Side effects are not only limited to data changes; interacting with input/output (I/O) operations can also introduce side effects:

```
def print_message(message):
    print(message)
```

```
Hello, World!
```

The print_message function affects the standard output, a global state, thus carrying side effects. While unavoidable in some contexts, it is beneficial to minimize and control I/O operations. These can be managed separately to maintain the purity of core computational functions.

Another aspect is dealing with exceptions and logging, which can also introduce side effects. Consider:

```
import logging

def divide(a, b):
    try:
        return a / b
    except ZeroDivisionError as e:
        logging.error("Division by zero: %s", e)
```

Logging and exception handling impact the flow by performing operations beyond simply returning a value. Segregating these into pure and impure parts simplifies testing and reasoning.

Finally, returning to the example of managing states without mutation, one can use immutable data structures wherever possible:

```
def update_point(point, dx, dy):
    x, y = point
    return (x + dx, y + dy)
```

The function update_point operates on tuples, inherently immutable, ensuring state changes are confined within the function scope, thereby maintaining the predictability and reliability of pure functions.

Eliminating side effects transforms functions into self-contained units with predictable behavior, crucial for functional programming. These principles enhance code maintainability, allowing developers to reason about and test their code with greater confidence.

4.4 Immutability: Concepts and Importance

Immutability is a fundamental concept in functional programming that refers to the inability to alter data after its creation. Once an immutable object is instantiated, its state cannot be modified. This property has significant implications for writing clean, predictable code, particularly in concurrent and parallel programming environments. Understanding immutability and its importance is crucial for effective functional programming in Python.

Immutability offers several advantages:

- **Predictability**: As immutable data cannot be changed, it is easier to reason about program behavior.
- **Thread Safety**: Immutable objects are inherently thread-safe, as concurrent operations will not alter their state.
- **Debugging and Testing**: Immutable structures simplify debugging and testing because the state remains consistent and does not change unexpectedly.

To illustrate these benefits, consider the following example:

```
# Mutable List Example
numbers = [1, 2, 3, 4, 5]
def append_number(num_list, num):
    num_list.append(num)
    return num_list

new_numbers = append_number(numbers, 6)
print(new_numbers)
print(numbers)
```

```
Output:
[1, 2, 3, 4, 5, 6]
[1, 2, 3, 4, 5, 6]
```

The above code demonstrates how the function append_number mutates the original list numbers. This action might lead to unintended side effects if numbers is accessed in other parts of the code, potentially causing bugs that are difficult to trace. By adopting immutability, such side effects can be avoided.

Now, consider an immutable approach using tuples:

```
# Immutable Tuple Example
numbers = (1, 2, 3, 4, 5)
```

```
def add_number(num_tuple, num):
    return num_tuple + (num,)

new_numbers = add_number(numbers, 6)
print(new_numbers)
print(numbers)
```

```
Output:
(1, 2, 3, 4, 5, 6)
(1, 2, 3, 4, 5)
```

In this example, the function add_number creates a new tuple by concatenating the existing tuple with the new number. The original numbers tuple remains unchanged. Such immutability ensures that the function does not produce side effects, preserving the original data's integrity.

To ensure immutability in custom data structures, one can define classes where the instance variables are not allowed to change once set. This can be enforced using properties without setters or by using the namedtuple factory function from the collections module:

```
from collections import namedtuple

Point = namedtuple('Point', ['x', 'y'])
point = Point(1, 2)
print(point)

# Trying to change the value will raise an AttributeError
try:
    point.x = 3
except AttributeError as e:
    print(e)
```

```
Output:
Point(x=1, y=2)
can't set attribute
```

In addition to tuples and namedtuple, Python provides other immutable data structures such as frozenset, which is an immutable version of set.

```
# Immutable frozenset Example
fruit_set = frozenset(['apple', 'banana', 'cherry'])
print(fruit_set)

# Attempting to add an element will raise an AttributeError
try:
    fruit_set.add('date')
except AttributeError as e:
    print(e)
```

```
Output:
frozenset({'banana', 'apple', 'cherry'})
'frozenset' object has no attribute 'add'
```

Immutability's role extends beyond simply avoiding side effects. It fundamentally impacts how state and data flow are managed in a program. In functional programming, functions are expected to be pure, which means their output depends only on their input parameters and they perform no side effects. Immutability reinforces this purity by ensuring that input data remains unaltered.

An important concept related to immutability is persistent data structures. These are data structures that preserve the previous version of themselves when modified, thus providing immutable updates. This is crucial for maintaining consistent states across time without sacrificing performance.

In practical applications, immutability may involve trade-offs between performance and safety. While immutable objects guarantee predictability and thread safety, creating new copies of data can incur additional memory and processing overhead. Thus, understanding when and how to effectively use immutability is essential for writing efficient and robust functional programs.

Through practice and continual application of immutability principles, programmers can achieve more reliable software, with fewer hidden bugs and improved maintainability.

4.5 Immutable Data Structures in Python: Tuples, NamedTuples, and frozenset

Immutable data structures are fundamental in functional programming as they ensure that once a data structure is instantiated, it cannot be altered. This leads to predictable and robust code. In Python, common immutable data structures include tuples, namedtuples, and frozenset.

Tuples are a simple and efficient way to store multiple items in a single variable. Unlike lists, tuples cannot be modified after their creation. Tuples are created by placing a sequence of values separated by commas within parentheses.

```
# Example of creating a tuple
fruits = ('apple', 'banana', 'cherry')
```

Accessing elements in a tuple is similar to lists, using zero-based indexing:

```
print(fruits[0]) # Output: 'apple'
```

Attempting to change an element of the tuple will result in an error:

```
fruits[0] = 'orange' # Raises a TypeError
```

Because tuples are immutable, they can be used as keys in dictionaries, whereas lists cannot.

Namedtuples provide a way to give more context to the elements of a tuple and make the code more readable. They are defined in the collections module. Namedtuples allow accessing fields by name instead of index position, improving readability and maintainability.

```
from collections import namedtuple

# Define namedtuple
Point = namedtuple('Point', ['x', 'y'])

# Create an instance of Point
p = Point(10, 20)

# Access fields by name
print(p.x) # Output: 10
print(p.y) # Output: 20
```

Namedtuples retain the immutability characteristic of tuples, ensuring that once an instance is created, its fields cannot be altered.

Frozenset is the immutable variant of the set data structure. Sets are collections of unique elements, and the frozenset type provides the same functionality but disallows changes after creation. This immutability is beneficial in ensuring that sets remain constant.

```
# Create a frozenset
fs = frozenset([1, 2, 3, 4])

# Check membership
print(2 in fs) # Output: True

# Again, attempting to modify a frozenset will raise an error
fs.add(5) # Raises an AttributeError
```

Like tuples, frozensets can be used as dictionary keys and elements of other sets, promoting their use in hash-based collections.

The utilization of these immutable data structures promotes code predictability and reduces the likelihood of accidental side-effects. Tuples, namedtuples, and frozenset are powerful tools in the arsenal of Python programmers aiming to write functional, clean, and reliable code.

4.6 Comparing Mutable and Immutable Objects

In functional programming, understanding the distinction between mutable and immutable objects is paramount. The distinction significantly impacts how data can be managed, manipulated, and preserved across the lifecycle of a program. Python, being a versatile programming language, supports both mutable and immutable objects, which we'll delve into in this section.

Mutable Objects are those whose state or content can be modified after they are created. Common examples of mutable data structures in Python include lists, dictionaries, and sets. The primary benefit of mutable objects is their flexibility; however, this comes with potential pitfalls such as unintended side effects, increased complexity in state management, and challenges in concurrent computing scenarios.

Consider the following Python code that demonstrates mutability:

```
# Mutable object example: List
mutable_list = [1, 2, 3]
mutable_list[0] = 10 # Modifies the first element of the list
mutable_list.append(4) # Appends an element to the list
print(mutable_list)
```

The output of this code will illustrate the changes made to the list:

```
[10, 2, 3, 4]
```

In this case, each operation—whether it is altering an existing element or appending a new one—affects the state of the mutable_list object. This type of mutability can lead to unpredictable states if not properly managed, especially in complex applications.

On the other hand, **Immutable Objects** are those whose state cannot be altered once they are created. Python's primary immutable data types include tuples, strings, and frozensets. The primary benefits of immutable objects are their inherent thread safety, simplicity in state management, and guarantee that the object's state will remain constant throughout its lifetime.

Consider the following Python code that demonstrates immutability:

```
# Immutable object example: Tuple
```

```
immutable_tuple = (1, 2, 3)
# Attempting to modify an element will raise an error:
try:
    immutable_tuple[0] = 10
except TypeError as e:
    print(e)

# Creating a new tuple based on existing one
new_tuple = immutable_tuple + (4,)
print(immutable_tuple)
print(new_tuple)
```

The output of this code highlights the immutability of tuples:

```
'tuple' object does not support item assignment
(1, 2, 3)
(1, 2, 3, 4)
```

When attempting to modify an element of immutable_tuple, Python raises a TypeError, indicating that the assignment operation is not allowed. Instead, creating a new tuple by concatenating the existing tuple with another tuple results in a new object, thus preserving the original immutable_tuple.

Comparing mutable and immutable objects reveals several critical implications:

1. **State changes**: - Mutable: Direct modification of the object is allowed. - Immutable: A new object needs to be created to represent any change, leaving the original object unchanged.

2. **Memory usage**: - Mutable: Potentially more efficient in terms of memory, as modifications happen in place. - Immutable: Typically requires additional memory allocation for creating new objects. However, Python employs optimizations such as interning for small integers and strings to mitigate this overhead.

3. **Concurrency**: - Mutable: Managing access to mutable objects in multi-threaded or asynchronous environments increases complexity and risk of race conditions. - Immutable: Naturally thread-safe, as their state cannot change after creation, ensuring consistency in concurrent scenarios.

4. **Function Arguments**: - Mutable: Passing a mutable object as a function argument can lead to unintended side effects, as the called function may alter the original object. - Immutable: Passing an immutable object as a function argument is safe from side effects, as the object's state cannot be altered by the called function.

5. **Coding Paradigms**: - Mutable: More aligned with imperative programming paradigms where state changes are frequent. - Immutable:

Better suited for functional programming paradigms that emphasize immutability and encourage pure functions.

Understanding these differences is fundamental for a Python programmer, especially when writing functional programming style code. Choosing between mutable and immutable objects can significantly affect the program's maintainability, performance, and correctness. When designing systems, it is essential to weigh the trade-offs and select the appropriate data structures that align with the desired properties and constraints of the application.

4.7 Implementing Immutability in Custom Data Structures

Implementing immutability in custom data structures necessitates careful consideration of design principles and an understanding of Python's built-in mechanisms for maintaining immutability. Custom data structures should prevent any modification once they are instantiated, ensuring that their state remains constant. This section delves into methods for establishing immutability in user-defined classes, leveraging Python's syntactic constructs and libraries.

In Python, the primary method to create immutable objects is by leveraging the dataclasses module combined with certain strategies to prevent modification. To illustrate these concepts, consider the following steps to create an immutable data structure.

```
from dataclasses import dataclass

@dataclass(frozen=True)
class ImmutablePoint:
    x: float
    y: float
```

The dataclass decorator with the frozen=True parameter is a powerful tool to enforce immutability. This approach leverages Python's built-in functionality to automatically generate a class with initialized fields. The frozen parameter ensures all attributes are read-only after instantiation, raising an AttributeError if any modification attempt occurs.

```
point = ImmutablePoint(1.0, 2.0)
point.x = 3.0
```

The above code results in an error:

```
Traceback (most recent call last):
  File "<stdin>", line 1, in <module>
dataclasses.FrozenInstanceError: cannot assign to field 'x'
```

Python's dataclass with frozen=True is inherently limited to basic use cases. More complex scenarios require explicit control over attribute access and mutation. Consider incorporating custom methods and encapsulation to achieve this.

```
class ImmutableRectangle:
    def __init__(self, length, width):
        self._length = length
        self._width = width

    @property
    def length(self):
        return self._length

    @property
    def width(self):
        return self._width

    def __setattr__(self, key, value):
        if hasattr(self, key):
            raise AttributeError(f"{key} is immutable")
        super().__setattr__(key, value)
```

The custom ImmutableRectangle class employs properties to encapsulate access to its attributes, preventing direct modification. The __setattr__ method is overridden to allow setting attributes only during initialization, effectively freezing their state. Any attempt to modify the attributes thereafter results in an exception.

```
rectangle = ImmutableRectangle(10, 5)
rectangle.length
# Output: 10
rectangle.width
# Output: 5

rectangle.length = 15
```

The code snippet above results in an error:

```
Traceback (most recent call last):
  File "<stdin>", line 1, in <module>
AttributeError: length is immutable
```

Further strengthening immutability can be achieved using the collections.namedtuple along with subclassing to introduce custom behavior while keeping mutability constraints.

```
from collections import namedtuple

class ImmutableShape(namedtuple('Shape', 'sides angles')):
    __slots__ = ()
    def __new__(cls, sides, angles):
        return super(ImmutableShape, cls).__new__(cls, sides, angles)
```

By using namedtuple, we define a lightweight, immutable data structure called ImmutableShape. This structure cannot be altered once instantiated, while still allowing the benefit of subclassing to incorporate additional methods or validation.

```
shape = ImmutableShape(4, [90, 90, 90, 90])
shape.sides
# Output: 4
shape.angles
# Output: [90, 90, 90, 90]

shape.sides = 5
```

Attempting to reassign the sides attribute results in the following error:

```
Traceback (most recent call last):
  File "<stdin>", line 1, in <module>
AttributeError: can't set attribute
```

Moreover, the __slots__ attribute in ImmutableShape prevents the creation of instance dictionaries, thereby ensuring efficient memory usage and further reinforcing immutability by limiting the addition of new attributes.

Incorporating immutability within custom data structures promotes robustness and consistency in program state management. By preventing inadvertent state changes, developers can avert a variety of logical errors, enhancing predictability and enforceability of business rules set within the application.

4.8 Managing State without Mutation

In functional programming, an often challenging paradigm shift lies in managing state without resorting to mutable constructs. Unlike imperative programming, where state is frequently mutated in place, functional programming promotes immutability. This ensures that functions remain pure, contributing to predictable and verifiable code.

A principal strategy in managing state without mutation is to leverage immutable data structures. By utilizing such structures, any alteration in state results in the creation of a new state rather than modifying the existing one. This makes it possible to precisely track changes and maintain the integrity of data.

Consider the following Python code, which demonstrates state management using immutable data structures:

```
from typing import Tuple
```

```
def increment_counter(counter: Tuple[int]) -> Tuple[int]:
    return (counter[0] + 1,)

# Initial state
initial_counter = (0,)

# Derived state after increment
new_counter = increment_counter(initial_counter)

print(f"Initial Counter: {initial_counter}") # Output: (0,)
print(f"New Counter: {new_counter}") # Output: (1,)
```

In the example above, the state is represented by a tuple, an immutable data structure. Invoking the increment_counter function does not alter the original initial_counter. Instead, it produces a new tuple representing the updated state. This approach adheres to the principles of functional programming, maintaining immutability and ensuring that state transitions are explicit and traceable.

Another method involves the use of functional constructs like closures. Closures can capture and carry state through function calls without direct mutation. The following example illustrates how closures can be utilized:

```
def make_counter():
    counter = 0

    def increment():
        nonlocal counter
        counter += 1
        return counter

    return increment

counter = make_counter()
print(counter()) # Output: 1
print(counter()) # Output: 2
print(counter()) # Output: 3
```

Here, the make_counter function defines a local variable counter and an increment function. The increment function captures the counter variable from its enclosing scope, updating and returning its value without exposing direct mutation to the outside. The nonlocal keyword is employed to indicate that counter belongs to the enclosing lexical scope, achieving state management without external mutation.

Functional programming also emphasizes the importance of higher-order functions and persistent data structures to handle state effectively. Persistent data structures offer versioned snapshots of data, allowing each version to coexist safely with others.

Consider the following example using the pyrsistent library:

```
from pyrsistent import pvector

# Initial state
vec = pvector([0, 1, 2])

# Create a new state
new_vec = vec.set(1, 10)

print(f"Original Vector: {vec}") # Output: pvector([0, 1, 2])
print(f"New Vector: {new_vec}") # Output: pvector([0, 10, 2])
```

The pyrsistent library provides persistent data structures like pvector, which facilitate immutability. Here, the set method does not modify the original vector but creates a new vector with the specified change, ensuring that the original state remains intact.

Furthermore, managing state in an application often requires handling more complex scenarios. State monads, an advanced functional programming technique, encapsulate stateful computations within a functional framework, maintaining purity and immutability. Although Python does not natively support monads as directly as languages like Haskell, similar concepts can be modeled using classes or decorators to simulate behavior.

Consider the following example:

```
class StateMonad:
    def __init__(self, value, state):
        self.value = value
        self.state = state

    def fmap(self, func):
        new_value, new_state = func(self.value, self.state)
        return StateMonad(new_value, new_state)

    def __repr__(self):
        return f"StateMonad(value={self.value}, state={self.state})"

def increment(value, state):
    return (value + 1, state + 1)

initial_state = StateMonad(0, 0)
new_state = initial_state.fmap(increment).fmap(increment)

print(initial_state) # Output: StateMonad(value=0, state=0)
print(new_state) # Output: StateMonad(value=2, state=2)
```

In this example, the StateMonad class encapsulates the value and state. The fmap method applies a function, producing a new state monad without altering the original. This allows for chaining stateful computations while maintaining immutability.

Employing these functional techniques enables effective state management, fostering code that is robust and free from unintended side effects. This ensures consistency and predictability in functional programming, aligning with its core principles.

4.9 Avoiding Global State

In functional programming, global state is a source of side effects that can significantly complicate the reasoning and debugging of programs. Global state refers to variables or states that are accessible from any part of the code, leading to dependencies that can result in unintended interactions, making the behavior of functions unpredictable. The elimination of global state contributes to the purity of functions, thereby enhancing modularity, testability, and clarity of the code. In Python, several strategies can be employed to avoid the use of global state effectively.

A common way to inadvertently introduce global state is through the use of global variables. Consider the following example:

```
counter = 0

def increment():
    global counter
    counter += 1
    return counter

print(increment()) # Output: 1
print(increment()) # Output: 2
```

In this example, the function increment modifies the global state variable counter. Such modification leads to side effects because the function's behavior depends on the global variable's current state. To avoid this, one can design functions to be pure by ensuring they do not rely on or modify global state.

Passing State as Parameters

One effective approach is to pass the state as parameters and return the new state. This technique ensures that functions are stateless and only produce outputs based on their inputs:

```
def increment(counter):
    return counter + 1

counter = 0
counter = increment(counter) # Output: 1
counter = increment(counter) # Output: 2
```

By explicitly passing the state, the function increment becomes pure, facilitating a more predictable and testable function without side effects.

Encapsulation and Closures

Encapsulation using closures is another strategy. Closures allow functions to enclose variables within their scope, without exposing them as global:

```
def counter_closure():
    counter = 0

    def increment():
        nonlocal counter
        counter += 1
        return counter

    return increment

increment = counter_closure()
print(increment()) # Output: 1
print(increment()) # Output: 2
```

In this example, the variable counter is encapsulated within the closure's scope, eliminating the need for a global variable, while retaining the state in a controlled manner.

Using Immutable Data Structures

Employing immutable data structures further helps in avoiding global state. Immutable objects, such as tuples or namedtuples, ensure that once created, their state cannot be altered. This immutability property prevents inadvertent side effects:

```
from collections import namedtuple

Point = namedtuple('Point', ['x', 'y'])

def move_point(point, dx, dy):
    return Point(point.x + dx, point.y + dy)

point = Point(0, 0)
point = move_point(point, 5, 3)
```

In the above code, the function move_point returns a new Point instance, preserving the immutability of the original Point object.

Functional Programming Patterns

Standard functional programming patterns, such as monads, can effectively encapsulate state. However, in Python, simpler constructs such as higher-order functions and the previously mentioned methods are typically sufficient. Generators and comprehensions also offer ways to work with sequences without maintaining global state.

For example, using a generator to produce a sequence of numbers:

```
def counter_generator():
    counter = 0
    while True:
        yield counter
        counter += 1

counter_gen = counter_generator()
print(next(counter_gen)) # Output: 0
print(next(counter_gen)) # Output: 1
```

Avoiding Dependency on Global State

In practice, avoiding global state requires deliberate design choices. Functions and methods should be designed to accept all necessary data as arguments and return new data, rather than altering shared states. When designing class-based systems, instance variables should be used instead of class variables unless the latter are strictly immutable.

For instance, the use of instance variables instead of global or class variables in a class:

```
class Counter:
    def __init__(self):
        self.counter = 0

    def increment(self):
        self.counter += 1
        return self.counter

counter_instance = Counter()
print(counter_instance.increment()) # Output: 1
print(counter_instance.increment()) # Output: 2
```

In this code, each Counter instance maintains its own state, avoiding the complications of global state.

Conclusion

By adhering to the principles of functional programming and avoiding the pitfalls of global state, one can create more robust, maintainable, and testable code. The methods outlined provide a diverse toolkit for managing state locally, ensuring that functions remain pure and predictable.

4.10 Practical Examples of Pure Functions and Immutability

To solidify the understanding of pure functions and immutability in functional programming, this section provides practical examples. These examples demonstrate the principles and highlight the advantages of adopting a functional approach.

Consider a simple mathematical function that adds two numbers. This pure function can be defined as follows:

```
def add(a, b):
    return a + b
```

The function add is pure because it always produces the same output for the same inputs, and it causes no side effects. To demonstrate the immutability aspect, consider the following example using immutable tuples:

```
def swap_elements(tup):
    return (tup[1], tup[0])

original_tuple = (1, 2)
swapped_tuple = swap_elements(original_tuple)
print(original_tuple) # Output: (1, 2)
print(swapped_tuple) # Output: (2, 1)
```

```
(1, 2)
(2, 1)
```

In this case, the original_tuple remains unchanged, showcasing immutability. The swap_elements function operates purely, generating a new tuple rather than modifying the original one.

Next, let's explore a pure function that processes a list of numbers by doubling each element:

```
def double_elements(numbers):
    return [x * 2 for x in numbers]

original_list = [1, 2, 3]
doubled_list = double_elements(original_list)
print(original_list) # Output: [1, 2, 3]
print(doubled_list) # Output: [2, 4, 6]
```

```
[1, 2, 3]
[2, 4, 6]
```

The function double_elements is pure, as it computes a new list and does not alter the original_list. This illustrates how pure functions can manipulate data without side effects, maintaining immutability.

Moreover, consider a scenario in which we need to update an element within an immutable data structure. For instance, using namedtuple:

```
from collections import namedtuple

Person = namedtuple('Person', ['name', 'age'])

def increment_age(person):
    return person._replace(age=person.age + 1)

original_person = Person(name='Alice', age=30)
older_person = increment_age(original_person)
print(original_person) # Output: Person(name='Alice', age=30)
print(older_person) # Output: Person(name='Alice', age=31)
```

```
Person(name='Alice', age=30)
Person(name='Alice', age=31)
```

Using the _replace method of namedtuple, increment_age generates a new Person instance while the original_person remains unchanged. This example underscores how immutability paired with pure functions benefits functional programming.

For handling more complex transformations, let's navigate an example involving frozenset for immutable sets. Assume we are tasked with ensuring no duplicates in a collection of data:

```
def unique_elements(items):
    return frozenset(items)

original_items = [1, 2, 2, 3, 4, 4, 5]
unique_items = unique_elements(original_items)
print(original_items) # Output: [1, 2, 2, 3, 4, 4, 5]
print(unique_items) # Output: frozenset({1, 2, 3, 4, 5})
```

```
[1, 2, 2, 3, 4, 4, 5]
frozenset({1, 2, 3, 4, 5})
```

The function unique_elements creates a frozenset, ensuring elements' uniqueness while preserving immutability. The original_items list remains untarnished, exemplifying the core functional programming tenet.

Incorporating these principles into a more sophisticated example, consider implementing a recursive factorial function, ensuring it remains pure:

```
def factorial(n):
    if n == 0:
        return 1
    else:
        return n * factorial(n-1)

result = factorial(5)
print(result) # Output: 120
```

This recursive definition of factorial manifests purity: it recalls itself with decremented values until the base case (0) is met, producing consistent outputs for given inputs without side effects.

Finally, addressing the concept of immutability in custom data structures, consider a class-based approach:

```
class ImmutablePoint:
    def __init__(self, x, y):
        self._x = x
        self._y = y

    @property
    def x(self):
        return self._x

    @property
    def y(self):
        return self._y

    def move(self, dx, dy):
        return ImmutablePoint(self._x + dx, self._y + dy)

point = ImmutablePoint(2, 3)
moved_point = point.move(1, -1)
print((point.x, point.y)) # Output: (2, 3)
print((moved_point.x, moved_point.y)) # Output: (3, 2)
```

```
(2, 3)
(3, 2)
```

The ImmutablePoint class exemplifies how immutability can be enforced in custom objects. The move method returns a new instance rather than modifying the existing one. As a result, the original point retains its values, adhering to immutability principles.

These examples collectively demonstrate how pure functions and immutability can be effectively utilized within Python to maintain consistent and predictable behavior, aligning with functional programming paradigms.

Chapter 5

Recursion and Recursive Data Structures

This chapter delves into recursion and recursive data structures, starting with the basics of defining and understanding recursion. It explains the concepts of base and recursive cases, along with the benefits and drawbacks of recursive approaches. The chapter discusses tail recursion and optimization techniques, explores common recursive data structures like lists, trees, and graphs, and illustrates how to implement recursive algorithms in Python. Practical problems like factorial, Fibonacci, and Hanoi are covered, as well as advanced techniques such as memoization and dynamic programming.

5.1 Introduction to Recursion

Recursion is a fundamental concept in computer science and functional programming. It involves a function calling itself directly or indirectly, allowing problems to be solved in a naturally divide-and-conquer manner. In essence, recursion breaks a problem down into smaller, more manageable sub-problems that resemble the original problem. This concept underpins many algorithms and data structures and is essential for writing clear, elegant, and efficient code.

To understand recursion, consider the process of defining functions.

In a non-recursive (iterative) approach, a function executes a series of steps to reach a goal. However, in recursion, a function solves a portion of the problem and then makes a call to itself to address the remaining part. The key elements in recursion are the base case and the recursive case. The base case provides a means to terminate the recursion, preventing it from continuing indefinitely. The recursive case decomposes the problem and makes the recurrent function call.

An example often cited to illustrate recursion is the computation of factorial numbers. The factorial of a non-negative integer n, denoted as $n!$, is the product of all positive integers less than or equal to n. This can be expressed recursively as:

$$n! = \begin{cases} 1 & \text{if } n = 0 \\ n \times (n-1)! & \text{if } n > 0 \end{cases}$$

This definition consists of a base case ($0! = 1$) and a recursive case ($n! = n \times (n-1)!$). The recursive case reduces the problem size progressively until the base case is reached, halting the recursion.

Here is a Python implementation of the factorial function using recursion:

```
def factorial(n):
    if n == 0:
        return 1
    else:
        return n * factorial(n-1)
```

When 'factorial(5)' is called, it performs a series of recursive calls:

```
factorial(5)
-> 5 * factorial(4)
  -> 4 * factorial(3)
    -> 3 * factorial(2)
      -> 2 * factorial(1)
        -> 1 * factorial(0)
          -> 1
```

Each recursive step decrements the argument 'n' until it reaches 0, invoking the base case and returning 1. The intermediate results are then multiplied as the recursion unwinds, resulting in '5 * 4 * 3 * 2 * 1 * 1 = 120'.

Another quintessential example of recursion is generating Fibonacci numbers. The Fibonacci sequence is defined by the recurrence relation:

$$F(n) = \begin{cases} 0 & \text{if } n = 0 \\ 1 & \text{if } n = 1 \\ F(n-1) + F(n-2) & \text{if } n > 1 \end{cases}$$

Here is a Python implementation of the Fibonacci function using recursion:

```
def fibonacci(n):
    if n == 0:
        return 0
    elif n == 1:
        return 1
    else:
        return fibonacci(n-1) + fibonacci(n-2)
```

Calling 'fibonacci(5)' results in a series of nested calls:

```
fibonacci(5)
-> fibonacci(4) + fibonacci(3)
  -> (fibonacci(3) + fibonacci(2)) + (fibonacci(2) + fibonacci(1))
    -> ((fibonacci(2) + fibonacci(1)) + (fibonacci(1) + fibonacci(0))) + ((fibonacci(1) + fibonacci(0)) + 1)
      -> (((fibonacci(1) + fibonacci(0)) + 1) + (1 + 0)) + ((1 + 0) + 1)
        -> (((1 + 0) + 1) + (1 + 0)) + ((1 + 0) + 1)
```

Recursive solutions often offer clarity and simplicity in expressing algorithms, especially when the problem has an inherent recursive structure. However, they can also lead to performance issues due to the overhead of numerous function calls and possible repeated calculations, such as in the naive Fibonacci implementation.

Understanding the principles of recursion and recognizing when it is appropriate are critical skills in functional programming. Mastering recursion enables the construction of sophisticated algorithms and data structures that are both efficient and intuitive.

5.2 Understanding the Base Case and Recursive Case

The cornerstone of any recursive function lies in the careful and precise definition of its base case and recursive case. These cases collectively enable a function to execute correctly and efficiently.

Base Case: A base case is a condition under which the recursive function returns a value without making any further recursive calls. It is the simplest, smallest instance of the problem, and acts as a terminating condition for the recursion. Absence of a properly defined base case often results in infinite recursion, causing a stack overflow.

Recursive Case: In the recursive case, the function calls itself with a subset or a reduction of the original problem. This reduction continues until it matches the base case. Ensuring each recursive call brings the problem closer to the base case is critical in recursive function design.

Consider the classic example of computing the factorial of a non-negative integer n:

```
def factorial(n):
    if n == 0: # Base case
        return 1
    else: # Recursive case
        return n * factorial(n - 1)
```

Here, $\text{factorial}(0) = 1$ is the base case. For any $n > 0$, the function makes a recursive call to factorial(n - 1), thereby progressively reducing the problem until n reaches 0.

To further illustrate, let's define a function to compute the n-th Fibonacci number:

```
def fibonacci(n):
    if n == 0: # Base case
        return 0
    elif n == 1: # Base case
        return 1
    else: # Recursive case
        return fibonacci(n - 1) + fibonacci(n - 2)
```

The base cases here are $\text{fibonacci}(0) = 0$ and $\text{fibonacci}(1) = 1$. For $n > 1$, the function recursively calls itself to compute both fibonacci(n - 1) and fibonacci(n - 2).

Identifying the base and recursive cases may sometimes require deeper analysis, especially for more complex algorithms. Take for example the classic Merge Sort algorithm, which uses the principle of divide and conquer—dividing a list into sublists until single elements (base case) are reached, and then merging them back into a sorted list (recursive case):

```
def merge_sort(arr):
    if len(arr) <= 1: # Base case
        return arr
    mid = len(arr) // 2
    left_half = merge_sort(arr[:mid]) # Recursive case
    right_half = merge_sort(arr[mid:]) # Recursive case
    return merge(left_half, right_half)

def merge(left, right):
    result = []
    i = j = 0
    while i < len(left) and j < len(right):
        if left[i] < right[j]:
```

```
            result.append(left[i])
            i += 1
        else:
            result.append(right[j])
            j += 1
    result.extend(left[i:])
    result.extend(right[j:])
    return result
```

The merge_sort function's base case checks if the list length is less than or equal to one. The recursive cases involve splitting the list recursively until individual elements, then merging them in a sorted manner.

Understanding these cases extends beyond simple mathematical functions. Recursive data structures such as linked lists and binary trees inherently follow recursive principles. For instance, consider a binary tree traversal:

```
class Node:
    def __init__(self, key):
        self.left = None
        self.right = None
        self.val = key

def inorder_traversal(root):
    if root:
        inorder_traversal(root.left) # Recursive case
        print(root.val)
        inorder_traversal(root.right) # Recursive case
```

In tree traversals, the base case checks if the node is null (end of a branch), while the recursive case continues traversing the left and right subtrees.

Correctly framing the base and recursive cases assures the recursive method's termination, correctness, and efficiency. Such principles are pivotal in not only writing precise and effective recursive functions but also in understanding more complex recursive algorithms and data structures.

5.3 Benefits and Drawbacks of Recursion

When discussing recursion, it is essential to assess both the benefits and drawbacks to provide a balanced perspective on when and how to apply recursive techniques effectively.

Benefits of Recursion

- **Simpler Code and Enhanced Readability**

Recursion allows for simpler and more intuitive code when dealing with problems naturally suited to recursive approaches. Problems like traversing trees or generating permutations are more straightforward when a recursive solution mirrors the problem's inherent recursive nature. Consider the example of traversing a binary tree:

```
class Node:
    def __init__(self, value):
        self.value = value
        self.left = None
        self.right = None

def in_order_traversal(node):
    if node is not None:
        in_order_traversal(node.left)
        print(node.value)
        in_order_traversal(node.right)
```

The recursive nature of this function reflects the structure of the binary tree, making the code easier to understand and maintain.

- **Modularity**

  Recursive functions tend to be modular. Each recursive call handles a simpler or different sub-problem, promoting separation of concerns. This modularity makes the code easier to test and debug since each function call can be inspected independently.

- **Solving Complex Problems**

  Certain complex problems, especially those involving divide-and-conquer strategies, are more naturally addressed using recursion. For example, the merge sort algorithm divides the list into halves, recursively sorts each half, and then merges the sorted halves.

```
def merge_sort(arr):
    if len(arr) > 1:
        mid = len(arr) // 2
        L = arr[:mid]
        R = arr[mid:]

        merge_sort(L)
        merge_sort(R)

        i = j = k = 0
        while i < len(L) and j < len(R):
            if L[i] < R[j]:
                arr[k] = L[i]
                i += 1
            else:
                arr[k] = R[j]
                j += 1
            k += 1
```

```
    while i < len(L):
        arr[k] = L[i]
        i += 1
        k += 1

    while j < len(R):
        arr[k] = R[j]
        j += 1
        k += 1
```

- **Suitability for Recursive Data Structures**

  Recursive functions are ideal for manipulating recursive data structures like trees and graphs. These structures consist of smaller and similar substructures, perfectly suiting recursive algorithms that traverse or manipulate these subparts.

Drawbacks of Recursion

- **Performance Overhead**

  Recursion often involves function call overhead, which can be substantial in languages like Python. Each recursive call consumes stack space, leading to increased memory usage. This overhead can be mitigated using techniques such as tail recursion optimization, although Python does not inherently support it.

- **Risk of Stack Overflow**

  Uncontrolled recursion can lead to excessive growth of the call stack, culminating in a stack overflow. This issue is common in deep recursions or infinite recursions. For example, a naively implemented Fibonacci function:

```
def fibonacci(n):
    if n <= 0:
        return 0
    elif n == 1:
        return 1
    else:
        return fibonacci(n-1) + fibonacci(n-2)
```

  The above function will quickly exhaust the stack for larger values of n. Therefore, recursion depth must be carefully managed.

- **Debugging Complexity**

  Debugging recursive functions can sometimes be challenging. Tracing the flow of recursive calls and unwinding the call stack to understand the flow of execution, especially in complex recursions, can be non-trivial.

- **Inefficient Without Optimization**

  Certain recursive solutions are inefficient without optimization techniques. For instance, the naive Fibonacci implementation above has exponential time complexity because it recalculates results for the same inputs multiple times. Using memoization or dynamic programming improves efficiency.

```
memo = {}
def fibonacci_optimized(n):
    if n in memo:
        return memo[n]
    if n <= 0:
        return 0
    elif n == 1:
        return 1
    else:
        memo[n] = fibonacci_optimized(n-1) + fibonacci_optimized(n-2)
        return memo[n]
```

Recursion has distinct advantages in simplicity, readability, and modularity but poses challenges such as performance overhead, potential for stack overflow, and complexity in debugging. Optimal use of recursion involves a careful balance of its benefits and drawbacks, complemented by suitable optimization techniques.

5.4 Tail Recursion and Optimization Techniques

Tail recursion is a specific form of recursion where the recursive call is the last operation in the function. This means that after the recursive call, there is no need to retain the current function's state, allowing certain optimizations that can improve performance and reduce the consumption of stack space.

In a tail-recursive function, the recursive call is positioned such that no computation or state update is needed post-recursion. This structure allows for a transformation known as tail call optimization (TCO), where the compiler can optimize calls to avoid adding a new stack frame for each recursive call. This optimization can convert a recursive process into an iterative one under the hood, thus preventing the typical drawbacks of recursion, such as stack overflow for deep recursion.

To understand how tail recursion functions, consider the canonical example of computing the factorial of a number. A standard recursive factorial function might look like this:

```
def factorial(n):
    if n == 0:
        return 1
    else:
        return n * factorial(n-1)
```

In this function, after the recursive call factorial(n-1), the result is multiplied by n. This multiplication occurs after the recursion, making it a non-tail recursive function. Next, let's transform this function into a tail-recursive version:

```
def tail_recursive_factorial(n, accumulator=1):
    if n == 0:
        return accumulator
    else:
        return tail_recursive_factorial(n-1, n*accumulator)
```

In the tail-recursive version, the function carries an additional parameter, accumulator, which accumulates the result as the recursion progresses. Here, the recursive call is the last operation in the function, making it suitable for tail call optimization.

Tail call optimization allows the interpreter or compiler to reuse the current function's stack frame for the next call, effectively transforming the recursion into an iterative loop. However, it is important to note that Python, by default, does not implement tail call optimization. Despite this, writing tail-recursive functions can still provide clarity and potentially facilitate easier translation to other languages or environments that do support TCO.

Alongside conceptualizing tail recursion, it is beneficial to employ optimization techniques to enhance the efficiency of recursive solutions. These techniques include memoization and dynamic programming, which can significantly reduce the time complexity of recursive algorithms.

Memoization involves caching the results of expensive function calls and reusing the cached result when the same inputs occur again. This approach can convert exponential time complexity into polynomial time by avoiding redundant computations. Here is an example of a memoized recursive function to compute Fibonacci numbers:

```
def memoized_fibonacci(n, memo={}):
    if n in memo:
        return memo[n]
```

```
    if n <= 1:
        return n
    memo[n] = memoized_fibonacci(n-1, memo) + memoized_fibonacci(n-2, memo)
    return memo[n]
```

In this example, a dictionary memo is used to store the Fibonacci values as they are calculated. Subsequent calls check this dictionary first to see if the value has already been computed, thereby avoiding redundant calculations.

Dynamic programming extends the idea of memoization and is particularly effective for optimization problems. It involves breaking down a problem into simpler subproblems and solving each subproblem only once. Unlike memoization, which is typically top-down (solving the main problem by solving subproblems as needed), dynamic programming often employs a bottom-up approach, solving smaller problems first and using their solutions to build up to the solution of the larger problem.

Consider the dynamic programming approach to the Fibonacci sequence:

```
def dp_fibonacci(n):
    if n <= 1:
        return n
    fib = [0] * (n + 1)
    fib[1] = 1
    for i in range(2, n + 1):
        fib[i] = fib[i-1] + fib[i-2]
    return fib[n]
```

In this dynamic programming solution, an array fib is used to store the computed values of Fibonacci numbers up to n. This method iteratively computes each Fibonacci number based on the previously computed values, thus ensuring efficient computation.

Using these optimization techniques, recursion can be effectively managed and utilized to solve complex problems efficiently. Tail recursion, memoization, and dynamic programming are powerful tools that, when combined, can optimize recursive algorithms to achieve significant performance improvements, even making recursive solutions viable for otherwise intractable problems.

5.5 Recursive Data Structures: Lists, Trees, and Graphs

Recursive data structures are pivotal in advanced computational problems, offering elegant solutions through their intrinsic recursive properties. In this section, we will explore three essential recursive data structures: lists, trees, and graphs. These structures are not only fundamental but also exhibit natural recursive characteristics that make them ideal candidates for recursive algorithmic techniques.

Recursive Lists

A list is a collection of elements arranged in a linear sequence. In recursive terms, a list can be defined based on a simple recursive rule: a list is either empty or consists of an element followed by another list. This definition can be succinctly represented in Python as follows:

```
class ListNode:
    def __init__(self, value=0, next=None):
        self.value = value
        self.next = next

def recursive_length(head):
    if head is None:
        return 0
    return 1 + recursive_length(head.next)
```

The above code snippet defines a singly linked list node ('ListNode') and computes the length of the list using recursion. The base case is when the head is None (indicating the end of the list), and the recursive case counts the current node and proceeds to the next node in the list.

Recursive Trees

Trees are hierarchical structures composed of nodes, where each node has zero or more children nodes. The recursive nature of trees allows us to design algorithms that process tree structures by recursively processing subtrees. Below is a basic example of a binary tree where each node has at most two children:

```
class TreeNode:
    def __init__(self, value=0, left=None, right=None):
        self.value = value
        self.left = left
        self.right = right

def recursive_tree_sum(root):
    if root is None:
        return 0
    return root.value + recursive_tree_sum(root.left) + recursive_tree_sum(root.right)
```

In this example, we define a binary tree node ('TreeNode') and a recursive function to compute the sum of all node values. The base case is when the root is None, returning a sum of zero. The recursive case adds the root's value to the sums obtained from the left and right subtrees.

Recursive Graphs

Graphs consist of a set of nodes (vertices) connected by edges and can be either directed or undirected. Unlike linear lists or hierarchical trees, graphs allow for complex relationships between nodes. A graph can be traversed recursively using algorithms like Depth-First Search (DFS). Here is an example of performing DFS on a graph:

```
def depth_first_search(graph, start, visited=None):
    if visited is None:
        visited = set()
    visited.add(start)

    for neighbor in graph[start]:
        if neighbor not in visited:
            depth_first_search(graph, neighbor, visited)
    return visited
```

In this code, depth_first_search takes a graph represented as an adjacency list, the starting node, and a set of visited nodes. The recursion explores each neighbor that has not been visited yet. The base case is implicitly defined by checking if a neighbor has already been visited.

Common Patterns in Recursive Data Structures

The recursive handling of lists, trees, and graphs often follows a similar pattern:

- **Base Case:** Determine the simplest scenario where the function can return an immediate result without further recursion. For lists, this could be an empty list; for trees, a None node; and for graphs, an already visited node.

- **Recursive Case:** Break the problem down into smaller subproblems, typically by making one recursive call for each component or child of the current structure. In lists, proceed to the next node; in trees, to each child node; in graphs, to each connected neighbor.

Understanding and leveraging these patterns enhances our ability to design efficient recursive algorithms for complex data structures. The recursive approach not only simplifies the logic but also aligns naturally with the inherent properties of these structures.

5.6 Implementing Recursive Algorithms in Python

Recursive algorithms are fundamental to functional programming and are essential for solving problems where the solution can be defined in terms of smaller instances of the same problem. In Python, recursion is a natural way to express such solutions, leveraging Python's function-calling capabilities. This section explores the implementation of recursive algorithms in Python, discussing practical aspects and providing detailed examples.

A recursive function is characterized by defining its behavior in terms of itself. It typically consists of one or more base cases, which provide terminating conditions, and one or more recursive cases, which reduce the problem toward the base case. Each invocation of the recursive case should make progress towards reaching a base case to ensure termination.

Factorial Function:

The factorial of a non-negative integer n, denoted by $n!$, is the product of all positive integers less than or equal to n. It can be recursively defined as:

$$n! = \begin{cases} 1 & \text{if } n = 0 \\ n \cdot (n-1)! & \text{if } n > 0 \end{cases}$$

In Python, this can be implemented as follows:

```
def factorial(n):
    if n == 0:
        return 1
    else:
        return n * factorial(n - 1)
```

```
>>> factorial(5)
120
```

Fibonacci Sequence:

The Fibonacci sequence is defined by the recurrence relation:

$$F(n) = \begin{cases} 0 & \text{if } n = 0 \\ 1 & \text{if } n = 1 \\ F(n-1) + F(n-2) & \text{if } n > 1 \end{cases}$$

A direct recursive implementation in Python looks like this:

```
def fibonacci(n):
    if n <= 1:
        return n
    else:
        return fibonacci(n - 1) + fibonacci(n - 2)
```

```
>>> fibonacci(6)
8
```

Hanoi Towers:

The Tower of Hanoi problem is a classic example of recursion. It involves moving a set of disks from one peg to another, with certain rules. The recursive method defines moving n disks from a source peg to a target peg using an auxiliary peg.

The algorithm:

```
def hanoi(n, source, target, auxiliary):
    if n == 1:
        print(f"Move disk 1 from {source} to {target}")
        return
    hanoi(n - 1, source, auxiliary, target)
    print(f"Move disk {n} from {source} to {target}")
    hanoi(n - 1, auxiliary, target, source)
```

```
>>> hanoi(3, 'A', 'C', 'B')
Move disk 1 from A to C
Move disk 2 from A to B
Move disk 1 from C to B
Move disk 3 from A to C
Move disk 1 from B to A
Move disk 2 from B to C
Move disk 1 from A to C
```

Recursive Depth and Stack Limitations:

Python's default recursion limit can be restrictive for deep recursion. The limit can be inspected and adjusted using the following:

```
import sys
print(sys.getrecursionlimit())
sys.setrecursionlimit(1500)
```

However, this should be done cautiously to avoid stack overflow errors. An alternative is to implement algorithms iteratively or use techniques such as memoization to optimize recursion.

Recursive Data Structures:

Recursive algorithms naturally fit recursive data structures such as lists, trees, and graphs. For example, recursively traversing a binary tree:

A binary tree node is defined as:

```
class TreeNode:
    def __init__(self, value=0, left=None, right=None):
        self.value = value
        self.left = left
        self.right = right
```

A recursive function to sum all nodes in a binary tree:

```
def sum_tree(node):
    if node is None:
        return 0
    return node.value + sum_tree(node.left) + sum_tree(node.right)
```

```
>>> root = TreeNode(1, TreeNode(2), TreeNode(3))
>>> sum_tree(root)
6
```

These examples highlight the fundamental approach to implementing recursive algorithms in Python. Each recursive function is crafted to break down the problem, ensuring it converges towards a base case, thereby solving the problem effectively and elegantly.

5.7 Common Recursive Problems: Factorial, Fibonacci, and Hanoi

Examining common recursive problems provides foundational understanding and hands-on practice in applying recursion. Three classic examples are often discussed: the factorial function, the Fibonacci sequence, and the Tower of Hanoi puzzle. Each of these problems emphasizes different aspects of recursion, including base and recursive cases, performance considerations, and the nature of recursive definitions.

Factorial Function

The factorial function is one of the simplest and most cited examples of recursion in computer science. By definition, the factorial of a non-negative integer n, denoted as $n!$, is the product of all positive integers less than or equal to n. The recursive definition is based on the observation that $n! = n \times (n-1)!$ with the base case defined as $0! = 1$.

The recursive implementation in Python can be expressed as follows:

```
def factorial(n):
    if n == 0:
        return 1
    else:
        return n * factorial(n - 1)
```

This function comprises two main components: the base case ('if n == 0: return 1'), which terminates the recursion, and the recursive case ('return n * factorial(n - 1)'), which reduces the problem into a smaller instance.

Let's consider the function call 'factorial(5)':

```
factorial(5)
5 * factorial(4)
5 * (4 * factorial(3))
5 * (4 * (3 * factorial(2)))
5 * (4 * (3 * (2 * factorial(1))))
5 * (4 * (3 * (2 * (1 * factorial(0)))))
5 * (4 * (3 * (2 * (1 * 1))))
5 * (4 * (3 * (2 * 1)))
5 * (4 * (3 * 2))
5 * (4 * 6)
5 * 24
120
```

The stack frames unfold, eventually computing $5! = 120$.

Fibonacci Sequence

The Fibonacci sequence is another essential recursive problem. This sequence is defined as follows:

$$F(0) = 0,$$
$$F(1) = 1,$$
$$F(n) = F(n-1) + F(n-2) \quad \text{for} \quad n > 1.$$

Thus, each term is the sum of the two preceding ones. The recursive implementation in Python is given below:

```python
def fibonacci(n):
    if n == 0:
        return 0
    elif n == 1:
        return 1
    else:
        return fibonacci(n - 1) + fibonacci(n - 2)
```

This function features two base cases ('if n == 0: return 0' and 'elif n == 1: return 1') and one recursive case.

Let's illustrate the function call 'fibonacci(5)':

```
fibonacci(5)
fibonacci(4) + fibonacci(3)
(fibonacci(3) + fibonacci(2)) + (fibonacci(2) + fibonacci(1))
((fibonacci(2) + fibonacci(1)) + (fibonacci(1) + fibonacci(0))) + ((fibonacci(1) + fibonacci(0)) + 1)
...
5
```

This tracing shows the repeated computations, leading to exponential time complexity $O(2^n)$. Optimization techniques such as memoization or dynamic programming can mitigate this inefficiency by storing previously computed results.

Tower of Hanoi

The Tower of Hanoi is a mathematical puzzle consisting of three rods and multiple disks of different sizes that can slide onto any rod. The puzzle's objective is to move the entire stack to another rod following these rules:

- Only one disk can be moved at a time.
- Each move involves taking the top disk from one stack and placing it on top of another stack or an empty rod.
- No disk may be placed on a smaller disk.

The recursive solution involves moving $n-1$ disks from the source rod to an auxiliary rod, then moving the nth disk directly to the destination rod, and finally moving the $n-1$ disks from the auxiliary rod to the destination rod. Here's the Python implementation:

```
def hanoi(n, source, target, auxiliary):
    if n == 1:
        print(f"Move disk 1 from rod {source} to rod {target}")
    else:
        hanoi(n - 1, source, auxiliary, target)
        print(f"Move disk {n} from rod {source} to rod {target}")
        hanoi(n - 1, auxiliary, target, source)
```

This function call 'hanoi(n, 'A', 'C', 'B')' for $n = 3$ produces the following sequence of moves:

```
Move disk 1 from rod A to rod C
Move disk 2 from rod A to rod B
Move disk 1 from rod C to rod B
Move disk 3 from rod A to rod C
Move disk 1 from rod B to rod A
Move disk 2 from rod B to rod C
Move disk 1 from rod A to rod C
```

The solution leverages the recursive decomposition of the problem into smaller subproblems, demonstrating the power and elegance of recursion in problem-solving.

5.8 Handling Deep Recursion: Stack Overflow and Limits

Deep recursion can lead to a significant problem known as stack overflow. In computer science, a stack overflow occurs when too much memory is used on the call stack, which typically results in a program crash. The call stack is a special type of memory storage that keeps track of active subroutines or function calls in a program. Each time a function calls another function, a new stack frame is added to the call stack. When the function returns, the stack frame is removed. This section explores the causes of stack overflow due to deep recursion, how to detect and mitigate it in Python, and discusses limitations imposed by the Python interpreter.

Understanding the causes of stack overflow requires knowledge of how recursion works. When a function calls itself repeatedly without reaching a base case within a reasonable number of calls, it leads to deep recursion. Each function call consumes a small amount of stack space, so an excessive number of calls will eventually exhaust the available stack space.

To illustrate the concept, let's consider a simple Python example where deep recursion leads to a stack overflow:

```
def deep_recursion(n):
    if n == 0:
        return 0
    else:
        return deep_recursion(n - 1) + 1

deep_recursion(100000) # This will likely cause a stack overflow
```

Upon executing this code snippet, Python raises a RecursionError:

```
RecursionError: maximum recursion depth exceeded in comparison
```

This error indicates that the recursion limit has been exceeded. By default, Python imposes a recursion limit to prevent stack overflow, which can be queried and modified using functions from the sys module:

```
import sys
print(sys.getrecursionlimit()) # Prints the current recursion limit
sys.setrecursionlimit(2000) # Sets a new recursion limit of 2000
```

While increasing the recursion limit can mitigate stack overflow for slightly deeper recursions, it is not a viable solution for significantly deep recursions due to inherent memory constraints. Instead, alternative approaches must be considered.

One such approach is converting the recursive algorithm to an iterative one. Iterative solutions use loops instead of recursive function calls, eliminating the risk of stack overflow. For instance, the following iterative version of the previous recursive example avoids deep recursion:

```
def iterative_version(n):
    count = 0
    while n > 0:
        n -= 1
        count += 1
    return count

iterative_version(100000)
```

This code avoids stack overflow by not using recursive calls.

Another approach is tail call optimization (TCO), an optimization technique that allows some forms of recursion to be executed without increasing the call stack size. Unfortunately, Python does not support TCO natively. However, we can restructure some recursive algorithms to take advantage of TCO by mimicking its behavior with loops and accumulator variables. Here is an example:

```
def tail_recursive(n, acc=0):
    if n == 0:
        return acc
    else:
        return tail_recursive(n - 1, acc + 1)

# Converting the tail-recursive function to an iterative equivalent
def iterative_tail_recursive(n):
    acc = 0
    while n > 0:
        n -= 1
        acc += 1
    return acc

iterative_tail_recursive(100000)
```

This iterative equivalent achieves the same outcome without the risk of stack overflow.

Memoization and dynamic programming also help manage deep recursion by storing intermediate results, thus reducing the number of recursive calls. However, these techniques are more suited for problems with overlapping subproblems and are addressed in the subsequent section.

The key to handling deep recursion lies in understanding the limitations of the stack and employing techniques to minimize excessive stack usage. Converting recursive algorithms to iterative ones, restructuring code to use TCO, and adopting memoization and dynamic programming approaches are effective strategies against stack overflow.

5.9 Memoization and Dynamic Programming Techniques

Memoization and dynamic programming (DP) are techniques used to optimize recursive algorithms. These strategies are essential to tackle problems that exhibit optimal substructure and overlapping subproblems. By storing results of expensive function calls and reusing them when the same inputs occur again, these techniques significantly reduce computation time and avoid redundant work.

Memoization involves augmenting a recursive function so that it keeps a record of results from previous computations. This method uses a data structure, often a dictionary or array, to store these intermediate results. When a function is called with a particular set of parameters, the memoized version first checks if the result is already stored. If so, it returns the cached result instead of recalculating it.

Consider the example of computing Fibonacci numbers. The naive recursive approach is computationally expensive due to the overlapping subproblems:

```
def fibonacci(n):
    if n <= 1:
        return n
    else:
        return fibonacci(n - 1) + fibonacci(n - 2)
```

In this implementation, 'fibonacci(2)' is recalculated multiple times. Memoization can remedy this inefficiency by storing calculated results, allowing the function to avoid redundant calculations.

```
def fibonacci_memo(n, memo={}):
    if n in memo:
        return memo[n]
    if n <= 1:
        return n
    memo[n] = fibonacci_memo(n - 1, memo) + fibonacci_memo(n - 2, memo)
    return memo[n]
```

Memoization transforms the exponential time complexity $O(2^n)$ of the naive approach into a linear time complexity $O(n)$. The key idea is to trade space for time, efficiently using available memory to store intermediate results.

Dynamic Programming extends the concept of memoization by solving problems bottom-up. Whereas memoization works well with a top-down recursive approach, DP is typically implemented iteratively. It's particularly useful in scenarios where the problem can be broken down into smaller interdependent subproblems.

To see how dynamic programming works, we can again consider the Fibonacci sequence. Instead of solving the problem recursively, we can build up the solution iteratively from the base cases.

```
def fibonacci_dp(n):
    if n <= 1:
        return n
    dp = [0 for _ in range(n + 1)]
    dp[1] = 1
    for i in range(2, n + 1):
        dp[i] = dp[i - 1] + dp[i - 2]
    return dp[n]
```

In this DP approach, we use an array dp to store the Fibonacci values from $dp[0]$ to $dp[n]$. Thus, each value is computed only once, resulting in a linear time complexity $O(n)$ and space complexity $O(n)$. Further optimization can reduce the space complexity to $O(1)$ by keeping track of only the last two values as follows:

```
def fibonacci_dp_optimized(n):
    if n <= 1:
        return n
    a, b = 0, 1
    for _ in range(2, n + 1):
        a, b = b, a + b
    return b
```

Comparison of Memoization and Dynamic Programming: - **Memoization** is suitable when the problem is more naturally expressed top-down. It maintains the recursive structure while optimizing for performance. - **Dynamic Programming** is favorable in problems where bottom-up construction is more intuitive or when excessive recursion depth could lead to stack overflow issues.

Both techniques can be applied to a variety of problems, such as:

- **Knapsack Problem**: Optimize the total value in a knapsack without exceeding the weight limit.
- **Longest Common Subsequence**: Find the longest subsequence common to two sequences.
- **Matrix Chain Multiplication**: Determine the most efficient way to multiply a given sequence of matrices.

Dynamic programming is rooted in principles that ensure efficient computation by combining the solutions of subproblems. Both techniques exemplify the power of using memory to enhance computational efficiency, highlighting the synergy between algorithm design and data structures in modern computer science.

5.10 Practical Examples of Recursive Data Structures

Recursive data structures are central to both the theory and practice of computer science, especially within the context of functional programming and Python. This section provides practical examples of recursive data structures, elucidating their implementations and applications.

Recursive Lists

A list is one of the most common data structures and can be defined recursively. A list is either empty, or it consists of an element followed by another list. This simple recursive definition can be implemented in Python as follows:

```
class RecursiveList:
    def __init__(self, head=None, tail=None):
        self.head = head
        self.tail = tail

    def is_empty(self):
        return self.head is None

    def prepend(self, value):
        return RecursiveList(value, self)

# Example usage:
rl1 = RecursiveList(1, RecursiveList(2, RecursiveList(3)))
print(rl1.head) # Output: 1
print(rl1.tail.head) # Output: 2
```

The output of this example is:

```
1
2
```

This implementation encapsulates the essential recursive nature of the list. Each element points to another list, which may be empty or may itself contain more elements.

Recursive Trees

A tree is another classical recursive data structure. A tree can be empty, or it can consist of a node (the root) that contains a value and references to zero or more child trees. This definition is naturally suited to a recursive implementation.

```
class TreeNode:
    def __init__(self, value=None, children=None):
        self.value = value
        self.children = children if children is not None else []

    def add_child(self, node):
        self.children.append(node)

# Example usage:
root = TreeNode(1)
child1 = TreeNode(2)
child2 = TreeNode(3)
root.add_child(child1)
root.add_child(child2)
print(root.value) # Output: 1
print(root.children[0].value) # Output: 2
```

The output of this example is:

```
1
2
```

This implementation showcases the recursive nature of trees, where each node can have multiple children, each of which is itself a tree. Functions operating on trees, such as traversals, can naturally be defined recursively.

Recursive Graphs

Graphs are a step further in complexity, as they introduce cycles and can be undirected or directed. A graph can be described recursively as a collection of nodes, each containing a value and references to other nodes.

```
class GraphNode:
    def __init__(self, value):
        self.value = value
        self.neighbors = []

    def add_neighbor(self, node):
        self.neighbors.append(node)

# Example usage:
node1 = GraphNode(1)
node2 = GraphNode(2)
node3 = GraphNode(3)
node1.add_neighbor(node2)
node2.add_neighbor(node3)
node3.add_neighbor(node1)
print(node1.value) # Output: 1
print(node1.neighbors[0].value) # Output: 2
```

The output of this example is:

This Python class captures the essence of recursive structures in graphs, enabling the representation of nodes that can point to other nodes, thus forming a complex, interconnected network.

Traversing Recursive Data Structures

Traversing these recursive data structures is also done using recursion. Consider the traversal of a tree:

```
def preorder_traversal(node):
    if not node:
        return
    print(node.value)
    for child in node.children:
        preorder_traversal(child)

# Example usage:
root = TreeNode(1, [TreeNode(2), TreeNode(3)])
preorder_traversal(root)
```

The output of this traversal is:

```
1
2
3
```

This recursive function prints the value of each node in a pre-order traversal, demonstrating how recursion simplifies the process of exploring complex data structures.

Benefits and Practicality

Employing these recursive data structures can significantly enhance readability and maintainability. Their recursive nature aligns well with functional programming paradigms present in Python, making them indispensable tools for developers. However, attention to stack depth and careful management of base cases ensure that operations on these structures remain efficient and executable within Python's constraints on recursion depth.

Chapter 6

Lambda Expressions and Anonymous Functions

This chapter introduces lambda expressions and anonymous functions in Python. It covers the syntax, structure, and appropriate use cases for lambda functions, while highlighting their limitations. The chapter examines using lambdas with functions like map, filter, and reduce, as well as in sorting and ordering data. It also explores anonymous functions as closures and compares them with named functions, offering best practices and practical examples to illustrate their utility.

6.1 Introduction to Lambda Expressions

Lambda expressions, often referred to as anonymous functions, are a core feature of Python that enable the definition of small, unnamed function objects in a concise way. This capability provides increased flexibility for certain programming tasks, particularly those involving higher-order functions such as $\mathrm{map}()$, $\mathrm{filter}()$, and $\mathrm{reduce}()$. At a fundamental level, a lambda expression allows you to encapsulate functionality within a single, line-of-code construct, facilitating clear and functional programming styles.

A lambda expression in Python is defined using the lambda keyword, followed by a list of parameters, a colon, and an expression. The general form is:

```
lambda arguments: expression
```

The return value of the lambda function is the result of the expression provided. Unlike a standard function defined using the def keyword, lambda functions are limited to a single expression and implicitly return its value. This characteristic makes them suitable for simple operations that can be expressed succinctly.

Consider an example where you want to create a function that adds 10 to its input. Traditionally, using the def keyword, you would write:

```
def add_ten(x):
    return x + 10

print(add_ten(5)) # Output: 15
```

The equivalent lambda expression for this function is:

```
add_ten = lambda x: x + 10
print(add_ten(5)) # Output: 15
```

Lambda expressions are commonly used in conjunction with Python's built-in higher-order functions. For instance, the map() function applies a given function to all items in an input list:

```
numbers = [1, 2, 3, 4, 5]
squared = map(lambda x: x**2, numbers)
print(list(squared)) # Output: [1, 4, 9, 16, 25]
```

In this example, the lambda expression lambda x: x**2 is used to succinctly define a function that squares each element of the list numbers.

Similarly, lambda functions simplify use cases where functions are required by other higher-order functions such as filter() and reduce(). For instance:

```
# Using lambda with filter to get even numbers
evens = filter(lambda x: x % 2 == 0, numbers)
print(list(evens)) # Output: [2, 4]

# Using lambda with reduce to compute the product of all elements
from functools import reduce
product = reduce(lambda x, y: x * y, numbers)
print(product) # Output: 120
```

The filter() function filters the elements of the list numbers by applying the lambda function lambda x: x % 2 == 0, whereas reduce(), which is available in the functools module, reduces the list numbers to a single value by applying the lambda function lambda x, y: x * y. These concise lambda expressions simplify the code without sacrificing readability.

While lambda expressions excel in brevity and are invaluable in many scenarios, their usage comes with certain limitations, which we will address in a subsequent section. For now, it is key to note that lambda expressions play a vital role in Python by enabling a functional, expressive, and versatile coding style. When appropriately employed, they augment the capability to write more readable and maintainable code.

Thus, lambda expressions introduce a powerful yet straightforward mechanism to define small, anonymous functions directly within your code, ensuring that the logical structure of the program remains clear and concise.

6.2 Syntax and Structure of Lambda Functions

Lambda functions, also referred to as anonymous functions, provide a succinct and expressive way to define small, unnamed functions in Python. They are particularly useful in contexts where a function is required temporarily or within a limited scope. The syntax and structure of lambda functions are fundamental for understanding how they differ from regular function definitions.

The basic form of a lambda function follows the structure:

```
lambda arguments: expression
```

Here, lambda is the keyword used to indicate the creation of a lambda function. The arguments section is a comma-separated list of input parameters, and the expression is the computation or operation that the lambda function performs.

To illustrate this with a simple example, consider a lambda function that adds two numbers:

```
add = lambda x, y: x + y
result = add(3, 5)
print(result)
```

8

In this code, lambda x, y: x + y defines an anonymous function that takes two arguments, x and y, and returns their sum. This lambda function is then assigned to the variable add, enabling its invocation with specific arguments (3 and 5 in this case) to produce the result 8.

Lambda functions are inherently limited to single expressions, which distinguishes them from regular functions defined using the def keyword. They cannot contain multiple statements or handle complex procedural logic directly. This constraint, however, is conducive to their role in functional programming patterns where concise, single-operation functions are essential.

Consider the necessity of using a lambda function within a sorting operation to sort a list of tuples by their second element:

```
data = [(1, 2), (3, 1), (5, 4)]
sorted_data = sorted(data, key=lambda x: x[1])
print(sorted_data)
```

```
[(3, 1), (1, 2), (5, 4)]
```

In this example, sorted() utilizes a lambda function as the key argument. The lambda function takes each tuple x and returns its second element, x[1]. Consequently, the sorted list is ordered based on the second elements of its tuples.

Lambda functions are also prevalent within the map, filter, and reduce functions, which facilitate functional programming paradigms in Python. For instance, consider using lambda with map:

```
numbers = [1, 2, 3, 4]
squared = map(lambda x: x ** 2, numbers)
print(list(squared))
```

```
[1, 4, 9, 16]
```

Here, map() applies the lambda function lambda x: x ** 2 to each element of the numbers list, resulting in a new list of squared values.

Similarly, lambda functions are utilized in filter to select elements from an iterable based on a condition:

```
numbers = [1, 2, 3, 4]
even = filter(lambda x: x % 2 == 0, numbers)
print(list(even))
```

```
[2, 4]
```

In this application, filter() retains only the elements for which the lambda function lambda x: x % 2 == 0 returns True.

Although lambda functions provide compact syntax, they are not a replacement for regular function definitions. Their utility is optimal in scenarios demanding brief, in-place functionality, especially within higher-order functions or constructing short-lived logic. These functions align with the principles of functional programming by promoting immutability and stateless operations. However, for more complex or reusable logic, using def to define standard functions is preferable to ensure clarity and maintainability in code.

6.3 When and Why to Use Lambda Functions

Lambda functions in Python offer an efficient and concise way to represent small anonymous functions. While they are not universally suitable for every situation, their utility in specific contexts makes them a valuable tool in the arsenal of a Python programmer. This section elucidates the circumstances under which lambda functions are particularly advantageous and the rationale behind their usage.

Lambda functions are particularly useful in scenarios where quick, throwaway functions are necessary. These are often functions that are passed as arguments to higher-order functions or used in places where a complete function definition would be syntactically verbose or disrupt the flow of code logic. Here are some common use cases and justifications for employing lambda functions.

- **Higher-Order Functions:** A higher-order function is a function that takes another function as an argument, returns a function, or both. Common higher-order functions such as map, filter, and reduce frequently exploit lambda functions for their first-class function inputs.

  ```
  numbers = [1, 2, 3, 4, 5, 6]
  squared_numbers = list(map(lambda x: x**2, numbers))
  print(squared_numbers)
  ```

  ```
  [1, 4, 9, 16, 25, 36]
  ```

  In this example, map() is used to apply a lambda function that squares each element in the list numbers. Using a lambda function here avoids the need to define a separate, named function for such a straightforward operation.

- **Inline Usage:** Lambda functions are extremely useful for short-lived operations within functions or methods, particularly when defining small functions inline, thereby keeping the code concise and readable.

```
def incrementor(n):
    return lambda x: x + n

add_five = incrementor(5)
print(add_five(10))
```

15

Here, incrementor returns a lambda function that increments its input x by n. The use of the lambda function keeps the additional logic concise and encapsulated within the higher-order function.

- **Sorting and Ordering:** Lambda functions are commonly employed within sorting and ordering methods, such as sorted or sort, where a custom key function can be succinctly expressed with a lambda.

```
data = [('apple', 2), ('banana', 3), ('pear', 1)]
sorted_data = sorted(data, key=lambda item: item[1])
print(sorted_data)
```

[('pear', 1), ('apple', 2), ('banana', 3)]

In this scenario, the lambda function specifies that sorting should be based on the second element of each tuple, a task elegantly handled without the need for a separate function definition.

- **Event Handling:** In graphical user interfaces (GUIs) and callback-based systems, lambda functions are often utilized to embed simple operations in the event-triggering code directly.

```
import tkinter as tk

root = tk.Tk()
button = tk.Button(root, text="Click me",
                   command=lambda: print("Button clicked"))
button.pack()
root.mainloop()
```

This example demonstrates attaching a lambda function to a button's command attribute in a Tkinter-based GUI application. The lambda function prints a message when the button is clicked.

- **Avoiding Pollution of Namespace:** Defining small functions using the standard def keyword can clutter the namespace with numerous functions that are unlikely to be reused. Lambda functions provide a means to prevent this by enabling the definition of compact, single-use functions on the fly.

```
nums = [1, -2, 3, -4, 5, -6]
positive_nums = list(filter(lambda x: x > 0, nums))
print(positive_nums)
```

```
[1, 3, 5]
```

Here, the lambda function is employed within the filter() function to extract positive numbers from the list nums, avoiding the creation of an additional named function.

Lambda functions exemplify Python's flexibility and ease of use for functional programming constructs. By circumspectly applying them where appropriate, one can write code that is both concise and expressive. These small anonymous functions enable developers to embed functionality directly within the calling constructs, streamlining the codebase while maintaining readability and functionality.

6.4 Limitations of Lambda Expressions

While lambda expressions offer a concise and powerful alternative to traditional function definitions in Python, they come with several limitations. Awareness of these restrictions is crucial to effectively use lambda functions without encountering pitfalls.

Lambda expressions in Python are subject to the following constraints:

1. **Single Expression Restriction**: A lambda function is limited to a single expression. This constraint means that only one operation or computation can be performed within a lambda expression. Compound statements are not permissible. This characteristic renders lambda expressions less suitable for functions requiring multiple logical steps or more complex operations.

```
# Valid Lambda Expression
square = lambda x: x * x

# Invalid Lambda Expression
# lambda x: (x = x + 1; x * x) # SyntaxError: invalid syntax
```

The inability to contain multiple expressions or statements restricts lambda expressions to fairly simple operations.

2. **Readability Concerns**: Lambda functions, while concise, can result in reduced code readability, especially for more complex operations. The compact syntax, while advantageous for brief and straightfor-

ward tasks, can become opaque, leading to difficulties in understanding and maintaining the code.

```
# Lambda function example
sum_product = lambda x, y: (x + y, x * y)

# Equivalent named function for better readability
def sum_and_product(x, y):
    return (x + y, x * y)
```

Named functions, with their ability to use descriptive names, often provide better clarity for complex operations as compared to lambdas.

3. **Lack of Annotations and Documentation**: Lambda functions do not support annotations or inline documentation (docstrings). This lack makes it harder to document lambda functions properly, thereby reducing the overall understandability and maintainability of the code.

```
# Lambda function without annotations
concat = lambda a, b: a + b

# Named function with annotations and docstring
def concatenate_strings(a: str, b: str) -> str:
    """
    Concatenates two input strings.
    """
    return a + b
```

Annotations and docstrings often provide crucial information about the input parameters and expected output, which is absent in lambdas.

4. **No Support for Statements**: Statements such as return, assert, try, and others are not allowed inside lambda expressions. This limitation confines the actions that can be performed within a lambda to purely expression-based operations.

```
# Invalid Lambda Expression
# lambda x: return x * 2 # SyntaxError: 'return' outside function
```

Any situation requiring such statements must utilize a named function instead.

5. **Scoping and Bindings**: Lambdas capture variables by reference, not by value. This behavior can lead to unexpected results, particularly in the context of loops or mutable variables.

```
functions = []
for i in range(5):
    functions.append(lambda : i)

# All elements in functions will contain the same lambda returning the final value of
     i
results = [f() for f in functions]
```

```
print(results) # Output: [4, 4, 4, 4, 4]
```

This scoping issue can be circumvented using default argument values or enclosing the lambda in another function, but such workarounds can complicate the code.

6. **Limited Error Handling**: Error handling within lambda expressions is inherently limited because they cannot contain multiple statements, including try and except blocks. Consequently, introducing robust error handling mechanisms often necessitates the use of named functions.

```
# Named function with error handling
def divide(a, b):
    try:
        return a / b
    except ZeroDivisionError:
        return 'Error: Division by zero'

# Lambda function can't handle errors
safe_divide = lambda a, b: a / b # Potential ZeroDivisionError
```

The described limitations should guide the decision-making process when considering lambda expressions. For simple, short-lived uses like quick calculations or small operations, lambdas can be very effective. However, for more complex functions requiring multiple operations, error handling, or clear documentation, standard function definitions are often the better choice.

6.5 Using Lambdas with map, filter, and reduce

The map, filter, and reduce functions are pivotal in Python's functional programming paradigm. They allow for concise and expressive data transformation and reduction. Lambda functions, due to their brevity and straightforward syntax, seamlessly integrate with these higher-order functions.

The map Function:

The map function applies a given function to all items in an input list (or any iterable) and returns an iterable of the results. The underlying mechanism can be described as mapping a transformation over a collection of elements. The syntax for map with a lambda function is as follows:

```
map(function, iterable)
```

Consider a scenario where you have a list of integers and you want to obtain their squares:

```
numbers = [1, 2, 3, 4, 5]
squared_numbers = map(lambda x: x**2, numbers)
print(list(squared_numbers))
```

```
[1, 4, 9, 16, 25]
```

In this code snippet, the lambda function `lambda x: x**2` is applied to each element in the `numbers` list, producing a new list of squared values.

The filter Function:

The `filter` function constructs a new iterable containing those elements of the initial iterable for which the provided function returns `True`. The syntax is:

```
filter(function, iterable)
```

For example, to filter out all even numbers from a list:

```
numbers = [1, 2, 3, 4, 5, 6, 7, 8, 9, 10]
even_numbers = filter(lambda x: x % 2 == 0, numbers)
print(list(even_numbers))
```

```
[2, 4, 6, 8, 10]
```

Here, the lambda function `lambda x: x % 2 == 0` identifies elements divisible by 2, thereby filtering out the even numbers.

The reduce Function:

The `reduce` function from the `functools` module applies a binary function cumulatively to the items of an iterable, reducing the iterable to a single accumulated value. Importantly, `reduce` produces a single output value, unlike `map` and `filter`. The syntax is:

```
from functools import reduce
reduce(function, iterable[, initializer])
```

A simple use case could be summing all elements in a list:

```
from functools import reduce

numbers = [1, 2, 3, 4, 5]
sum_numbers = reduce(lambda x, y: x + y, numbers)
print(sum_numbers)
```

15

In this example, the lambda function lambda x, y: x + y adds pairs of elements cumulatively.

Extending this to a more complex example, consider finding the product of all elements:

```
numbers = [1, 2, 3, 4, 5]
product_numbers = reduce(lambda x, y: x * y, numbers)
print(product_numbers)
```

120

The lambda function lambda x, y: x * y multiplies elements cumulatively.

Combining map, filter, and reduce:

These functions can be combined for more sophisticated data transformations. For instance, consider obtaining the sum of squares of only the odd numbers in a list:

```
numbers = [1, 2, 3, 4, 5]
odd_squares_sum = reduce(
    lambda x, y: x + y,
    map(lambda x: x**2, filter(lambda x: x % 2 != 0, numbers))
)
print(odd_squares_sum)
```

35

Here, the filter function first isolates the odd numbers (1, 3, 5), map then squares these numbers (1, 9, 25), and reduce computes the sum of these squares (1 + 9 + 25).

Each function adheres to a clear, single responsibility. map transforms elements, filter selects elements, and reduce aggregates elements. Properly leveraging these functions with lambda expressions can significantly streamline data processing pipelines in Python.

The use of lambda with these functions, while sometimes causing a decrease in code readability for complex operations, offers powerful options for succinctly handling routine data manipulation tasks.

6.6 Lambda Functions in Sorting and Ordering Data

Sorting and ordering data efficiently is a common requirement in many programming tasks. The sorted() function and the sort() method in Python are often utilized for this purpose. By leveraging lambda functions as key functions within these sorting utilities, developers can customize the sorting behavior in powerful and concise ways.

The sorted() function returns a new list containing all items from the iterable in ascending order. Its syntax allows for optional parameters that include a key function and a Boolean reverse, as shown below:

```
sorted(iterable, key=None, reverse=False)
```

Similarly, the sort() method modifies the list in place. Its syntax is identical in terms of parameters:

```
list.sort(key=None, reverse=False)
```

Both sorted() and sort() take a key parameter that specifies a function of one argument to be applied to each element for sorting purposes. Using a lambda function in this context allows for concise and flexible expressions without the need to define a separate function.

To illustrate, consider sorting a list of tuples representing students, where each tuple contains a name and a grade. To sort the list by grade, we use a lambda function to extract the second element of each tuple:

```
students = [('John', 88), ('Emma', 92), ('Sam', 90)]

# Sort by grade
sorted_students = sorted(students, key=lambda x: x[1])
print(sorted_students)
```

The resultant output is:

```
[('John', 88), ('Sam', 90), ('Emma', 92)]
```

In this example, lambda x: x[1] specifies that sorting should be based on the second element of each tuple, which represents the student's grade. The versatility of lambda functions enables more complex sorts, such as sorting by multiple criteria. Suppose we want to sort primarily by grade and secondarily by name in cases where grades are identical. This requirement can be addressed using a tuple as the key:

```
students = [('John', 88), ('Emma', 92), ('Sam', 90), ('Chris', 90)]

# Sort by grade, then by name
sorted_students = sorted(students, key=lambda x: (x[1], x[0]))
print(sorted_students)
```

The resultant output is:

```
[('John', 88), ('Chris', 90), ('Sam', 90), ('Emma', 92)]
```

Here, the lambda function `lambda x: (x[1], x[0])` instructs Python to sort primarily by grade and use name as a tie-breaker.

Another practical application involves sorting dictionaries. Suppose we have a list of dictionaries representing products, and each dictionary contains 'name', 'price', and 'quantity' fields. We can sort by price in ascending order as follows:

```
products = [
    {'name': 'Laptop', 'price': 900, 'quantity': 10},
    {'name': 'Smartphone', 'price': 600, 'quantity': 30},
    {'name': 'Tablet', 'price': 300, 'quantity': 50}
]

# Sort by price
sorted_products = sorted(products, key=lambda x: x['price'])
print(sorted_products)
```

The resultant output is:

```
[{'name': 'Tablet', 'price': 300, 'quantity': 50},
 {'name': 'Smartphone', 'price': 600, 'quantity': 30},
 {'name': 'Laptop', 'price': 900, 'quantity': 10}]
```

Lambda functions allow transforming the data into sortable structures seamlessly within the `key` parameter. If we need to sort the products by name in descending order, we set the `reverse` parameter to `True`:

```
# Sort by name in descending order
sorted_products = sorted(products, key=lambda x: x['name'], reverse=True)
print(sorted_products)
```

The resultant output is:

```
[{'name': 'Tablet', 'price': 300, 'quantity': 50},
 {'name': 'Smartphone', 'price': 600, 'quantity': 30},
 {'name': 'Laptop', 'price': 900, 'quantity': 10}]
```

The effective use of lambda functions in sorting tasks not only achieves concise code but also gives the flexibility to handle sophisticated sorting requirements. Whether working with lists of tuples, dictionaries, or complex objects, lambda functions provide a dynamic way to define sorting keys that are both efficient and readable.

6.7 Anonymous Functions as Closures

Closures are a powerful concept in Python, and anonymous functions, or lambda expressions, can be utilized effectively to create them. A closure is essentially an inner function that remembers and has access to variables in the local scope in which it was created, even after the outer function has finished executing.

To understand how lambda functions operate as closures, consider the following example:

```
def make_multiplier(factor):
    return lambda x: x * factor

double = make_multiplier(2)
print(double(5)) # Output: 10
```

In the above example, the function make_multiplier returns an anonymous function that multiplies its input by factor. The variable factor is captured by the lambda, creating a closure. Even after the execution of make_multiplier has completed, the lambda function retains access to the variable factor. This allows the lambda function to remember the value of factor when it was created.

Further inspect the output produced:

```
10
```

Closures maintain their state over time, hence, each time make_multiplier is called, it produces a new function that closes over a different instance of the variable factor. For instance:

```
triple = make_multiplier(3)
print(triple(5)) # Output: 15
print(double(5)) # Output: 10
```

This code demonstrates that double and triple are distinct closures, maintaining their respective captured values of factor.

The output from the aforementioned code is:

```
15
10
```

Anonymous functions as closures can be particularly powerful when used in factory functions, enhancing modular and clean designs. Consider another example:

```
def power_factory(exp):
    return lambda base: base ** exp
```

```
square = power_factory(2)
cube = power_factory(3)

print(square(4)) # Output: 16
print(cube(2)) # Output: 8
```

In the above example, power_factory creates anonymous functions that compute the power of a number. These functions remember the value of exp, with which they were instantiated.

Outputs from this example are:

```
16
8
```

Moreover, it is critical to understand how lambda expressions behave inside loops as closures. When a lambda expression closes over a variable in a loop, it does not capture the variable's value at each iteration. Instead, it captures a reference to the variable, which may lead to unexpected results:

```
functions = []
for i in range(5):
    functions.append(lambda: i)

for f in functions:
    print(f())
```

Upon inspection of the above code's output, we find:

```
4
4
4
4
4
```

This output occurs because each lambda function captured a reference to the variable i, which ended with a value of 4 after the loop. To ensure each lambda function captures the current value of i during the loop, default arguments can be used:

```
functions = []
for i in range(5):
    functions.append(lambda i=i: i)

for f in functions:
    print(f())
```

This modification ensures that each lambda captures the intended value of i at each iteration, producing the correct output:

```
0
1
2
3
4
```

Anonymous functions as closures, therefore, offer a versatile tool for maintaining state across function executions and are especially useful in designing concise and expressive functional constructs in Python. Understanding their behavior and application can significantly enhance the functional programming capability of a Python developer.

6.8 Comparison with Named Functions

Lambda expressions, despite their concise syntax, serve a specific purpose in Python's ecosystem that sometimes overlaps with named functions. This section dissects the functional and operational differences between lambda expressions and named functions.

Lambda functions are anonymous, which means they are defined without a name. They are often used for short-term use cases where a small function is required temporarily. The typical syntax for a lambda function is:

```
lambda arguments: expression
```

Consider the following lambda function for adding two numbers:

```
add = lambda x, y: x + y
# Usage
result = add(3, 5)
```

Here, add acts as a function adding two numbers, but it is defined without the traditional def keyword. On the contrary, named functions use the def keyword and include a function name. This allows for better readability and reusability, especially when the function's logic is complex or likely to be reused multiple times.

```
def add(x, y):
    return x + y
# Usage
result = add(3, 5)
```

Named functions can also accept optional parameters, have more complex expressions, and support a range of Python features, such as decorators.

When examining performance, there is no significant difference between lambda functions and named functions, as they both compile to a function object. However, lambda functions are syntactically limited to a single expression and cannot contain statements or multiple expressions. For example, the following attempts to create a multi-line lambda function will fail:

```
# This will raise a SyntaxError
lambda x:
    x += 1
    return x
```

Named functions, on the other hand, can include multiple statements, making them more suitable for complex operations:

```
def increment_and_return(x):
    x += 1
    return x
```

Another key comparison aspect is readability. In more extensive and collaborative codebases, named functions are often preferred due to their self-descriptive nature. Here's an example where readability can be enhanced with a named function:

```
# Using a lambda function
sorted_list = sorted(my_list, key=lambda x: x.lower())

# Using a named function
def lower_case_key(x):
    return x.lower()
sorted_list = sorted(my_list, key=lower_case_key)
```

The named function lower_case_key clearly explains that the sorting key involves converting elements to lowercase, which might not be immediately obvious with the inline lambda expression.

Named functions are also inherently more testable due to their named references, whereas lambdas are mainly suitable for simple operations that fit into a single logical line. For unit testing, a named function can be more easily isolated and tested:

```
def test_add():
    assert add(3, 5) == 8
```

Named functions allow using decorators, which can modify their behavior in sophisticated ways that lambdas cannot. For example:

```
def my_decorator(func):
    def wrapper(*args, **kwargs):
        print("Something is happening before the function is called.")
        result = func(*args, **kwargs)
        print("Something is happening after the function is called.")
        return result
```

```
    return wrapper

@my_decorator
def say_hello():
    print("Hello!")

say_hello()

# Output:
\begin{verbatim}
Something is happening before the function is called.
Hello!
Something is happening after the function is called.
\end{verbatim}
```

Finally, while lambdas are suited for simple tasks, named functions encapsulate more expressive logic and support decorations, annotations, and various Pythonic constructs, providing a balance of readability and functionality that facilitates code maintenance and collaboration.

By appreciating these differences, developers can better decide when to use lambda expressions and when to opt for named functions, optimizing their code for both functionality and clarity.

6.9 Best Practices for Using Lambda Expressions

When leveraging lambda expressions, it is crucial to adhere to certain best practices to ensure code clarity, efficiency, and maintainability. Understanding these practices can help avoid common pitfalls and effectively utilize lambda functions in Python programming.

Firstly, lambda functions should be concise. They are designed for small, simple operations and should not encompass complex logic. A lambda function should typically fit on one line and execute a straightforward operation. The following example demonstrates a clear and concise lambda function for adding two numbers:

```
add = lambda x, y: x + y
result = add(3, 4)
print(result)
```

The output is:

```
7
```

This lambda expression is readable and performs a simple addition operation, aligning with the principle of keeping lambda functions concise.

Another best practice is to use lambda functions contextually, meaning they should be employed where their succinct syntax provides an advantage, such as in the context of higher-order functions like map, filter, and reduce. Here is an example using map:

```
squared_numbers = map(lambda x: x**2, range(10))
print(list(squared_numbers))
```

The output is:

```
[0, 1, 4, 9, 16, 25, 36, 49, 64, 81]
```

In this case, using a lambda function within map enhances the code's readability and accomplishes the task succinctly.

Lambda expressions can also enhance data sorting tasks by providing a clear and quick method for specifying the key for sorting. An example involving a list of tuples demonstrates this advantage:

```
students = [("John", 75), ("Emma", 90), ("Sam", 82)]
# Sort by the second item in each tuple
sorted_students = sorted(students, key=lambda student: student[1])
print(sorted_students)
```

The output is:

```
[('John', 75), ('Sam', 82), ('Emma', 90)]
```

Here, the lambda function provides a straightforward mechanism for defining the sorting criteria.

Despite these benefits, lambdas should not replace regular functions when the logic is more complex or requires documentation. Named functions should be preferred in such cases for improved readability and maintainability. Consider the following, where a named function is more appropriate:

```
def complex_operation(x):
    # Multiple operations with explanatory comments
    if x % 2 == 0:
        return x**2
    else:
        return x**3

numbers = [1, 2, 3, 4]
complex_results = list(map(complex_operation, numbers))
print(complex_results)
```

This example outlines the importance of named functions in scenarios requiring elaborate logic or explanations.

To further improve code clarity, combining lambdas with other concise syntactic structures should be avoided. Excessively nested or chained lambda expressions can obscure the logic, reducing readability and maintainability. For instance, instead of chaining lambdas in the following convoluted manner:

```
result = (lambda x: (lambda y: y**2)(x) + 3)(2)
print(result)
```

It is preferable to simplify the expressions and use intermediate results as shown here:

```
inner_lambda = lambda y: y**2
outer_lambda = lambda x: inner_lambda(x) + 3
result = outer_lambda(2)
print(result)
```

Finally, it is essential to be aware of and respect the scope limitations in lambda functions. Lambdas inherently rely on their enclosing environment for variable resolution, a concept known as lexical scoping. Consequently, variable bindings might lead to unexpected results in different contexts. Here, understanding closures profoundly can prevent such issues:

```
def make_multiplier(factor):
    return lambda x: x * factor

double = make_multiplier(2)
triple = make_multiplier(3)

print(double(5))
print(triple(5))
```

The lambda functions generated here correctly capture the factor from their respective calling environments, enabling the correct multiplier behavior as demonstrated:

```
10
15
```

By adhering to these best practices, developers can effectively utilize lambda functions, ensuring their code remains both efficient and comprehensible.

6.10 Practical Examples of Lambda Functions in Python

The utility of lambda expressions in Python extends beyond simple theoretical constructs; their power is best understood through practical applications. This section explores various scenarios where lambda functions are not only useful but also enhance the functionality and readability of code.

Consider a situation where we need to manipulate data within a list. For example, given a list of numerical values, we may wish to compute their squares. Using a lambda function with the map function provides a concise solution:

```
numbers = [1, 2, 3, 4, 5]
squared_numbers = list(map(lambda x: x ** 2, numbers))
print(squared_numbers)
```

```
[1, 4, 9, 16, 25]
```

In this example, the lambda function lambda x: x ** 2 computes the square of each element in the numbers list. The map function applies this lambda function to each element, and the use of list converts the result back to a list of squared numbers.

Lambda functions are also particularly powerful when combined with the filter function to extract elements that meet specific criteria. Consider filtering a list to include only even numbers:

```
numbers = [1, 2, 3, 4, 5, 6, 7, 8, 9, 10]
even_numbers = list(filter(lambda x: x % 2 == 0, numbers))
print(even_numbers)
```

```
[2, 4, 6, 8, 10]
```

Here, the lambda function lambda x: x % 2 == 0 returns True for even numbers and False otherwise, and filter constructs a list containing only the numbers for which the lambda function returns True.

Lambda functions find meaningful applications in more complex scenarios such as sorting. Suppose we need to sort a list of tuples based on the second element of each tuple:

```
tuples = [(1, 'one'), (3, 'three'), (2, 'two')]
sorted_tuples = sorted(tuples, key=lambda x: x[1])
print(sorted_tuples)
```

```
[(1, 'one'), (3, 'three'), (2, 'two')]
```

In this case, lambda x: x[1] is used as the key argument in the sorted function to specify that sorting should be based on the second element of each tuple. The result is a list of tuples sorted alphabetically by the string values 'one', 'three', and 'two'.

More advanced usages of lambda functions involve mathematical computation and data aggregation. Consider computing the product of all elements in a list using the reduce function from the functools module:

```
from functools import reduce

numbers = [1, 2, 3, 4, 5]
product = reduce(lambda x, y: x * y, numbers)
print(product)
```

```
120
```

The lambda function here, lambda x, y: x * y, multiplies each pair of elements from the list successively.

Lambda functions also play a significant role in creating simple, on-the-fly functions for use in data structures where larger, named functions might be cumbersome. For instance, a dictionary of mathematical operations can be created where each operation is represented by a lambda function:

```
operations = {
    'add': lambda x, y: x + y,
    'subtract': lambda x, y: x - y,
    'multiply': lambda x, y: x * y,
    'divide': lambda x, y: x / y if y != 0 else float('inf')
}

print(operations['add'](2, 3))
print(operations['divide'](10, 2))
```

```
5
5.0
```

In this setup, the dictionary operations contains keys for each arithmetic operation, where the values are lambda functions implementing the operations. This allows for dynamically calling operations based on dictionary keys.

Another practical scenario involves using lambdas as custom sort criteria. For instance, sorting a list of dictionaries by a specific key:

```
students = [
    {'name': 'John', 'grade': 88},
    {'name': 'Emma', 'grade': 92},
    {'name': 'Ava', 'grade': 95},
    {'name': 'Sophia', 'grade': 89}
]

sorted_students = sorted(students, key=lambda student: student['grade'])
print(sorted_students)
```

```
[{'name': 'John', 'grade': 88}, {'name': 'Sophia', 'grade': 89}, {'name': 'Emma', 'grade': 92}, {'name': 'Ava', 'grade': 95}]
```

Here, the lambda function lambda student: student['grade'] sorts the list of students by their grades, demonstrating the versatility and expressive power of lambda functions in handling complex data structures.

By embedding short, single-use functions directly into larger expressions or function calls, lambda functions serve as an essential tool for writing concise and readable code. Such practical examples clearly illustrate the value lambda expressions add to Python programming.

Chapter 7

Functional Programming Libraries in Python

This chapter provides an overview of essential functional programming libraries in Python. It discusses the functools, itertools, and operator modules, alongside third-party libraries such as toolz, fn.py, funcy, and multipledispatch. The chapter also covers libraries for immutable data structures, like pyrsistent and immutables, and concludes with a comparative summary and practical examples of using these libraries to enhance functional programming in Python.

7.1 Introduction to Functional Programming Libraries

Functional programming is a paradigm that treats computation as the evaluation of mathematical functions and avoids changing-state and mutable data. Python, though primarily an imperative and object-oriented language, offers robust support for functional programming through a variety of built-in and third-party libraries. These libraries enable developers to leverage functional programming techniques and principles in Pythonic ways. The focus of this section is to introduce the fundamental libraries that aid in functional programming within Python.

One of the core libraries for functional programming in Python is the

functools module. This module provides higher-order functions which can act on or return other functions. Key functions include reduce, partial, and lru_cache, which facilitate the creation, optimization, and combination of functions.

```
from functools import reduce

def factorial(n):
    return reduce(lambda x, y: x * y, range(1, n + 1))

print(factorial(5)) # Output: 120
```

Another indispensable module is **itertools**. This module provides a collection of fast and memory-efficient tools for working with iterators. Common functions include count, cycle, repeat, permutations, and combinations, all of which are useful for creating iterators for efficient looping.

```
from itertools import permutations

perm = permutations([1, 2, 3])
for p in perm:
    print(p)
```

```
(1, 2, 3)
(1, 3, 2)
(2, 1, 3)
(2, 3, 1)
(3, 1, 2)
(3, 2, 1)
```

The **operator** module functions as a collection of efficient functions that correspond to standard operators. These can be used to replace function objects which are otherwise defined using lambda. Functions like itemgetter, attrgetter, and methodcaller simplify accessing elements, attributes, or methods.

```
from operator import itemgetter

students = [('John', 'A', 15), ('Jane', 'B', 12), ('Dave', 'B', 10)]
sorted_students = sorted(students, key=itemgetter(2))

print(sorted_students) # Output: [('Dave', 'B', 10), ('Jane', 'B', 12), ('John', 'A', 15)]
```

In addition to the built-in modules, third-party libraries like **toolz**, **fn.py**, **funcy**, and **multipledispatch** extend functional programming capabilities in Python.

toolz is a library designed to handle high-performance, functional data manipulation tasks. It includes functions for processing iterators, functions, and dictionaries efficiently.

```
from toolz import compose

def double(x):
    return x * 2

def increment(x):
    return x + 1

f = compose(double, increment)
print(f(3)) # Output: 8
```

fn.py offers anonymous functions and other tools specifically targeting functional programming.

```
from fn import reduce

def factorial(n):
    return reduce(lambda x, y: x * y, range(1, n + 1))

print(factorial(5)) # Output: 120
```

funcy provides a suite of versatile functional tools for better manipulation and processing of data.

```
from funcy import partial

def power(base, exponent):
    return base ** exponent

square = partial(power, exponent=2)
print(square(5)) # Output: 25
```

multipledispatch is designed for function overloading and supports multiple dispatch by allowing functions to be defined for specific types of input parameters.

```
from multipledispatch import dispatch

@dispatch(int, int)
def add(a, b):
    return a + b

@dispatch(str, str)
def add(a, b):
    return a + b

print(add(1, 2)) # Output: 3
print(add('a', 'b')) # Output: 'ab'
```

Libraries such as **pyrsistent** and **immutables** provide immutable data structures, which are essential in functional programming for avoiding side effects and maintaining pure functions. These libraries offer persistent data structures like persistent lists and dictionaries.

```
from pyrsistent import pvector
```

```
v = pvector([1, 2, 3])
v2 = v.append(4)

print(v) # Output: pvector([1, 2, 3])
print(v2) # Output: pvector([1, 2, 3, 4])
```

Python's rich ecosystem of functional programming libraries significantly augments its ability to support and promote the principles of functional programming, allowing developers to write more expressive, efficient, and maintainable code.

7.2 The functools Module

The functools module in Python provides higher-order functions that act on or return other functions. It is a set of tools for creating and working with functions and callable objects, useful for implementing and enhancing functional programming paradigms in Python. Key functions within the functools module include partial, reduce, lru_cache, cmp_to_key, and singledispatch, alongside decorators such as wraps. This section delves into these functions and decorators, illustrating their use with practical examples.

The partial Function

The partial function allows for the adaptation of existing functions by fixing a certain number of arguments, resulting in a new function with fewer arguments. This is particularly useful when a function that takes multiple arguments needs to be called repeatedly with some of the same arguments.

```
from functools import partial

def multiply(x, y):
    return x * y

# Create a new function that multiplies by 2
double = partial(multiply, 2)
print(double(4)) # Output: 8
```

Here, partial creates a new function double that multiplies its input by 2. This reduces the need to specify the multiplication factor each time the function is called.

The reduce Function

The reduce function, which is also available in the functools module in

Python 3 (previously in the functools module in Python 2), applies a rolling computation to sequential pairs of values in a list. It reduces a list to a single value by applying a binary function.

```
from functools import reduce

def add(x, y):
    return x + y

numbers = [1, 2, 3, 4, 5]
sum_of_numbers = reduce(add, numbers)
print(sum_of_numbers) # Output: 15
```

In this example, reduce applies the add function cumulatively to the items of the numbers list, effectively summing the list's values.

The lru_cache Decorator

The lru_cache decorator is used to cache the results of expensive or I/O bound function calls. This can significantly enhance performance by avoiding redundant computations. The lru_cache retains a maximum size specified by the user and discards the least recently used items when the cache is full.

```
from functools import lru_cache

@lru_cache(maxsize=32)
def fibonacci(n):
    if n < 2:
        return n
    return fibonacci(n-1) + fibonacci(n-2)

print([fibonacci(n) for n in range(10)])
# Output: [0, 1, 1, 2, 3, 5, 8, 13, 21, 34]
```

The lru_cache decorator caches the results of the fibonacci function calls, reusing them when the same n value is passed, thus improving the performance.

The cmp_to_key Function

The cmp_to_key function converts an old-style comparison function to a key function. This is useful in transitioning from Python 2, which used comparison functions, to Python 3, which utilizes key functions.

```
from functools import cmp_to_key

def compare(a, b):
    return (a > b) - (a < b)

numbers = [3, 2, 5, 4, 1]
sorted_numbers = sorted(numbers, key=cmp_to_key(compare))
print(sorted_numbers) # Output: [1, 2, 3, 4, 5]
```

Here, cmp_to_key enables the transition from the comparison function compare to a key function, facilitating sorting.

The singledispatch Decorator

The singledispatch decorator transforms a function into a single-dispatch generic function, enabling the development of polymorphic functions. The dispatch happens based on the type of the first argument.

```
from functools import singledispatch

@singledispatch
def fun(arg):
    print('Default action:', arg)

@fun.register(int)
def _(arg):
    print('Integer action:', arg)

@fun.register(str)
def _(arg):
    print('String action:', arg)

fun(10) # Output: Integer action: 10
fun("Hello") # Output: String action: Hello
fun([1, 2]) # Output: Default action: [1, 2]
```

The singledispatch decorator allows the function fun to behave differently based on the type of argument passed, making it a powerful tool for writing polymorphic code.

The wraps Decorator

The wraps decorator is typically used for writing decorators. It helps in preserving the original function's metadata when it is decorated, such as the function's name, docstring, and the module it belongs to.

```
from functools import wraps

def decorator(func):
    @wraps(func)
    def wrapper(*args, **kwargs):
        print("Before function call")
        result = func(*args, **kwargs)
        print("After function call")
        return result
    return wrapper

@decorator
def say_hello(name):
    """This function says hello"""
    print(f"Hello, {name}")

say_hello("Alice")
print(say_hello.__name__) # Output: say_hello
print(say_hello.__doc__) # Output: This function says hello
```

The wraps decorator ensures that the decorated say_hello function retains its original name and docstring, which is useful for introspection and debugging.

These functions and decorators in the functools module facilitate the application of functional programming concepts in Python, substantially improving code clarity, performance, and maintainability.

7.3 The itertools Module

The itertools module in Python is a collection of tools for building and working with iterators. Iterators are fundamental to achieving lazy evaluation, an important concept in functional programming. The itertools module provides a standard interface for working with combinatorial constructs such as Cartesian products, permutations, and combinations, as well as for performing many fundamental operations like filtering, mapping, and accumulating. This section delves into the most frequently used functions within the itertools module, elaborating on their purposes and practical applications.

Product

The product function computes the Cartesian product of input iterables. This means it generates all possible pairs (or tuples) of elements taken from multiple collections. The function is invoked as follows:

```
import itertools

result = itertools.product('AB', [1, 2])
print(list(result))
```

The output will be:

```
[('A', 1), ('A', 2), ('B', 1), ('B', 2)]
```

Permutations

Permutations refer to all possible arrangements of elements of a given iterable. The permutations function from itertools is adept at generating these arrangements. Consider the following code:

```
result = itertools.permutations('ABC', 2)
print(list(result))
```

The output will be:

```
[('A', 'B'), ('A', 'C'), ('B', 'A'), ('B', 'C'), ('C', 'A'), ('C', 'B')]
```

Combinations

The combinations function generates all possible combinations of a specified length from the elements of an iterable. For instance:

```
result = itertools.combinations('ABC', 2)
print(list(result))
```

The output will be:

```
[('A', 'B'), ('A', 'C'), ('B', 'C')]
```

Combinations With Replacement

The combinations_with_replacement function is similar to combinations, but it allows individual elements to be repeated. Here's how it works:

```
result = itertools.combinations_with_replacement('AB', 2)
print(list(result))
```

The output will be:

```
[('A', 'A'), ('A', 'B'), ('B', 'B')]
```

Count

The count function generates an infinite sequence of evenly spaced values. Typically, it is used to create counters or to generate index values. The following example demonstrates its usage:

```
counter = itertools.count(start=10, step=2)
print(next(counter))
print(next(counter))
```

The output will be:

```
10
12
```

Cycle

The cycle function endlessly repeats an iterable. This is particularly useful in scenarios where one needs to loop over a collection indefinitely.

```
cycler = itertools.cycle('AB')
print(next(cycler))
print(next(cycler))
print(next(cycler))
```

The output will be:

```
A
B
A
```

Repeat

The repeat function allows the repetition of a single element multiple times. This is straightforward when one needs a constant stream of the same value.

```
repeater = itertools.repeat('X', 3)
print(list(repeater))
```

The output will be:

```
['X', 'X', 'X']
```

Accumulate

The accumulate function returns accumulated sums or the result of other aggregation functions over an iterable. By default, it performs addition.

```
result = itertools.accumulate([1, 2, 3, 4, 5])
print(list(result))
```

The output will be:

```
[1, 3, 6, 10, 15]
```

One can also use this function with other binary functions to produce different accumulation results.

```
import operator

result = itertools.accumulate([1, 2, 3, 4], operator.mul)
print(list(result))
```

The output will be:

```
[1, 2, 6, 24]
```

Chain

The chain function takes multiple iterables and returns a single iterator that produces values from those iterables consecutively.

```
result = itertools.chain('ABC', 'DEF')
print(list(result))
```

The output will be:

```
['A', 'B', 'C', 'D', 'E', 'F']
```

Compress

The compress function filters one iterable with another iterable of booleans. Elements from the data iterable are included in the output if the corresponding value in selectors is True.

```
result = itertools.compress('ABCDEF', [1, 0, 1, 0, 1, 0])
print(list(result))
```

The output will be:

```
['A', 'C', 'E']
```

Dropwhile

The dropwhile function returns elements of an iterable after a predicate becomes False. This function is useful for filtering out the initial part of an iterable where elements meet a condition.

```
result = itertools.dropwhile(lambda x: x < 5, [1, 4, 6, 4, 1])
print(list(result))
```

The output will be:

```
[6, 4, 1]
```

Takewhile

The takewhile function returns elements from an iterable as long as the predicate is True. Once the predicate becomes False, the iterator is exhausted.

```
result = itertools.takewhile(lambda x: x < 5, [1, 4, 6, 4, 1])
print(list(result))
```

The output will be:

```
[1, 4]
```

Filterfalse

The filterfalse function returns only those elements of an iterable for which a predicate is False, i.e., it is the complement of the built-in filter function.

```
result = itertools.filterfalse(lambda x: x % 2, range(10))
print(list(result))
```

The output will be:

```
[0, 2, 4, 6, 8]
```

Groupby

The groupby function returns consecutive keys and groups from an iterable. This function is particularly useful for grouping elements based on a certain key function.

```
data = sorted([('apple', 1), ('banana', 2), ('apple', 3)], key=lambda x: x[0])
for key, group in itertools.groupby(data, key=lambda x: x[0]):
    print(key, list(group))
```

The output will be:

```
apple [('apple', 1), ('apple', 3)]
banana [('banana', 2)]
```

Tee

The tee function splits one iterator into multiple independent iterators, which can be used to consume the values of the original iterator in parallel.

```
it1, it2 = itertools.tee([1, 2, 3, 4])
print(list(it1))
print(list(it2))
```

The output will be:

```
[1, 2, 3, 4]
[1, 2, 3, 4]
```

The itertools module is an invaluable toolkit for functional programmers in Python, enabling complex operations in a concise and efficient manner.

7.4 The operator Module

The operator module in Python provides a comprehensive suite of functions that correspond to intrinsic operators in Python. These functions are designed to facilitate functional programming by making it possible to perform operations using functions rather than operators, thereby allowing for more abstract and flexible code.

An essential feature of the operator module is its support for various types of operations, including arithmetic, logical, bitwise, and comparison operations. This module is ideal for scenarios where lambda functions might otherwise be used, offering a more readable and often more efficient alternative.

Arithmetic Operators

Arithmetic operations are fundamental in both functional and procedural programming. The operator module encapsulates these as functions:

```
import operator
```

```
# Addition
print(operator.add(2, 3)) # Output: 5

# Subtraction
print(operator.sub(5, 2)) # Output: 3

# Multiplication
print(operator.mul(2, 3)) # Output: 6

# Division
print(operator.truediv(7, 2)) # Output: 3.5
```

These functions mirror the behavior of their corresponding arithmetic operators, encapsulating additions, subtractions, multiplications, and divisions.

Logical Operators

Logical operations such as AND, OR, and NOT are also available within the operator module. These operators are converted into functions to facilitate use in higher-order functions or functional constructs:

```
# Logical AND
print(operator.and_(True, False)) # Output: False

# Logical OR
print(operator.or_(True, False)) # Output: True

# Logical NOT
print(operator.not_(False)) # Output: True
```

The addition of an underscore suffix (e.g., and_ instead of and) is necessary due to the fact that the logical operators themselves are reserved keywords in Python.

Bitwise Operators

Bitwise operations manipulate the individual bits of integer values. These are frequently used in low-level programming, cryptography, and graphics. The operator module provides functional counterparts for operations like AND, OR, XOR, and shifts:

```
# Bitwise AND
print(operator.and_(7, 3)) # Output: 3 (0b111 & 0b011 = 0b011)

# Bitwise OR
print(operator.or_(4, 1)) # Output: 5 (0b100 | 0b001 = 0b101)

# Bitwise XOR
print(operator.xor(4, 1)) # Output: 5 (0b100 ^ 0b001 = 0b101)

# Left Shift
print(operator.lshift(3, 2)) # Output: 12 (0b0011 << 2 = 0b1100)

# Right Shift
```

```
print(operator.rshift(8, 2)) # Output: 2 (0b1000 >> 2 = 0b0010)
```

These functions enable concise and readable implementations of complex bitwise operations that would otherwise require manually constructed lambda expressions.

Comparison Operators

The operator module also includes functions for all standard comparison operations:

```
# Less than
print(operator.lt(3, 5)) # Output: True

# Less than or equal to
print(operator.le(3, 3)) # Output: True

# Equal to
print(operator.eq(3, 3)) # Output: True

# Not equal to
print(operator.ne(3, 5)) # Output: True

# Greater than
print(operator.gt(5, 3)) # Output: True

# Greater than or equal to
print(operator.ge(5, 5)) # Output: True
```

These functional equivalents of comparison operators are particularly useful in sorting and filtering operations within higher-order functions like sorted and filter.

Item and Attribute Getters/Setters

Another powerful aspect of the operator module is its support for item and attribute manipulation through functions such as itemgetter, attrgetter, and methodcaller:

```
# itemgetter
import operator

a = [1, 2, 3]
print(operator.itemgetter(1)(a)) # Output: 2

# attrgetter
class Person:
    def __init__(self, name, age):
        self.name = name
        self.age = age

p = Person("Alice", 30)
print(operator.attrgetter('name')(p)) # Output: Alice

# methodcaller
s = "hello"
print(operator.methodcaller('upper')(s)) # Output: HELLO
```

itemgetter is useful for extracting values from sequences, attrgetter is instrumental in attribute access from objects, and methodcaller allows calling methods with specified arguments.

Through the usage of these functional abstractions, the operator module enables more succinct and expressive functional code, which is both easier to read and to maintain. This makes it a valuable tool for developers seeking to leverage functional programming paradigms within the Python ecosystem.

7.5 The toolz Library

The **toolz** library is a collection of functional utilities for iterators, functions, and dictionaries. It is designed for high performance and to promote concise, readable code. Unlike Python's built-in libraries, **toolz** aims to provide a more comprehensive and functional approach to common programming tasks.

The **toolz** library is divided primarily into three submodules: *itertoolz*, *functoolz*, and *dicttoolz*. Each submodule targets a specific type of operation:

- **itertoolz**: Operations on iterators, such as transformations, aggregations, and filtering.
- **functoolz**: Functions for higher-order functional programming, such as function composition and currying.
- **dicttoolz**: Tools for manipulating dictionaries, like merging, key filtering, and value mapping.

toolz is particularly useful for functional programming as it allows for the composition of complex transformations and operations in a readable and efficient manner.

To begin using **toolz**, it needs to be installed via pip:

```
pip install toolz
```

itertoolz Submodule

The *itertoolz* submodule offers various functions to work with iterators. Here are some of the most commonly used functions:

map and **filter** are already familiar to most Python developers, but *itertoolz* extends this functionality with additional features:

```
from toolz import itertoolz

numbers = [1, 2, 3, 4, 5, 6]

# map function
squares = itertoolz.map(lambda x: x**2, numbers)
print(list(squares))
# Output: [1, 4, 9, 16, 25, 36]

# filter function
even_numbers = itertoolz.filter(lambda x: x % 2 == 0, numbers)
print(list(even_numbers))
# Output: [2, 4, 6]
```

Another notable function is **reduce**, which applies a binary function cumulatively to the items of a sequence:

```
from toolz import itertoolz

numbers = [1, 2, 3, 4, 5, 6]

# reduce function
sum_numbers = itertoolz.reduce(lambda x, y: x + y, numbers)
print(sum_numbers)
# Output: 21
```

Operations like **groupby** and **partition** are especially useful for data processing tasks:

```
from toolz import itertoolz

data = [('fruit', 'apple'), ('fruit', 'banana'), ('vegetable', 'carrot'), ('fruit', 'pear')]

# groupby function
grouped = itertoolz.groupby(lambda x: x[0], data)
print(grouped)
# Output: {'fruit': [('fruit', 'apple'), ('fruit', 'banana'), ('fruit', 'pear')], 'vegetable': [('
    vegetable', 'carrot')]}

# partition function
partitions = itertoolz.partition(2, data)
print(list(partitions))
# Output: [(('fruit', 'apple'), ('fruit', 'banana')), (('vegetable', 'carrot'), ('fruit', 'pear'))
    ]
```

functoolz Submodule

The *functoolz* submodule focuses on higher-order functions which are central to functional programming:

One of the most powerful tools provided by **functoolz** is **compose**, which allows for the composition of multiple functions:

```
from toolz import functoolz

def increment(x):
    return x + 1

def square(x):
    return x ** 2

# compose function
composed_func = functoolz.compose(square, increment)
print(composed_func(4)) # Execution of square(increment(4))
# Output: 25
```

Another useful feature is **curry**, enabling partial function application:

```
from toolz import functoolz

@functoolz.curry
def multiply(x, y):
    return x * y

double = multiply(2)
print(double(5))
# Output: 10
```

memoize is another function that caches the results of expensive function calls:

```
from toolz import functoolz

@functoolz.memoize
def factorial(n):
    if n == 0:
        return 1
    else:
        return n * factorial(n-1)

print(factorial(5))
# Output: 120
```

dicttoolz Submodule

The *dicttoolz* submodule offers tools for dictionary manipulation:

One common task is to merge multiple dictionaries. **merge** simplifies this task:

```
from toolz import dicttoolz

dict1 = {'a': 1, 'b': 2}
dict2 = {'b': 3, 'c': 4}

merged_dict = dicttoolz.merge(dict1, dict2)
print(merged_dict)
# Output: {'a': 1, 'b': 3, 'c': 4}
```

Filtering a dictionary's keys or values can be accomplished with the **keyfilter** and **valfilter** functions:

```
from toolz import dicttoolz

data = {'a': 1, 'b': 2, 'c': 3, 'd': 4}

# keyfilter
filtered_by_key = dicttoolz.keyfilter(lambda k: k in 'ab', data)
print(filtered_by_key)
# Output: {'a': 1, 'b': 2}

# valfilter
filtered_by_value = dicttoolz.valfilter(lambda v: v > 2, data)
print(filtered_by_value)
# Output: {'c': 3, 'd': 4}
```

itemmap allows applying a function to each key-value pair in the dictionary:

```
from toolz import dicttoolz

data = {'a': 1, 'b': 2, 'c': 3, 'd': 4}

mapped_items = dicttoolz.itemmap(lambda kv: (kv[0], kv[1] * 2), data)
print(mapped_items)
# Output: {'a': 2, 'b': 4, 'c': 6, 'd': 8}
```

The **toolz** library provides an extensive toolkit for anyone looking to leverage functional programming patterns in Python, enhancing code readability and reusability through modular, higher-order functions.

7.6 The fn.py Library

The fn.py library is designed to elevate functional programming capabilities in Python. By providing a range of functional programming utilities, fn.py facilitates a more expressive and declarative code style. This section delves into its core functionalities, illustrating its utility with practical examples to enhance comprehension.

First, we install the library using pip:

```
pip install fn
```

One of the significant highlights of fn.py is its support for function composition. Function composition allows for the combining of multiple functions into a single function, where the output of one function becomes the input to the next. This is implemented through the compose function.

Consider the following example:

```
from fn import F

def double(x):
    return x * 2

def increment(x):
    return x + 1

composed_function = F(double) * increment
result = composed_function(3)
print(result) # Output will be 8
```

8

In this example, increment first increases the input value by 1, and then double multiplies the result by 2. The order of execution follows the reverse order of composition, ensuring that increment runs before double.

fn.py also includes a powerful curry function that enables partial application of functions. Currying converts a function that takes multiple arguments into a sequence of functions, each accepting a single argument.

Let us illustrate currying with an example:

```
from fn import curry

@curry
def add(x, y):
    return x + y

add_5 = add(5)
result = add_5(3)
print(result) # Output will be 8
```

8

Here, the @curry decorator transforms the add function, allowing it to be partially applied. The intermediate function add_5 is created, which automatically applies 5 as the first argument.

Mapping and reducing operations are also streamlined using fn.py.

Combining map and filter can be done succinctly:

```
from fn.op import map, filter

numbers = range(10)
result = list(filter(lambda x: x % 2 == 0, map(lambda x: x + 1, numbers)))
print(result) # Output will be [1, 3, 5, 7, 9]
```

```
[1, 3, 5, 7, 9]
```

In this example, each number is incremented by 1, and then only the even results are retained. The operation is declaratively expressed without intermediate variables, keeping code concise and clear.

Functional pipelines are another powerful feature provided by fn.py. These pipelines streamline data processing by chaining operations together. An example of creating a pipeline that multiplies, filters, and sums elements can be written as:

```
from fn import F
from fn.op import add, mul, is_even

pipeline = F(range) * (map, lambda x: x * 2) * (filter, is_even) * sum
result = pipeline(10)
print(result) # Output will be 90
```

```
90
```

The pipeline takes in a range of numbers from 0 to 9, doubles each number, filters for even numbers, and sums the results, producing the final result of 90.

Moreover, fn.py supports advanced pattern matching, which allows for more readable and concise conditions by leveraging the match, case, and default functions. Here is a simple demonstration:

```
from fn.match import match, when

@match(when(int))
def describe(value):
    return "This is an integer"

@describe.when(str)
def describe(value):
    return "This is a string"

result = describe(42)
print(result) # Output will be "This is an integer"

result = describe("Hello")
print(result) # Output will be "This is a string"
```

```
This is an integer
This is a string
```

In this example, the type of value is matched, allowing describe to return a description based on the input type.

The fn.py library enriches Python with functional programming constructs, making it an essential tool for anyone looking to embrace a functional approach in Python programming. By enhancing readability and reducing boilerplate, fn.py paves the way to write more expressive and maintainable code.

7.7 The funcy Library

The funcy library is a powerful and versatile tool for functional programming in Python, providing a rich collection of utilities and data structures designed to enhance and simplify code written in a functional style. funcy emphasizes conciseness and elegance, making it an excellent choice for both beginners and experienced functional programmers.

At its core, funcy offers a variety of higher-order functions such as map, filter, reduce, and their enhanced counterparts. Additionally, it provides functions for working with sequences, dictionaries, sets, and even for dealing with exceptions and side effects gracefully. Let's explore some of the key functionalities offered by the funcy library.

Installation

To begin using funcy, it must be installed via pip. The command to install it is straightforward:

```
pip install funcy
```

Functional Iterators

One of the primary features of funcy is its powerful and flexible iterators. These iterators provide an enhanced functional interface for handling iterable collections.

```
import funcy as fy

numbers = [1, 2, 3, 4, 5]

squared = fy.map(lambda x: x**2, numbers)
filtered = fy.filter(lambda x: x % 2 == 0, numbers)
reduced = fy.reduce(lambda x, y: x + y, numbers)

print(list(squared)) % Output: [1, 4, 9, 16, 25]
print(list(filtered)) % Output: [2, 4]
print(reduced) % Output: 15
```

The fy.map function applies a given function to each element of the iterable, making it a direct analog to Python's native map but with additional features, such as support for multiple iterables. The fy.filter function yields all items from the iterable that satisfy a predicate. The fy.reduce function applies a binary function cumulatively to the items of an iterable, from left to right, reducing the iterable to a single value.

Sequences

The funcy library extends predefined sequence operations and introduces additional ones that are highly practical.

```
import funcy as fy

numbers = [1, 2, 3, 4, 5]

# Drop first "n" elements
dropped = fy.drop(2, numbers)

# Take first "n" elements
taken = fy.take(2, numbers)

# Partition sequence into chunks of n elements
chunks = fy.chunks(2, numbers)

print(list(dropped)) % Output: [3, 4, 5]
print(list(taken)) % Output: [1, 2]
print(list(chunks)) % Output: [[1, 2], [3, 4], [5]]
```

fy.drop omits the first n elements, fy.take retrieves the first n elements, and fy.chunks splits the sequence into chunks of specified sizes. These are invaluable for sequence manipulation in a clean and expressive manner.

Working with Dictionaries

Manipulating dictionaries is a common task in Python programming, and funcy simplifies this by offering comprehensive functions tailored to dictionary operations.

```
import funcy as fy

data = {'a': 1, 'b': 2, 'c': 3}

# Map over dictionary values
mapped_values = fy.walk_values(lambda v: v * 2, data)

# Filter dictionary by values
filtered_dict = fy.keep(lambda x: x > 1, data)

print(mapped_values) % Output: {'a': 2, 'b': 4, 'c': 6}
print(filtered_dict) % Output: {'b': 2, 'c': 3}
```

fy.walk_values applies a function to each value in the dictionary, producing a new dictionary with the results. fy.keep is used to retain key-value pairs for which the condition holds.

Handling Exceptions

The funcy library includes utilities for managing exceptions in a more functional way. These tools allow for better control over error handling and recovery processes in your code.

```
import funcy as fy

def divide(a, b):
    return a / b

safely_divide = fy.safe(divide, default=0)

result1 = safely_divide(4, 2) % Output: 2.0
result2 = safely_divide(4, 0) % Output: 0

print(result1)
print(result2)
```

fy.safe wraps a function so that, in case of errors, it returns a default value rather than propagating the exception. This results in more robust and fault-tolerant programs.

Lazy Evaluation

funcy supports lazy evaluation, which allows for deferred computation until the value is actually needed. This is particularly useful in scenarios dealing with large datasets to optimize memory and processing time.

```
import funcy as fy

lazy_squares = fy.lazy(lambda: (x**2 for x in range(10)))

print(list(lazy_squares))
```

fy.lazy constructs a generator-based lazy sequence, computing values only as they are iterated over.

Bag Datatype

The funcy library introduces the Bag datatype, a lazy iterable with several enhanced methods not available in standard Python iterators.

```
import funcy as fy

numbers = [1, 2, 3, 4, 5]

bag = fy.make_bag(numbers)

# Bag supports standard functional operations
multiplied_bag = bag.map(lambda x: x * 10)
filtered_bag = bag.filter(lambda x: x % 2 == 0)
```

```
print(list(multiplied_bag)) % Output: [10, 20, 30, 40, 50]
print(list(filtered_bag)) % Output: [2, 4]
```

Bag operations return new lazy bags, which postpone computation until required, delivering effective management of resources for large collections.

The extensive utility provided by the funcy library represents an invaluable asset to Python programmers aiming for concise and functional code. Combining ease of use with high efficiency, funcy stands out as a quintessential tool for functional programming in Python.

7.8 The multipledispatch Library

Multipledispatch is a library that brings the notion of method overloading to Python. It allows for multiple functions to carry the same name but differ in their signature, determined by the number and type of arguments. This feature is not native to Python, which neither supports method overloading nor implements multiple dispatch intrinsically. The multipledispatch library fills this gap by enabling multiple dispatch, a form of method dispatching from which the invoked function implementation is selected based on the runtime types of more than one of its arguments.

The core of the multipledispatch library is the dispatch decorator. By utilizing this decorator, one can register multiple functions with the same name but different type annotations for their parameters. When a function call is made, the library uses the types of the passed arguments to determine which specific function implementation should be invoked.

To begin using the multipledispatch library, it must be installed via pip:

```
pip install multipledispatch
```

Here is an illustrative example that demonstrates how the multipledispatch library can be utilized:

```
from multipledispatch import dispatch

@dispatch(int, int)
def add(x, y):
    return x + y

@dispatch(str, str)
def add(x, y):
    return x + y
```

```
@dispatch(list, list)
def add(x, y):
    return x + y

# The calls below will resolve to different add implementations
print(add(1, 2)) # Output: 3
print(add("Hello, ", "World!")) # Output: "Hello, World!"
print(add([1, 2], [3, 4])) # Output: [1, 2, 3, 4]
```

In the example above, we define the function add three times, each for a different type signature. The dispatch decorator registers each of these definitions, and based on the types of arguments passed during the function call, the appropriate implementation is selected at runtime.

Implicit Type Conversion

The multipledispatch library also supports implicit type conversions. If a more specific method is not available for the argument types, it will attempt to convert the arguments to a more general type that matches one of the registered functions.

```
@dispatch(float, float)
def add(x, y):
    return x + y

print(add(1, 2.0)) # Output: 3.0
print(add(1.5, 2)) # Output: 3.5
```

In this scenario, when calling add with an int and a float, a conversion occurs so that the float, float method can be invoked, demonstrating the flexibility of multipledispatch.

Dispatching With Custom Types

Multipledispatch is not limited to primitive data types but can also work with user-defined types. Consider the following example with custom types:

```
class Dog:
    def __init__(self, name):
        self.name = name

class Cat:
    def __init__(self, name):
        self.name = name

@dispatch(Dog, Cat)
def make_friends(dog, cat):
    return f"{dog.name} and {cat.name} are friends!"

@dispatch(Cat, Dog)
def make_friends(cat, dog):
    return f"{cat.name} and {dog.name} are friends!"

dog = Dog("Rex")
```

```
cat = Cat("Whiskers")

print(make_friends(dog, cat)) # Output: "Rex and Whiskers are friends!"
print(make_friends(cat, dog)) # Output: "Whiskers and Rex are friends!"
```

This code demonstrates how the multipledispatch library can handle user-defined classes, facilitating operations that depend on the interaction between different object types.

Performance Considerations

While powerful, it is essential to recognize that use of multipledispatch can introduce overhead due to the dynamic determination of the appropriate function implementation at runtime. This overhead is acceptable in many cases but could be a bottleneck in performance-critical applications. It is advisable to profile the performance in relevant scenarios to ensure that the flexibility provided by multiple dispatch does not negatively impact the application's performance.

By leveraging the multipledispatch library, Python's functional programming capabilities are significantly enhanced, allowing for clear, concise, and flexible code that can handle various input types and combinations seamlessly.

7.9 Libraries for Immutable Data Structures: pyrsistent and immutables

In functional programming, immutability is a core principle. Immutable data structures do not change once they are created, which leads to safer and more predictable programs. Two prominent libraries in Python that facilitate immutable data structures are pyrsistent and immutables. Both libraries offer a variety of constructs to work with immutable objects, streamlining functional programming practices.

Pyrsistent is a library that provides functional, immutable data structures based on persistent data structures. It supports various collection types including PVector, PMap, PSet, and PRecord. These collections behave similarly to their mutable counterparts in the standard Python library, but with immutability.

To illustrate the use of pyrsistent, consider the following example where we utilize a persistent vector (PVector):

```
from pyrsistent import pvector
```

```
# Creating an immutable PVector
immutable_vector = pvector([1, 2, 3])
print("Original PVector:", immutable_vector)

# Attempting to "modify" the PVector - a new PVector is returned
new_vector = immutable_vector.append(4)
print("New PVector after append:", new_vector)
print("Confirmation of immutability - Original PVector:", immutable_vector)
```

Output:

```
Original PVector: pvector([1, 2, 3])
New PVector after append: pvector([1, 2, 3, 4])
Confirmation of immutability - Original PVector: pvector([1, 2, 3])
```

In the example above, appending an element to the PVector does not alter the original vector but creates a new one instead, highlighting its immutability.

PMap is another data structure provided by pyrsistent, akin to the standard Python dictionary, but immutable:

```
from pyrsistent import pmap

# Creating an immutable PMap
immutable_map = pmap({"a": 1, "b": 2, "c": 3})
print("Original PMap:", immutable_map)

# Modifying the PMap - a new PMap is returned
new_map = immutable_map.set("d", 4)
print("New PMap after set:", new_map)
print("Confirmation of immutability - Original PMap:", immutable_map)
```

Output:

```
Original PMap: pmap({'a': 1, 'b': 2, 'c': 3})
New PMap after set: pmap({'a': 1, 'b': 2, 'c': 3, 'd': 4})
Confirmation of immutability - Original PMap: pmap({'a': 1, 'b': 2, 'c': 3})
```

The PMap maintains immutability by ensuring any updates to the map result in the creation of a new instance.

Immutables is another library catering to immutable data, offering types such as Map and Set. It is known for its performance-oriented design, leveraging Trie data structures to achieve efficient immutability.

To see immutables in action, consider the following example using an immutable Map:

```
from immutables import Map

# Creating an immutable Map
immutable_map = Map({"x": 10, "y": 20})
print("Original Map:", immutable_map)

# Modifying the Map - a new Map is returned
new_map = immutable_map.set("z", 30)
```

```
print("New Map after set:", new_map)
print("Confirmation of immutability - Original Map:", immutable_map)
```

Output:

```
Original Map: Map({'x': 10, 'y': 20})
New Map after set: Map({'x': 10, 'y': 20, 'z': 30})
Confirmation of immutability - Original Map: Map({'x': 10, 'y': 20})
```

In this example, similar to pyrsistent, the immutables library ensures immutability by returning a new instance of Map when attempting to modify the original.

Both libraries also support nested structures, enabling complex, hierarchical data management while maintaining immutability. This is particularly crucial in functional programming, where the integrity of data transformations and state consistency are paramount.

By utilizing pyrsistent and immutables, one can effectively manage immutable data structures within Python, fostering a more functional programming paradigm. These libraries contribute to maintaining predictable state and facilitating safer concurrency in applications. The provision of familiar APIs makes transitioning to immutable data structures straightforward for those accustomed to Python's built-in collections.

7.10 Comparative Summary of Functional Libraries

When approaching functional programming in Python, the plethora of available libraries can present a bewildering landscape. This section aims to demystify the functional programming ecosystem by offering a meticulous comparative summary of key libraries: functools, itertools, operator, toolz, fn.py, funcy, and multipledispatch, along with libraries for immutable data structures like pyrsistent and immutables. By evaluating these libraries on various parameters such as functionality, usability, performance, and community support, we can better understand how they complement one another and when each is most appropriately employed.

Functionality Comparison

- functools: Primarily provides tools that aid in higher-order functions and function operations such as partial application, function memoization with lru_cache, and combinatorial utilities like reduce.

- itertools: Offers efficient iterators for looping constructs, including infinite iterators (count, cycle), finite iterators (chain, compress), and combinatorial generators (product, permutations).
- operator: Exposes a set of efficient functions corresponding to standard operator symbols, facilitating the creation of higher-order functions and enhancing code clarity.
- toolz: Extends the built-in modules with a collection of utility functions for functional programming, covering function composition, partial application, and lazy evaluation.
- fn.py: Emphasizes simplicity and readability, offering constructs for function composition, as well as functional collections such as sequences and maps.
- funcy: Aims for a rich set of utilities that emphasize lazy evaluation, function composition, and higher-order functions.
- multipledispatch: Simple interface to multiple function dispatching, allowing function overloading based on types rather than merely argument counts.
- pyrsistent and immutables: Provide efficient immutable data structures, crucial for side-effect-free programming. pyrsistent offers a broader range of data structures including persistent lists and maps, while immutables focuses on immutable mappings.

Usability and Interface

- functools, itertools, and operator: Being part of the Python Standard Library, they provide highly optimized and well-documented functionalities. Their interfaces are consistent with Python's design philosophy.
- toolz: Emphasizes a functional style with a large collection of utilities that encourage functional composition and chaining. Provides extensions for both standard data types and NumPy arrays.
- fn.py: Designed with a clean syntax that emphasizes readability. However, it is less feature-rich compared to toolz and funcy.
- funcy: Offers a comprehensive set of utilities with an emphasis on lazy evaluation, ensuring memory efficiency for large datasets.

- multipledispatch: Provides an intuitive API for overloading functions based on argument types, beneficial for polymorphic behavior without excessive boilerplate code.

- pyrsistent and immutables: Offer interfaces mimicking native Python collections, ensuring ease of migration from mutable to immutable data structures.

Performance Considerations

- functools, itertools, and operator: Being part of the Standard Library, they are highly optimized for performance and are typically the most performant.

- toolz: Strikes a balance between performance and convenience. While slightly slower than built-in modules, it is optimized for common functional tasks.

- fn.py: Designed for simplicity over raw performance, suitable for scripts where readability is prioritized over execution speed.

- funcy: Focuses on lazy evaluation to optimize memory usage and processing time for large datasets.

- multipledispatch: Efficient for its purpose of type-based function dispatch, although overhead might be noticeable in performance-critical applications.

- pyrsistent and immutables: Both libraries offer high-performance immutable collections, with pyrsistent particularly noted for its fast read and moderate update speeds, and immutables providing competitive performance for immutable mapping structures.

Community and Documentation

- functools, itertools, operator: Extensive and high-quality documentation is provided as part of the official Python documentation. Community support is strong due to their widespread use.

- toolz: Comprehensive documentation and a relatively active community. It is frequently updated and supported by contributors.

- fn.py: Simplistic documentation compared to toolz, with a smaller although dedicated user base.

- funcy: Well-documented and regularly maintained with a moderate community size that actively contributes to problem-solving.
- multipledispatch: Sufficiently documented with clear examples, enjoying moderate community support.
- pyrsistent and immutables: Both libraries maintain good documentation, with pyrsistent having a slight edge in terms of supplemental tutorials and community-driven examples.

By understanding these functional libraries' strengths and use cases, practitioners can choose appropriate tools tailored to the specific requirements of their functional programming tasks in Python.

7.11 Practical Examples with Functional Libraries

To illustrate the power and applicability of functional programming libraries in Python, this section explores practical examples. These examples utilize the concepts and libraries discussed previously, showcasing how these tools can simplify and enhance code.

Example 1: Data Processing Pipeline with toolz

In this example, we will create a data processing pipeline using the toolz library. Consider a list of dictionaries representing user data. We aim to filter users based on age, extract their names, and convert names to uppercase.

```
from toolz import compose, map, filter

# Sample data
users = [
    {'name': 'Alice', 'age': 30},
    {'name': 'Bob', 'age': 15},
    {'name': 'Charlie', 'age': 35},
]

# Function to filter users older than 20
def filter_adults(user):
    return user['age'] > 20

# Function to extract names
def get_name(user):
    return user['name']

# Function to convert names to uppercase
def to_uppercase(name):
    return name.upper()
```

```
# Composing the data processing pipeline
pipeline = compose(list, map(to_uppercase), map(get_name), filter(filter_adults))

# Applying the pipeline to the user data
processed_users = pipeline(users)
print(processed_users)
```

Running this code yields:

```
['ALICE', 'CHARLIE']
```

The use of compose enables the combination of multiple operations into a single pipeline, making the code more readable and functional.

Example 2: Using functools.reduce for Summation

The functools library's reduce function can be used to accumulate values in a collection. Here, we will sum a list of numbers using reduce.

```
from functools import reduce
from operator import add

# Sample data
numbers = [1, 2, 3, 4, 5]

# Summing the numbers using reduce
total_sum = reduce(add, numbers)
print(total_sum)
```

The output is:

```
15
```

The reduce function applies the add operator cumulatively, resulting in the total sum of the list elements.

Example 3: Lazy Evaluation with itertools

The itertools module provides tools for creating iterators, enabling lazy evaluation which can be more memory-efficient for large datasets. We will use itertools to generate an infinite sequence of natural numbers and extract a subset of it.

```
import itertools

# Infinite sequence of natural numbers
natural_numbers = itertools.count(start=1)

# Take the first 10 natural numbers
first_ten = list(itertools.islice(natural_numbers, 10))
print(first_ten)
```

Executing the above code generates:

```
[1, 2, 3, 4, 5, 6, 7, 8, 9, 10]
```

The islice function allows us to obtain a slice of the infinite sequence efficiently.

Example 4: Dispatching Functions with multipledispatch

The multipledispatch library facilitates function overloading. Using this library, different code paths can be executed based on the type of arguments. Here, we will dispatch functions based on input types.

```
from multipledispatch import dispatch

# Function for integer input
@dispatch(int)
def process(data):
    return data + 10

# Function for string input
@dispatch(str)
def process(data):
    return data.upper()

# Applying the dispatch functions
result_int = process(5)
result_str = process('hello')

print(result_int)
print(result_str)
```

The output is:

```
15
HELLO
```

This example demonstrates how multipledispatch can be used to create flexible and type-specific functions.

Example 5: Immutable Data Structures with pyrsistent

The pyrsistent library provides immutable data structures. Here, we will use a PVector to maintain an immutable list.

```
from pyrsistent import v

# Creating an immutable list
immutable_list = v(1, 2, 3)

# Attempting to modify the list
new_list = immutable_list.append(4)
print(immutable_list)
print(new_list)
```

Running this code produces:

```
pvector([1, 2, 3])
pvector([1, 2, 3, 4])
```

The original list remains unchanged, and a new list is created with the appended element, demonstrating immutability.

These practical examples highlight the versatility and efficiency of functional programming libraries in Python. Employing these libraries can lead to more concise, readable, and maintainable code, essential for modern software development.

Chapter 8

Functional Design Patterns and Strategies

This chapter explores functional design patterns and strategies, focusing on their application in Python. It covers common patterns such as the Strategy, Decorator, Factory, Singleton, Command, Observer, and Adapter patterns. Additionally, it examines functional composition, pipelines, and advanced concepts like monads and functors. Practical examples are provided to illustrate these patterns, along with best practices for implementing functional design in Python.

8.1 Introduction to Functional Design Patterns

Functional design patterns play a crucial role in structuring and organizing code written in a functional programming style. These patterns facilitate the development of software by providing proven solutions to common problems. They also help with maintaining and scaling applications by promoting code reuse and enhancing readability. In this section, we will explore the key concepts that underpin functional design patterns, examine their benefits, and provide a foundation for understanding the patterns explored in subsequent sections.

Functional programming (FP) is often associated with a declarative approach where functions are first-class citizens. This implies that functions can be passed as arguments, returned from other functions, and assigned to variables. FP encourages immutability, higher-order functions, and pure functions, which ensure that functions have no side effects and always produce the same output given the same input. These principles are the basis on which functional design patterns are built.

A common thread through functional design patterns is the emphasis on the composition of functions. Function composition allows for building complex operations by combining simpler functions. This compositionality leads to modular and highly reusable code. Let's briefly review some core concepts that facilitate understanding these patterns.

Higher-Order Functions: Higher-order functions are functions that take other functions as arguments or return them as results. They are fundamental in functional programming and serve as building blocks for many patterns. An example in Python is the map function, which applies a given function to each item in an iterable:

```
def square(x):
    return x * x

numbers = [1, 2, 3, 4]
squared_numbers = map(square, numbers)
print(list(squared_numbers))

# Output:
# [1, 4, 9, 16]
```

Pure Functions: Pure functions are deterministic and side-effect-free. This property ensures that the function's output is always the same for the same input, making reasoning about the code easier and enabling optimizations such as memoization.

```
def pure_function(x, y):
    return x + y

result = pure_function(3, 5)
print(result)

# Output:
# 8
```

Immutability: Immutability implies that once a data structure is created, it cannot be modified. Instead of altering existing structures, new structures are created, preserving the original. This property aids in maintaining the integrity of data and avoiding unintended side effects.

```
from collections import namedtuple

Point = namedtuple('Point', ['x', 'y'])
```

```
p1 = Point(2, 3)

# Trying to modify will result in an error
# p1.x = 5 # AttributeError

# Create a new instance with the desired change
p2 = p1._replace(x=5)
print(p2)

# Output:
# Point(x=5, y=3)
```

Function Composition: Function composition is the process of combining two or more functions to produce a new function. This new function takes the output of one function as the input to another, creating a pipeline of operations.

```
def add_one(x):
    return x + 1

def multiply_by_two(x):
    return x * 2

def compose(f, g):
    return lambda x: f(g(x))

new_function = compose(multiply_by_two, add_one)
print(new_function(3))

# Output:
# 8
```

With these core concepts in mind, let's briefly enumerate some of the functional design patterns that we will discuss in this chapter:

- **Strategy Pattern:** Enables selecting an algorithm at runtime.
- **Decorator Pattern:** Allows adding behavior to functions in a modular way.
- **Factory Pattern:** Provides a method for creating instances without specifying the exact class of the object.
- **Singleton Pattern:** Ensures a class has only one instance and provides a global point of access to it.
- **Command Pattern:** Encapsulates a request as an object, allowing for parameterization and queuing.
- **Observer Pattern:** Defines a one-to-many dependency between objects.

- **Adapter Pattern:** Allows incompatible interfaces to work together.

Understanding these patterns and their implementation in a functional style will enhance your ability to write clean, efficient, and scalable Python code. As we proceed through this chapter, each pattern will be explained with practical examples, elucidating how Python's functional programming features facilitate their implementation.

8.2 The Strategy Pattern

The Strategy Pattern is a behavioral design pattern that enables the selection of an algorithm's behavior at runtime. This pattern defines a family of algorithms, encapsulates each one, and makes them interchangeable. The Strategy Pattern allows the algorithm to vary independently from clients that use it, promoting flexibility in the choice of behavior.

In Python, the Strategy Pattern is commonly implemented using higher-order functions or classes. The core components of the Strategy Pattern include the Context, Strategy, and ConcreteStrategy. Below is a detailed exploration of these components and their implementation.

The **Context** is the class that interacts with the strategies. It holds a reference to a Strategy object and delegates part of its behavior to the strategy. The context is not concerned with which strategy is being used, allowing it to support various behaviors.

The **Strategy** is an interface common to all concrete strategies. It declares a method that is common to all supported strategies, and the Context uses this method to execute the algorithm defined by a ConcreteStrategy.

The **ConcreteStrategy** classes implement the Strategy interface and define the algorithm for each type of strategy.

Let's start by defining a simple example where a TextProcessor can apply different formatting strategies to text. In this example, we implement two strategies: one for converting text to uppercase and one for converting text to lowercase.

We'll begin by defining the Strategy interface:

```
from abc import ABC, abstractmethod
```

```
class TextFormatter(ABC):
    @abstractmethod
    def format(self, text: str) -> str:
        pass
```

Next, we implement the ConcreteStrategy classes:

```
class UpperCaseFormatter(TextFormatter):
    def format(self, text: str) -> str:
        return text.upper()

class LowerCaseFormatter(TextFormatter):
    def format(self, text: str) -> str:
        return text.lower()
```

Now, we define the Context class that uses a TextFormatter:

```
class TextProcessor:
    def __init__(self, formatter: TextFormatter):
        self._formatter = formatter

    def set_formatter(self, formatter: TextFormatter):
        self._formatter = formatter

    def process(self, text: str) -> str:
        return self._formatter.format(text)
```

The TextProcessor class takes an instance of TextFormatter (or any of its subclasses) during initialization. The set_formatter method allows changing the strategy at runtime. The process method applies the strategy to the given text.

Here is how you can use the Strategy Pattern with the TextProcessor:

```
if __name__ == "__main__":
    text = "Hello, Strategy Pattern!"

    upper_case_processor = TextProcessor(UpperCaseFormatter())
    print(upper_case_processor.process(text)) # HELLO, STRATEGY PATTERN!

    lower_case_processor = TextProcessor(LowerCaseFormatter())
    print(lower_case_processor.process(text)) # hello, strategy pattern!
```

The output of this script will be:

```
HELLO, STRATEGY PATTERN!
hello, strategy pattern!
```

This example demonstrates how easy it is to switch between different formatting strategies without altering the TextProcessor class. This flexibility is the main advantage of the Strategy Pattern.

The Strategy Pattern is not limited to formatting text; it can be applied to various scenarios such as sorting algorithms, routing logic, or any situation where you need interchangeable behaviors. Consider the following example where we employ the Strategy Pattern to sort a list using different algorithms.

First, let's define the Strategy interface for a sorting algorithm:

```
class SortStrategy(ABC):
    @abstractmethod
    def sort(self, data: list) -> list:
        pass
```

Next, we implement two ConcreteStrategy classes: one for bubble sort and one for quicksort.

```
class BubbleSortStrategy(SortStrategy):
    def sort(self, data: list) -> list:
        n = len(data)
        for i in range(n):
            for j in range(0, n-i-1):
                if data[j] > data[j+1]:
                    data[j], data[j+1] = data[j+1], data[j]
        return data

class QuickSortStrategy(SortStrategy):
    def sort(self, data: list) -> list:
        if len(data) <= 1:
            return data
        pivot = data[len(data) // 2]
        left = [x for x in data if x < pivot]
        middle = [x for x in data if x == pivot]
        right = [x for x in data if x > pivot]
        return self.sort(left) + middle + self.sort(right)
```

We then define the Context class that uses a SortStrategy:

```
class Sorter:
    def __init__(self, strategy: SortStrategy):
        self._strategy = strategy

    def set_strategy(self, strategy: SortStrategy):
        self._strategy = strategy

    def sort(self, data: list) -> list:
        return self._strategy.sort(data)
```

Finally, here is how you can use different sorting strategies with the Sorter:

```
if __name__ == "__main__":
    data = [5, 3, 8, 6, 2]

    bubble_sorter = Sorter(BubbleSortStrategy())
    print(bubble_sorter.sort(data.copy())) # [2, 3, 5, 6, 8]

    quick_sorter = Sorter(QuickSortStrategy())
    print(quick_sorter.sort(data.copy())) # [2, 3, 5, 6, 8]
```

The output of this script will be:

```
[2, 3, 5, 6, 8]
[2, 3, 5, 6, 8]
```

This example uses two different sorting algorithms interchangeably without changing the Sorter class logic. This demonstrates the power of the Strategy Pattern in providing flexibility and maintaining code organization.

8.3 The Decorator Pattern

The Decorator Pattern is a structural pattern that allows behavior to be added to individual objects, either statically or dynamically, without affecting the behavior of other objects from the same class. In functional programming, decorators are higher-order functions that accept a function as an argument and return a new function that extends the behavior of the original function.

In Python, function decorators are implemented using the @decorator syntax, which can significantly improve code readability and reuse.

Basic Decorator Example

Consider a basic decorator that logs the execution time of a function:

```
import time

def log_execution_time(func):
    def wrapper(*args, **kwargs):
        start_time = time.time()
        result = func(*args, **kwargs)
        end_time = time.time()
        print(f"Function {func.__name__} took {end_time - start_time} seconds to
            execute.")
        return result
    return wrapper

@log_execution_time
def compute():
    sum([i**2 for i in range(10000)])

compute()
```

In this example, the compute function is decorated with log_execution_time. When compute is called, the log_execution_time decorator logs the execution time of compute. The decorator wraps the original function, thereby adding new behavior without modifying the function itself.

Parameterization of Decorators

Decorators can also be parameterized to provide more flexibility. For instance, consider a decorator that can log to a file instead of printing to the console:

```
def log_to_file(file_name):
    def decorator(func):
        def wrapper(*args, **kwargs):
            start_time = time.time()
            result = func(*args, **kwargs)
            end_time = time.time()
            with open(file_name, 'a') as f:
                f.write(f"Function {func.__name__} took {end_time - start_time}
                    seconds to execute.\n")
            return result
        return wrapper
    return decorator

@log_to_file('execution_log.txt')
def compute():
    sum([i**2 for i in range(10000)])

compute()
```

The log_to_file decorator is now parameterized to take a file_name argument, allowing it to log to any specified file. This shows the power and flexibility of decorators in extending functionalities dynamically.

Chaining Multiple Decorators

Multiple decorators can be chained together to compose complex behaviors. Each decorator is applied in the order specified before defining the function:

```
def uppercase(func):
    def wrapper(*args, **kwargs):
        result = func(*args, **kwargs)
        return result.upper()
    return wrapper

def exclamation(func):
    def wrapper(*args, **kwargs):
        result = func(*args, **kwargs)
        return result + "!"
    return wrapper

@exclamation
@uppercase
def greet(name):
    return f"Hello, {name}"

print(greet("World"))
```

In this example, the greet function is first decorated with uppercase and then with exclamation. When greet is called, it first produces the string "Hello, World", which is then converted to uppercase and finally an exclamation mark is added, resulting in "HELLO, WORLD!".

Class Decorators

Besides functions, decorators can also be applied to classes to modify their behavior:

```
def add_class_metadata(author):
    def decorator(cls):
        cls.author = author
        return cls
    return decorator

@add_class_metadata('John Doe')
class SampleClass:
    pass

print(SampleClass.author)
```

Here, the add_class_metadata decorator adds an author attribute to the SampleClass. This demonstrates how decorators can be utilized to extend or modify class functionalities in a clean and modular manner.

Practical Use Cases

Decorators are particularly useful in scenarios like logging, access control, memoization (caching results of expensive function calls), and pre/-post processing steps.

For logging, the decorator can capture function calls, parameters, and output values, which is crucial for debugging and monitoring:

```
def logger(func):
    def wrapper(*args, **kwargs):
        print(f"Calling function {func.__name__} with arguments {args} and keyword
              arguments {kwargs}")
        result = func(*args, **kwargs)
        print(f"Function {func.__name__} returned {result}")
        return result
    return wrapper

@logger
def add(a, b):
    return a + b

add(2, 3)
```

The logger decorator logs the function name, arguments, and return value, assisting in understanding the function's behavior during execution.

To optimize performance, decorators can be used to cache results of computationally expensive functions through memoization:

```
def memoize(func):
    cache = {}
    def wrapper(*args):
        if args in cache:
```

```
            return cache[args]
        result = func(*args)
        cache[args] = result
        return result
    return wrapper

@memoize
def fibonacci(n):
    if n < 2:
        return n
    return fibonacci(n-1) + fibonacci(n-2)

print(fibonacci(35))
```

The memoize decorator stores the results of function calls in a cache, reducing the need for redundant calculations, thereby speeding up repeated computations.

The Decorator Pattern in Python provides a powerful mechanism for enhancing functionalities in a clean, reusable, and decoupled manner.

8.4 The Factory Pattern

The Factory Pattern is an essential design pattern that enables object creation without specifying the exact class of object that will be created. This pattern is particularly useful in scenarios where the type of objects to be created is determined during runtime. By using factories, code becomes more modular, flexible, and easier to maintain.

In the context of functional programming in Python, the Factory Pattern adheres to the functional paradigm by abstracting the object creation process, allowing for more concise and readable code. This section elaborates on implementing the Factory Pattern in Python using functional constructs.

Basic Principles

At its core, the Factory Pattern involves a factory function responsible for creating objects. This function encapsulates the logic for instantiating objects and can decide which subclass to instantiate based on inputs or configuration. The key benefit is that the client code is decoupled from the specific classes it needs to instantiate.

```
class Dog:
    def speak(self):
        return "Woof!"
```

```
class Cat:
    def speak(self):
        return "Meow!"

def animal_factory(animal_type):
    if animal_type == 'dog':
        return Dog()
    elif animal_type == 'cat':
        return Cat()
    else:
        raise ValueError(f"Unknown animal type: {animal_type}")
```

In the above example, animal_factory is a simple factory function. It takes a parameter animal_type and returns an instance of the corresponding class. This approach allows client code to request objects without knowing the concrete classes.

```
>>> dog = animal_factory('dog')
>>> dog.speak()
'Woof!'
>>> cat = animal_factory('cat')
>>> cat.speak()
'Meow!'
```

Enhancing Flexibility with Higher-Order Functions

Python's support for higher-order functions enhances the flexibility of the Factory Pattern. By passing functions or lambdas as parameters, factories can be made more dynamic and extensible.

```
def dog_factory():
    return Dog()

def cat_factory():
    return Cat()

def enhanced_animal_factory(factory_function):
    return factory_function()

dog = enhanced_animal_factory(dog_factory)
cat = enhanced_animal_factory(cat_factory)

print(dog.speak()) # Output: Woof!
print(cat.speak()) # Output: Meow!
```

Here, enhanced_animal_factory accepts a factory function as an argument, which can be called to create the required object. This makes the factory itself more adaptable and modular.

Using Partial Functions for Configuration

The functools.partial function in Python can be leveraged to pre-configure factory functions, further enhancing the Factory Pattern.

```
from functools import partial

class Animal:
    def __init__(self, name, sound):
        self.name = name
        self.sound = sound

    def speak(self):
        return f"{self.sound}! My name is {self.name}."

dog_factory = partial(Animal, sound='Woof')
cat_factory = partial(Animal, sound='Meow')

dog = dog_factory(name='Buddy')
cat = cat_factory(name='Kitty')

print(dog.speak()) # Output: Woof! My name is Buddy.
print(cat.speak()) # Output: Meow! My name is Kitty.
```

By using functools.partial, the factory functions are configured with constant parameters, reducing boilerplate and improving readability. Factories can now focus on the varying parameters while maintaining pre-configured settings.

Advantages of the Factory Pattern in Functional Design

The Factory Pattern, when embraced within functional programming paradigms, offers several benefits:

- **Separation of Concerns**: Object creation logic is encapsulated within the factory, decoupling it from the client code.

- **Flexibility and Extensibility**: By utilizing higher-order functions and partial application, factories can be easily extended or modified without altering the client code.

- **Enhanced Readability**: The use of factory functions makes the client code more readable, as the object creation process is abstracted away.

- **Improved Code Maintenance**: Changes to object creation logic are localized within the factory, simplifying maintenance.

Functional programming in Python thus benefits significantly from applying the Factory Pattern, allowing for more modular and maintainable code structures.

8.5 The Singleton Pattern

The Singleton Pattern is a creational design pattern used to restrict the instantiation of a class to one single instance. The primary goal of this pattern is to ensure that a class has only one instance and provides a global point of access to that instance. This is particularly useful when exactly one object is needed to coordinate actions across the system.

In traditional Object-Oriented Programming (OOP), Singleton Pattern is implemented by creating a class with a method that creates a new instance of the class if one does not exist yet. In subsequent calls, the method returns the same instance created before.

In Python, the Singleton Pattern can be implemented in multiple ways. Here, we will explore various methods: using a decorator, using a metaclass, and using a module-level implementation.

```
def singleton(cls):
    instances = {}

    def get_instance(*args, **kwargs):
        if cls not in instances:
            instances[cls] = cls(*args, **kwargs)
        return instances[cls]

    return get_instance

@singleton
class SingletonClass:
    def __init__(self):
        self.value = "Singleton Value"

# Usage
instance1 = SingletonClass()
instance2 = SingletonClass()

print(instance1 is instance2) # Output: True
print(instance1.value) # Output: Singleton Value
```

In this example, the singleton decorator wraps the class. The decorator maintains a dictionary of instances. When the class is called, it checks if an instance of the class already exists. If it does not, it creates one; otherwise, it returns the existing instance. This ensures only one instance of the class is ever created.

Another method to implement the Singleton Pattern in Python is by using metaclasses. A metaclass in Python is a class of a class that defines how a class behaves. A class is itself an instance of metaclass.

```
class SingletonMeta(type):
    _instances = {}

    def __call__(cls, *args, **kwargs):
        if cls not in cls._instances:
            cls._instances[cls] = super(SingletonMeta, cls).__call__(*args, **kwargs)
        return cls._instances[cls]

class SingletonClass(metaclass=SingletonMeta):
    def __init__(self):
        self.value = "Singleton Value"

# Usage
instance1 = SingletonClass()
instance2 = SingletonClass()

print(instance1 is instance2) # Output: True
print(instance1.value) # Output: Singleton Value
```

In this example, the SingletonMeta metaclass overrides the __call__ method to control the instantiation process. It keeps a dictionary of instances and ensures that only one instance of the class exists.

The Singleton Pattern can also be implemented at the module level. Since Python modules are singletons by default, this approach leverages this feature.

```
# singleton_module.py
class SingletonClass:
    def __init__(self):
        self.value = "Singleton Value"

singleton_instance = SingletonClass()

# Usage
from singleton_module import singleton_instance

instance1 = singleton_instance
instance2 = singleton_instance

print(instance1 is instance2) # Output: True
print(instance1.value) # Output: Singleton Value
```

In this module-level approach, the singleton instance is created when the module is loaded. Importing the singleton instance from the module ensures that the same instance is used throughout the program.

The Singleton Pattern, when applied with care and caution, can be very effective in scenarios where a single point of control or a single instance is paramount, such as in managing configurations, logging, caching, or managing a connection pool. However, it is important to be aware of its potential downsides, such as difficulty in testing due to hidden dependencies.

In functional programming, where immutability and side-effect-free functions are emphasized, the need for singletons can often be reduced. Still, it's essential to understand this pattern and its implementation for cases where it aligns well with the system's architecture and requirements.

8.6 The Command Pattern

The Command Pattern is an essential design pattern that falls under the behavioral patterns category. It is particularly useful in scenarios where actions or operations need to be executed, undone, or queued. This pattern encapsulates a request as an object, thereby allowing for parameterization of clients with queues, requests, and operations. It supports the undoable operations and can also be used to implement transaction logs.

Structure of the Command Pattern:

In the Command Pattern, four primary components are involved:

1. **Command Interface**: This defines the interface for executing an operation. 2. **Concrete Command**: This implements the Command interface and defines the relationship between the Receiver object and an action. 3. **Invoker**: This asks the command to carry out the request. 4. **Receiver**: This performs the actual action.

To illustrate this in Python, consider the following example:

```
class Command:
    def execute(self):
        pass

class ConcreteCommand(Command):
    def __init__(self, receiver):
        self.receiver = receiver

    def execute(self):
        self.receiver.action()

class Receiver:
    def action(self):
        print("Action executed by the Receiver")

class Invoker:
    def __init__(self):
        self._commands = []
```

```
    def store_command(self, command):
        self._commands.append(command)

    def execute_commands(self):
        for command in self._commands:
            command.execute()
```

Operation of the Command Pattern:

- The Command interface declares a method for executing a command, which in this example is execute(). - The ConcreteCommand class implements this interface and maintains a reference to a Receiver object. When this method is executed, it invokes the corresponding operation(s) on the Receiver. - The Receiver object knows how to perform the operations associated with carrying out a request. - The Invoker object stores commands and later executes them. The Invoker does not need to know the specifics of the command or the receiver.

The following code runs the setup:

```
# Creating objects for receiver and invoker
receiver = Receiver()
invoker = Invoker()

# Creating command with its receiver
command = ConcreteCommand(receiver)

# Storing the command to invoker
invoker.store_command(command)

# Executing commands stored in invoker
invoker.execute_commands()
```

Action executed by the Receiver

Advantages and Applications:

1. **Decoupling Objects**: The Command Pattern decouples the classes that invoke the operation from the object that executes the operation. This separation allows for more flexibility in assigning responsibilities to objects.

2. **Command Queues and Logs**: Commands can be easily queued for later execution or stored for implementing a log of executed commands, which may be essential for various transactional operations.

3. **Support for Undo/Redo Mechanisms**: Because an executed command can be stored, it is relatively straightforward to implement undo and redo functionalities. The state before the command's execution can be saved, allowing the system to revert to that state if necessary.

Undo Functionality in Command Pattern:

Modifying the Command Pattern to incorporate undo functionality involves adding an unexecute() method to the Command interface and updating the ConcreteCommand class to implement this method.

```
class Command:
    def execute(self):
        pass

    def unexecute(self):
        pass

class ConcreteCommand(Command):
    def __init__(self, receiver, action, undo_action):
        self.receiver = receiver
        self._action = action
        self._undo_action = undo_action

    def execute(self):
        getattr(self.receiver, self._action)()

    def unexecute(self):
        getattr(self.receiver, self._undo_action)()
```

In this extended version, the command explicitly includes an undo action, thus supporting rollback mechanics.

To enhance the application further, implement context-aware functionality and strategies for prioritizing and scheduling commands. By doing so, the Command Pattern can be effectively employed in robust, scalable systems that require sophisticated command and operation handling functionalities.

8.7 The Observer Pattern

The Observer Pattern, commonly found in object-oriented programming, facilitates a one-to-many dependency between objects so that when one object, known as the subject, changes state, its dependent objects, referred to as observers, are notified and automatically updated. This pattern is especially useful in cases where an event must trigger updates in multiple components.

In a functional programming context, we leverage immutability and higher-order functions to implement the Observer Pattern. Instead of modifying state directly, we create new state representations and propagate them through functions.

To elaborate on the implementation, let us consider the components of the Observer Pattern: the Subject, the Observer, and the mechanism through which they interact. Here is a Pythonic approach using functional programming principles.

```
from typing import Callable, List

# Define the type for an observer function, which takes new state and performs some
    action
Observer = Callable[[int], None]

class Subject:
    def __init__(self):
        self._observers: List[Observer] = []
        self._state: int = 0

    def register(self, observer: Observer) -> None:
        """Registers an Observer to the Subject"""
        self._observers.append(observer)

    def unregister(self, observer: Observer) -> None:
        """Unregisters an Observer from the Subject"""
        self._observers.remove(observer)

    def notify(self) -> None:
        """Notifies all registered Observers"""
        for observer in self._observers:
            observer(self._state)

    def set_state(self, state: int) -> None:
        """Sets the new state and notifies Observers"""
        self._state = state
        self.notify()

    def get_state(self) -> int:
        """Returns the current state"""
        return self._state
```

The ‘Subject‘ class holds a list of observers and a state. It provides methods to register and unregister observers, set the state, and notify all observers when the state changes.

Each observer is a callable that takes the new state and performs some action with it. This functional approach abstracts the observer behavior into functions, making it easier to manage and test.

Consider the following observer functions:

```
def observer_a(state: int) -> None:
    print(f"Observer A: State updated to {state}")

def observer_b(state: int) -> None:
    print(f"Observer B: State updated to {state}")
```

These observers simply print the updated state when notified. Now, let’s see them in action:

```
# Create a Subject instance
subject = Subject()
```

```
# Register observers
subject.register(observer_a)
subject.register(observer_b)

# Change state, which should notify observers
subject.set_state(10)
subject.set_state(20)
```

The output of the above code will be:

```
Observer A: State updated to 10
Observer B: State updated to 10
Observer A: State updated to 20
Observer B: State updated to 20
```

This demonstrates how each observer is notified whenever the subject's state changes. The functional approach ensures that the state and behavior are clearly separated, making the system easier to understand and maintain.

Functional reactive programming (FRP) extends the Observer Pattern by incorporating advanced functional programming techniques, such as streams and monads, to handle events over time. Libraries such as RxPy (Reactive Extensions for Python) offer more advanced and flexible mechanisms to manage such scenarios.

For instance, using RxPy, we can reorganize our example as follows:

```
import rx
from rx import operators as ops
from rx.subject import BehaviorSubject

# Create a BehaviorSubject to act as the Subject
subject = BehaviorSubject(0)

# Define observer functions
def observer_a(state: int) -> None:
    print(f"Observer A: State updated to {state}")

def observer_b(state: int) -> None:
    print(f"Observer B: State updated to {state}")

# Subscribe observers to the subject
subject.subscribe(observer_a)
subject.subscribe(observer_b)

# Set new states
subject.on_next(10)
subject.on_next(20)
```

The output will again be:

```
Observer A: State updated to 10
Observer B: State updated to 10
Observer A: State updated to 20
Observer B: State updated to 20
```

RxPy simplifies handling sequences of events and offers various operators to manipulate these sequences declaratively. This approach further abstracts and decouples the implementation details, adhering to the functional programming paradigm's principles.

Understanding the Observer Pattern through both basic functional constructs and more advanced libraries like RxPy provides a solid foundation for integrating event-driven programming with functional design strategies in Python. The clarity and succinctness of functional code can lead to more robust and maintainable systems, especially in complex applications where state and behavior need to be managed consistently.

8.8 The Adapter Pattern

The Adapter Pattern, also termed as Wrapper Pattern, is a structural design pattern that allows objects with incompatible interfaces to collaborate. This pattern works as a bridge between two interfaces, enabling interaction between the two without modifying their existing code. In a functional programming context within Python, the Adapter Pattern is remarkably useful in scenarios where existing functions or objects need to interface with new systems or components requiring different methods or attributes.

The core idea behind the Adapter Pattern can be encapsulated through an Adapter class that wraps instances of the incompatible interface. This class translates method calls from the expected interface to the actual methods in the wrapped instance.

Consider a scenario where we have a legacy system with a specific interface that our current system needs to interact with. The Adapter Pattern can be implemented in a functional programming paradigm using higher-order functions, which are functions that operate on or return other functions.

Firstly, let us examine a simple example involving two classes with incompatible interfaces:

```
class LegacyRectangle:
    def __init__(self, width, height):
        self.width = width
        self.height = height

    def get_width(self):
        return self.width
```

```
    def get_height(self):
        return self.height
```

The new implementation expects a different interface:

```
class NewRectangle:
    def __init__(self, size):
        self.size = size # assuming size is a tuple (width, height)

    def get_size(self):
        return self.size
```

To enable objects of the LegacyRectangle class to be used where NewRectangle objects are expected, we can implement an adapter. In functional programming, this adaptation can be achieved using higher-order functions:

```
def rectangle_adapter(legacy_rect):
    def get_size():
        return legacy_rect.get_width(), legacy_rect.get_height()

    return get_size
```

With this implementation, we leverage the functional paradigm by creating higher-order functions that allow for the adaptation of interfaces. Usage of this adapter can be demonstrated as follows:

```
legacy_rect = LegacyRectangle(10, 5)
adapted_get_size = rectangle_adapter(legacy_rect)
print(adapted_get_size()) # Output: (10, 5)
```

```
(10, 5)
```

This approach retains function purity and immutability, aligning with functional programming principles. By wrapping the LegacyRectangle instance, we avoid modifying the original class while producing an interface compatible with the NewRectangle class.

Another idiomatic Python example extends the concept to a more complex domain, such as adapting data fetching from different data sources. Suppose we have a legacy JSON data provider and a new XML data provider. Each provider has a specific method to fetch data:

```
class JSONDataProvider:
    def fetch_json_data(self):
        return {"name": "John", "age": 30}

class XMLDataProvider:
    def fetch_xml_data(self):
        return "<person><name>John</name><age>30</age></person>"
```

Assuming our current system expects a unified interface to fetch data in a dictionary format, the adapter pattern can guide us in designing a functional solution.

```
import xml.etree.ElementTree as ET

def json_adapter(provider):
    return provider.fetch_json_data

def xml_adapter(provider):
    def fetch_data():
        data = provider.fetch_xml_data()
        root = ET.fromstring(data)
        return {child.tag: child.text for child in root}
    return fetch_data
```

This function-based adapter paradigm ensures that the fetch_data functions returned from each adapter conform to the expected dictionary interface. Here's how these adapters can be utilized:

```
json_provider = JSONDataProvider()
xml_provider = XMLDataProvider()

json_fetch = json_adapter(json_provider)
xml_fetch = xml_adapter(xml_provider)

print(json_fetch()) # Output: {'name': 'John', 'age': 30}
print(xml_fetch()) # Output: {'name': 'John', 'age': '30'}
```

```
{'name': 'John', 'age': 30}
{'name': 'John', 'age': '30'}
```

By applying the Adapter Pattern functionally, we provide flexibility and reusability in the codebase without altering existing implementations. This keeps the codebase maintainable and scalable, adhering to the principles of functional programming by using pure functions and minimizing side effects.

8.9 Functional Composition and Pipelines

Functional composition and pipelines are fundamental concepts in functional programming that promote code modularity, reusability, and clarity. These concepts allow developers to create complex functionality by combining simpler functions.

Functional composition is the process of combining two or more functions to produce a new function. This new function represents the application of the subsequent functions to the result of the previous functions.

In mathematical terms, if we have two functions f and g, their composition h can be expressed as $h(x) = g(f(x))$. In Python, this can be conveniently performed using higher-order functions.

Function Composition Example: Consider two simple functions, one that adds 2 to a number add_two, and another that squares a number square:

```
def add_two(x):
    return x + 2

def square(x):
    return x * x
```

Composing these functions manually can be done as follows:

```
result = square(add_two(3))
print(result) # Output is 25
```

To achieve more streamlined composition, we can create a composition function. The compose function takes two functions f and g and returns a new function that is their composition.

```
def compose(f, g):
    return lambda x: f(g(x))

composed_function = compose(square, add_two)
print(composed_function(3)) # Output is 25
```

A pipeline is a similar concept but involves a chain of functions applied in sequence to an initial value. Pipelines are particularly useful for data transformation operations, and they work well with iterators and generators.

Pipeline Example: Suppose we have a list of numbers and we want to apply a series of transformations: adding 2 to each number, then squaring each result, and finally converting the results to string representations. We can define individual transformation functions:

```
def add_two(x):
    return x + 2

def square(x):
    return x * x

def to_string(x):
    return str(x)
```

Using a pipeline approach, we can perform these operations in a sequence:

```
numbers = [1, 2, 3, 4, 5]
pipeline = map(square, map(add_two, numbers))
string_results = list(map(to_string, pipeline))

print(string_results) # Output is ['9', '16', '25', '36', '49']
```

In this approach, the map function helps to apply the transformations in sequence. The initial list of numbers is transformed by first applying add_two, then square, and finally converting to string with to_string.

Pipeline with List Comprehension: Alternatively, we can achieve the same result using list comprehensions for a more functional style:

```
numbers = [1, 2, 3, 4, 5]
result = [to_string(square(add_two(n))) for n in numbers]

print(result) # Output is ['9', '16', '25', '36', '49']
```

While this example is straightforward, it demonstrates the power of combining simple functions to build complex processing pipelines. It is essential to note that pipelines can be more flexible and reusable if implemented with higher-order functions, such as map and filter.

Advanced Pipelines: For more advanced use cases, such as data processing in large datasets or when handling streams of data, leveraging libraries like itertools for infinite iterators, or toolz for functional programming utilities, can be very powerful. Consider an example where we need a pipeline to process a large dataset by filtering and transforming the data:

```
from itertools import islice, count
from toolz import pipe

# Generate an infinite sequence of numbers
numbers = count(1)

# Define the pipeline transformations
pipeline = pipe(
    numbers,
    lambda x: islice(x, 10),
    lambda x: map(add_two, x),
    lambda x: filter(lambda n: n % 2 == 0, x),
    lambda x: map(square, x)
)

# Convert to list to visualize the processing result
result = list(pipeline)

print(result) # Output is [16, 36, 64, 100]
```

In this advanced example, count generates an infinite sequence of numbers starting from 1. This sequence is processed through a pipeline composed of slicing the first 10 elements, adding 2, filtering out odd numbers, and squaring the remaining values. Using pipe from the toolz library simplifies the syntax and integrates the transformations seamlessly.

Functional composition and pipelines are pivotal in writing clear, maintainable, and scalable Python code. By abstracting and chaining simple operations, developers can handle complex data transformations elegantly and efficiently.

8.10 Monads and Functors in Python

Monads and functors are advanced functional programming constructs that enable handling computations, effects, and data transformations in a consistent and composition-friendly manner. While these concepts originate from category theory, their practical applications in functional programming can greatly simplify complex computation pipelines. This section delves into the implementation and utility of monads and functors in Python, enhancing your proficiency in functional patterns.

A **functor** is a type that implements the map function, allowing you to apply a function to the values within a context. A **monad** builds upon functors by supporting an additional operation, typically called flatMap or bind, enabling the chaining of operations that return values wrapped in the same context.

To understand how to implement and use these constructs in Python, consider the following examples and principles.

Functor Implementation: A functor in Python can be represented by any class that implements a map method.

```
class Functor:
    def __init__(self, value):
        self.value = value

    def map(self, f):
        return Functor(f(self.value))

# Example usage
f = Functor(5)
result = f.map(lambda x: x + 1)
print(result.value) # Output: 6
```

In the above example:

- The Functor class encapsulates a value and provides a map method to apply a function to it.
- The map method returns a new Functor containing the transformed value.

Using this functor pattern, Python developers can build pipelines of transformations applied to encapsulated values.

Monad Implementation: A monad extends the concept of a functor by supporting a bind operation (or flatMap in some contexts).

```
class Monad(Functor):
    def flatMap(self, f):
        return f(self.value)

# Example usage
m = Monad(5)
result = m.flatMap(lambda x: Monad(x + 1))
print(result.value) # Output: 6
```

In this example:

- The Monad class inherits from the Functor class, inheriting the map method.
- It introduces a flatMap method to handle functions returning other monads.
- The flatMap method allows chaining of monad-returning functions seamlessly.

With these foundations, developers can construct more advanced use cases, such as managing computations that may fail.

Example: Maybe Monad for Optional Values:

The Maybe monad is a common pattern for handling computations that might fail or return nothing. This can be useful for avoiding NoneType errors in Python.

```
class Maybe(Monad):
    def __init__(self, value):
        self.value = value

    def flatMap(self, f):
        if self.value is None:
            return self
        return f(self.value)

    @classmethod
```

```
    def of(cls, value):
        return cls(value)

# Example usage
m = Maybe.of(5)
result = m.flatMap(lambda x: Maybe.of(x + 1))
print(result.value) # Output: 6

none_result = Maybe.of(None).flatMap(lambda x: Maybe.of(x + 1))
print(none_result.value) # Output: None
```

In this example:

- The Maybe monad handles values that might be None.
- The flatMap method checks for None values before applying the function.
- The static of method is a utility to create a Maybe instance conveniently.

By utilizing these constructs, you can build robust pipelines that handle cases where computations may not yield valid results without scattering null checks throughout your code.

Combining Monads and Functors:

Combining these constructs allows even more powerful abstractions. Consider an example where you may need to compose multiple functors and monads:

```
class ListFunctor(Functor):
    def map(self, f):
        return ListFunctor([f(x) for x in self.value])

class MaybeMonad(Monad):
    def __init__(self, value):
        self.value = value

    def flatMap(self, f):
        if self.value is None:
            return self
        return f(self.value)

    @staticmethod
    def maybe(value):
        return MaybeMonad(value)

# Example usage
f = ListFunctor([1, 2, 3])
mapped_result = f.map(lambda x: x + 1)
print(mapped_result.value) # Output: [2, 3, 4]

m = MaybeMonad.maybe(5)
flat_mapped_result = m.flatMap(lambda x: MaybeMonad.maybe(x + 1))
print(flat_mapped_result.value) # Output: 6
```

In this illustration:

- A ListFunctor class implements the map method to apply functions to lists.
- The MaybeMonad further encapsulates the Maybe monad logic.
- Functions can be applied to lists and Maybe values in a composable way.

Advanced Monad Usages: Handling Side Effects:

Monads are also useful for handling side effects, such as state management, logging, or I/O operations. One common monad used for this purpose is the IO monad, which abstracts side effects, thereby allowing pure functional transformations without executing the effects until necessary.

```
class IO(Monad):
    def __init__(self, effect):
        self.effect = effect

    def flatMap(self, f):
        def new_effect():
            result = self.effect()
            return f(result).effect()
        return IO(new_effect)

    def run(self):
        return self.effect()

# Example usage
def read_line():
    return "User input"

def process_input(value):
    return IO(lambda: value.upper())

io = IO(read_line).flatMap(process_input)
print(io.run()) # Output: USER INPUT
```

Here:

- The IO monad wraps an effectful computation in a function.
- The flatMap method chains these computations without executing them.
- The run method finally executes the wrapped computations.

This approach can be extended to more complex workflows involving multiple effects, managed in a clean and functional manner.

8.11 Practical Examples of Functional Design Patterns

In this section, we will delve into practical examples of functional design patterns within Python. These examples serve to reinforce the theoretical concepts presented in previous sections by providing concrete implementations. They are designed to help solidify your understanding and to showcase how these patterns can be applied for solving real-world problems.

To illustrate the practical applications, we will revisit some of the patterns already introduced: Strategy, Decorator, and Observer patterns. The examples will use Python code snippets and display the program outputs, offering a hands-on approach to learning these patterns.

Strategy Pattern: Example of Sorting Algorithms

The Strategy pattern is highly useful when you want to encapsulate different algorithms within a family and make them interchangeable. Here, we will consider a common example involving sorting algorithms.

Let's define three different sorting strategies: Bubble Sort, Quick Sort, and Merge Sort. We will create a Strategy interface and concrete implementations for each algorithm.

```
from typing import List, Callable

class SortStrategy:
    def sort(self, data: List[int]) -> List[int]:
        raise NotImplementedError("SortStrategy.sort is not implemented")

class BubbleSort(SortStrategy):
    def sort(self, data: List[int]) -> List[int]:
        n = len(data)
        for i in range(n):
            for j in range(0, n-i-1):
                if data[j] > data[j+1]:
                    data[j], data[j+1] = data[j+1], data[j]
        return data

class QuickSort(SortStrategy):
    def sort(self, data: List[int]) -> List[int]:
        if len(data) <= 1:
            return data
        pivot = data[len(data) // 2]
        left = [x for x in data if x < pivot]
        middle = [x for x in data if x == pivot]
        right = [x for x in data if x > pivot]
        return self.sort(left) + middle + self.sort(right)

class MergeSort(SortStrategy):
    def sort(self, data: List[int]) -> List[int]:
        if len(data) <= 1:
```

```
            return data
        middle = len(data) // 2
        left = self.sort(data[:middle])
        right = self.sort(data[middle:])
        return self._merge(left, right)

    def _merge(self, left: List[int], right: List[int]) -> List[int]:
        result = []
        i = j = 0
        while i < len(left) and j < len(right):
            if left[i] < right[j]:
                result.append(left[i])
                i += 1
            else:
                result.append(right[j])
                j += 1
        result.extend(left[i:])
        result.extend(right[j:])
        return result

class Context:
    def __init__(self, strategy: SortStrategy):
        self._strategy = strategy

    def set_strategy(self, strategy: SortStrategy):
        self._strategy = strategy

    def perform_sort(self, data: List[int]) -> List[int]:
        return self._strategy.sort(data)

# Usage example
data = [64, 34, 25, 12, 22, 11, 90]
context = Context(BubbleSort())
print("Bubble Sort:", context.perform_sort(data.copy()))

context.set_strategy(QuickSort())
print("Quick Sort:", context.perform_sort(data.copy()))

context.set_strategy(MergeSort())
print("Merge Sort:", context.perform_sort(data.copy()))
```

```
Bubble Sort: [11, 12, 22, 25, 34, 64, 90]
Quick Sort: [11, 12, 22, 25, 34, 64, 90]
Merge Sort: [11, 12, 22, 25, 34, 64, 90]
```

This implementation demonstrates how we can switch out different sorting strategies without altering the Context class. Each strategy adheres to the SortStrategy interface, making them interchangeable.

Decorator Pattern: Example of Text Formatting

The Decorator pattern is useful for adding behavior to objects dynamically. This example will show how to use decorators to add various formatting options to text.

First, define a base interface for text components and concrete implementations for basic text. Create decorators to add different formatting options like bold and italic.

```python
class Text:
    def render(self) -> str:
        raise NotImplementedError("Text.render is not implemented")

class PlainText(Text):
    def __init__(self, text: str):
        self._text = text

    def render(self) -> str:
        return self._text

class TextDecorator(Text):
    def __init__(self, wrapped: Text):
        self._wrapped = wrapped

    def render(self) -> str:
        return self._wrapped.render()

class BoldDecorator(TextDecorator):
    def render(self) -> str:
        return f'<b>{super().render()}</b>'

class ItalicDecorator(TextDecorator):
    def render(self) -> str:
        return f'<i>{super().render()}</i>'

class UnderlineDecorator(TextDecorator):
    def render(self) -> str:
        return f'<u>{super().render()}</u>'

# Usage example
basic_text = PlainText("Hello, world!")
bold_text = BoldDecorator(basic_text)
italic_text = ItalicDecorator(bold_text)
underlined_text = UnderlineDecorator(italic_text)

print("Plain:", basic_text.render())
print("Bold:", bold_text.render())
print("Bold and Italic:", italic_text.render())
print("Bold, Italic, and Underlined:", underlined_text.render())
```

```
Plain: Hello, world!
Bold: <b>Hello, world!</b>
Bold and Italic: <b><i>Hello, world!</i></b>
Bold, Italic, and Underlined: <b><i><u>Hello, world!</u></i></b>
```

This example shows how decorators can be stacked to add multiple layers of formatting to the text, demonstrating the flexibility and composability of this pattern.

Observer Pattern: Example of a Simple Event System

The Observer pattern is valuable when you need to notify multiple objects about state changes. Let's consider a simple event system where various observers respond to events.

Define an Observable class and an Observer interface. Implement concrete observers that respond to specific events.

```
from typing import List, Protocol

class Observer(Protocol):
    def update(self, event: str):
        pass

class Observable:
    def __init__(self):
        self._observers: List[Observer] = []

    def add_observer(self, observer: Observer):
        self._observers.append(observer)

    def remove_observer(self, observer: Observer):
        self._observers.remove(observer)

    def notify_observers(self, event: str):
        for observer in self._observers:
            observer.update(event)

class ConcreteObserverA:
    def update(self, event: str):
        if event == "event_A":
            print("ConcreteObserverA: Responding to event A")

class ConcreteObserverB:
    def update(self, event: str):
        if event == "event_B":
            print("ConcreteObserverB: Responding to event B")

# Usage example
observable = Observable()
observer_a = ConcreteObserverA()
observer_b = ConcreteObserverB()

observable.add_observer(observer_a)
observable.add_observer(observer_b)

observable.notify_observers("event_A")
observable.notify_observers("event_B")
```

```
ConcreteObserverA: Responding to event A
ConcreteObserverB: Responding to event B
```

This implementation defines an Observable class that can notify multiple observers of events. Concrete observers can subscribe and respond to specific events, showcasing the flexible and decoupled nature of the Observer pattern.

These practical examples illustrate how functional design patterns can be effectively utilized in Python to create flexible, maintainable, and extensible code. By understanding and applying these patterns, you can tackle a wide array of problems with a functional programming approach.

8.12 Best Practices for Functional Design

In this section, we delineate the best practices for implementing functional design in Python, focusing on principles and strategies that promote robust, maintainable, and scalable code. Leveraging functional programming paradigms in Python enables the creation of clear, concise, and declarative code. Adopting these best practices will enhance the quality of your functional Python code and improve its readability and performance.

Pure Functions

Pure functions are fundamental to functional programming. They follow these principles: they do not cause side effects, and their output depends solely on their input parameters. This determinism improves testability and debugging. Here's an example:

```
def add(a: int, b: int) -> int:
    return a + b
```

Using pure functions ensures that functions remain predictable and consistent.

Immutability

Immutability is the concept of not modifying data once it has been created. Instead, new data structures are returned from functions creating a more predictable and manageable state. Immutable types in Python include tuples, frozen sets, and strings. Whenever possible, prefer immutable data structures like 'namedtuple' or 'dataclass' with 'frozen=True'.

```
from collections import namedtuple

Point = namedtuple('Point', ['x', 'y'])
p1 = Point(1, 2)
p2 = Point(3, 4)

# Immutable, attempting to modify will raise an AttributeError
# p1.x = 10
```

This immutability reduces unintended side effects and promotes safer concurrent code.

First-Class and Higher-Order Functions

In Python, functions are first-class citizens, meaning they can be passed as arguments, returned from other functions, and assigned to variables. A higher-order function is a function that takes one or more functions as arguments or returns a function.

```
def apply_function(func, value):
    return func(value)

def square(x):
    return x * x

result = apply_function(square, 5) # returns 25
```

Utilizing higher-order functions aids in creating more abstract and reusable components.

Function Composition

Function composition allows the combination of simple functions to build more complex ones. This modular approach enhances code reusability.

```
def multiply_by_two(x):
    return x * 2

def add_five(x):
    return x + 5

def compose(f, g):
    return lambda x: f(g(x))

composed_function = compose(multiply_by_two, add_five)
result = composed_function(10) # returns 30
```

Through function composition, complex operations can be broken into smaller, maintainable functions.

Avoiding Side Effects

Minimizing side effects is crucial for achieving referential transparency. Functions should not modify external state or perform I/O operations.

```
# Not recommended
global_var = 0

def modify_global(x):
    global global_var
    global_var += x

# Recommended
def add(x, y):
    return x + y
```

Containing side effects helps in making functions more predictable and easier to test.

Lazy Evaluation

Lazy evaluation delays the computation of an expression until its value is needed. This approach optimizes performance, especially for large data sets. Python supports lazy evaluation through generators and the 'itertools' module.

```
def lazy_range(n):
    i = 0
    while i < n:
        yield i
        i += 1

for num in lazy_range(5):
    print(num)
```

Lazy evaluation conserves memory and improves performance by generating values on-the-fly.

Functional Data Structures

Functional data structures, such as those found in the 'collections' module, facilitate the implementation of functional programming techniques.

```
from collections import deque

# Functional queue
queue = deque()
queue.append(1)
queue.append(2)
queue.popleft() # returns 1
```

Choosing the right data structures supports efficient and idiomatic functional programming.

Using Map, Filter, and Reduce

The 'map', 'filter', and 'reduce' functions provide a functional approach to processing collections.

```
from functools import reduce

nums = [1, 2, 3, 4, 5]

# Map
squared_nums = list(map(lambda x: x * x, nums))

# Filter
even_nums = list(filter(lambda x: x % 2 == 0, nums))

# Reduce
sum = reduce(lambda x, y: x + y, nums)
```

These functions help to process collections in a declarative and concise manner.

Declarative Over Imperative

Emphasize the what over the how. Functional programming encourages declaring the desired outcome rather than explicitly coding each step. List comprehensions and generator expressions are excellent tools for this purpose.

```
# Imperative
result = []
for x in range(10):
    if x % 2 == 0:
        result.append(x * x)

# Declarative
result = [x * x for x in range(10) if x % 2 == 0]
```

Declarative code is often more readable and concise.

Using Functional Libraries

Leveraging libraries that support functional programming facilitates the adoption of best practices. Libraries such as 'toolz' and 'fn.py' provide additional functional programming utilities.

```
from toolz import curry

@curry
def sum_three(a, b, c):
    return a + b + c

add_five_to_sum = sum_three(5)
result = add_five_to_sum(3, 2) # returns 10
```

These libraries extend Python's functional programming capabilities, enabling more expressive and concise code.

By adhering to these best practices, Python developers can effectively implement functional programming techniques to enhance code quality, maintainability, and scalability.

Chapter 9

Handling State and Side Effects

This chapter addresses the challenges of handling state and side effects in functional programming. It explains the distinction between pure functions and side effects, and how to manage state using immutable data structures and closures. The chapter explores functional techniques for handling I/O operations, and introduces state monads for state management. Techniques for isolating side effects and refactoring imperative code to functional code are also discussed, with practical examples to solidify these concepts.

9.1 Introduction to State and Side Effects

State and side effects represent foundational concepts in programming, particularly as they pertain to functional programming paradigms. In essence, state refers to the stored information that a program can retrieve or update, while side effects describe any observable effects a function may have beyond calculating a return value. Understanding these concepts is crucial to leveraging the full power of functional programming in Python, as they challenge the traditional imperative approach and introduce a more declarative style of coding.

In imperative programming, state is commonly manipulated through variable assignments and modifications. For example:

```
counter = 0
counter += 1
```

Here, counter is a state variable whose value is being modified. This kind of state manipulation can make it difficult to maintain a consistent and predictable program flow because the state changes as the program executes.

In contrast, functional programming advocates for the use of immutable data structures. Immutable data ensures that once a data structure is created, it cannot be altered. Any modifications result in a new data structure, leaving the original one unchanged. This immutability facilitates reasoning about code by ensuring that functions do not produce unexpected side effects. Consider the following example:

```
from collections import namedtuple

Point = namedtuple('Point', ['x', 'y'])
p1 = Point(2, 3)
p2 = Point(p1.x, p1.y + 1)
```

In this example, p1 remains unchanged when p2 is created, providing a guarantee that the original state is preserved.

Side effects are another critical aspect when comparing imperative to functional programming. A side effect occurs when a function interacts with the outside world or its surrounding state. Common side effects include modifying a global variable, writing to a file, or sending data over a network. Consider the following function with a side effect:

```
log = []

def add_and_log(x, y):
    result = x + y
    log.append(result)
    return result
```

While this function returns the sum of the inputs, it also modifies the log list, producing a side effect. Such side effects can complicate testing and reasoning about the function, as it now depends on and alters an external state.

In functional programming, pure functions are highly valued. A pure function's output depends solely on its input and has no side effects. This ensures predictability and reusability, leading to more reliable and maintainable code. An imperative function, like the one modifying a global log, can be refactored into a pure function:

```
def add(x, y):
    return x + y
```

Pure functions offer significant advantages, including easier testing and parallelization. Since they do not rely on or alter external state, they can be executed concurrently without concerns about race conditions or synchronization issues.

Functional programming handles state through techniques such as closures and monads. Closures allow functions to capture variables from their surrounding scope, creating a form of state encapsulation without resorting to mutable global variables. Additionally, monads provide a structured approach to sequence computations and manage side effects while preserving function purity. These concepts will be elaborated upon in subsequent sections, where their implementation and benefits will be explored in depth.

Handling and managing state and side effects in a functional manner requires a shift in thinking from traditional approaches. By embracing immutability and pure functions, alongside leveraging advanced functional techniques, Python developers can produce code that is both more robust and easier to maintain.

9.2 Understanding State in Functional Programming

State in programming refers to the stored information that a program can access and modify as it runs. In imperative programming, handling state typically involves mutable variables that can be updated at any point within a piece of code. In contrast, functional programming takes a different approach by emphasizing immutability and avoiding side effects. This distinction fundamentally shapes how state is managed and manipulated in functional paradigms.

To comprehend how state is handled in functional programming, it is essential first to understand the core principles that differentiate it from imperative programming. Functional programming emphasizes pure functions, which are functions that do not cause side effects and always produce the same output given the same input. This paradigm shift changes how state transitions are approached and necessitates alternative strategies for maintaining and updating state.

Immutability is a cornerstone of functional programming. Immutable data structures, once created, cannot be changed. Instead of modifying existing data, new data structures are created to reflect changes. This immutability ensures that functions can remain pure, preventing them from altering the program state outside their defined scope.

The practical implication for state management is that, with immutability, one must consider how to represent state changes without altering existing variables. A common technique employed is to use recursive data structures or functions to generate new states based on old states. For example, consider a list where elements need to be added. Instead of appending an element to an existing list, a new list is created by combining the new element with the existing list.

```
# Using immutable data structures
def add_element(lst, element):
    return [element] + lst

# Initial list
original_list = [1, 2, 3]

# Adding an element
new_list = add_element(original_list, 4)

# The original list remains unchanged
print("Original List:", original_list)
print("New List:", new_list)
```

```
Output:
Original List: [1, 2, 3]
New List: [4, 1, 2, 3]
```

In this example, the function add_element generates a new list instead of modifying the original_list, adhering to the principles of immutability. The state change is represented by the creation of a new_list, leaving the original_list intact.

Another fundamental concept is the use of *recursive functions* to handle state transitions. Recursive functions break down problems into simpler sub-problems, solving each in its context and then combining the results. This technique aligns well with immutable data structures, as each recursive call can generate a new state without modifying the current state.

Consider a function that calculates the sum of elements in a list:

```
# Recursive function to sum elements of a list
def sum_list(lst):
    if not lst:
        return 0
    else:
```

```
        return lst[0] + sum_list(lst[1:])

# List of numbers
numbers = [1, 2, 3, 4]

# Calculating the sum
total = sum_list(numbers)

print("Sum of elements:", total)
```

Output:
Sum of elements: 10

This recursive function processes each element of the list by breaking the problem into smaller sub-problems, summing the first element with the result of the remaining elements. The state transitions are naturally handled by the function calls, maintaining immutability.

Closures also play a significant role in managing state in functional programming. A *closure* is a function that retains the bindings of free variables that exist when the function is created. This means that a closure can "remember" the state in which it was formed, and this encapsulated state can be used when the closure is invoked.

Consider the following example where a closure is used to create a counter:

```
# Function to create a counter
def make_counter():
    count = 0
    def counter():
        nonlocal count
        count += 1
        return count
    return counter

# Creating a new counter
counter = make_counter()

# Incrementing the counter
print(counter()) # Output: 1
print(counter()) # Output: 2
```

Here, the make_counter function returns a closure, counter, which maintains the count state. Each invocation of counter increments the count and returns the new value. The key aspect is that the state is encapsulated within the closure, providing controlled access and modification while adhering to the functional programming principles.

Functional programming languages often provide constructs such as *monads* to manage state in a clean and predictable manner. A monad is a design pattern used to handle program-wide concerns such as state, exceptions, or I/O, in a modular way. The state monad in particular encapsulates state transitions, allowing for sequential computation while maintaining immutability and purity.

In Python, using monads would require additional libraries or custom implementations, but the concept remains instrumental in understanding how state can be managed functionally. Monads provide a framework for combining stateful computations while keeping the results predictable and maintaining referential transparency.

Understanding state in functional programming involves recognizing the intrinsic differences from imperative paradigms, emphasizing immutability, and using functions, closures, and abstract constructs like monads to manage state transitions effectively. The approach ensures that state management is predictable, modular, and aligns with the fundamental principles of functional programming.

9.3 Pure Functions and Side Effects

Pure functions are a foundational concept in functional programming. The principle of purity dictates that a function's return value should be solely determined by its input arguments, without observable side effects. This characteristic renders pure functions referentially transparent, implying that a function call can be replaced with its output value without altering the program's behavior. This predictability and stability are advantageous when reasoning about code, optimizing, or debugging.

A formal definition of a pure function requires two conditions:

- **Deterministic Output:** For a given set of input values, a pure function always produces the same output.
- **No Side Effects:** A pure function does not cause any side effects, which include altering any state outside the function, modifying its arguments, or depending on any external state changes.

To illustrate this concept, consider the following example of a pure function in Python:

```
def add(a, b):
    return a + b

print(add(2, 3)) # Output: 5
```

In contrast, side effects occur when a function interacts with external state or system I/O, such as modifying a global variable, altering a data structure passed by reference, or performing operations like reading from a file or printing to the console. Side effects can complicate the comprehension and maintenance of code since they introduce dependencies on the external state and can lead to unintended consequences.

Here is an example of a function with a side effect:

```
total = 0

def add_with_side_effect(a, b):
    global total
    total += (a + b)
    return total

print(add_with_side_effect(2, 3)) # Output: 5
print(total) # Output: 5
```

In this example, the total variable is modified by the function add_with_side_effect, creating a dependency on the external state (total). This dependence makes the program's behavior harder to predict and reason about compared to the pure function shown earlier.

In functional programming, managing side effects is crucial to maintain code clarity and ensure the predictability of functions. This is typically achieved by adhering to immutability, utilizing pure functions as much as possible, and isolating side effects in controlled parts of the code.

Consider a scenario where we have a list of prices and we need to apply a discount to each price and compute the total discounted amount. A pure functional approach would involve using pure functions for each computational step:

```
def apply_discount(price, discount):
    return price - (price * discount)

def total_discounted(prices, discount):
    discounted_prices = map(lambda p: apply_discount(p, discount), prices)
    return sum(discounted_prices)

prices = [100, 200, 300]
discount = 0.1
print(total_discounted(prices, discount)) # Output: 540.0
```

Here, apply_discount is a pure function. The total_discounted function utilizes map and sum, both of which are functional constructs that do not alter the original list of prices but produce a new list with the discounted prices. By maintaining purity, these functions guarantee predictable behavior without side effects.

A significant challenge in practical functional programming is handling necessary side effects such as I/O operations. In cases where side effects cannot be avoided, it is beneficial to confine them to the outer layers of the application and preserve the inner core logic as pure. This approach, often called functional core, imperative shell, allows us to isolate and manage side effects more effectively.

The following example demonstrates how one might handle I/O operations functionally by separating pure logic from side effects:

```
def read_input():
    return input("Enter a number: ")

def write_output(result):
    print(f"The result is: {result}")

def process_input(user_input):
    return int(user_input) * 2

# Main execution logic
user_input = read_input() # Side Effect
result = process_input(user_input) # Pure Function
write_output(result) # Side Effect
```

By organizing the code in this manner, the pure logic (process_input) is decoupled from the side effects (read_input and write_output). This isolation simplifies testing and reasoning about the core logic while containing the complexity introduced by side effects to well-defined sections of the code.

Maintaining the purity of functions wherever feasible and judiciously managing side effects leads to more maintainable, testable, and reliable code in functional programming. This discipline forms the cornerstone of effective state management and side effect handling in functional programming paradigms.

9.4 Managing State with Immutable Data Structures

Handling state in functional programming requires approaches that do not rely on altering data in place. Instead, such approaches focus on the creation of new data structures that reflect the necessary changes while maintaining the original state unmodified. This technique ensures that functions remain pure and predictable.

Immutable data structures are the cornerstone of this methodology. Unlike mutable data structures that allow in-place modification, immutable data structures necessitate the creation of new structures upon modification. This practice avoids side effects and supports functional programming paradigms.

Consider a simple list in Python. Python's default list is mutable and allows operations that alter its state directly:

```
# Initial mutable list
lst = [1, 2, 3]
# Mutating the list
lst.append(4)
```

In this example, the 'append' operation directly modifies the original list. Conversely, to employ immutable data structures, one must utilize techniques that return new versions of the list rather than modifying the original.

Python's built-in tuple type provides a basic example of an immutable data structure. However, practical manipulations often need more sophisticated structures. One such example comes from the 'immutables' library, which provides a 'Map' that can be used similarly to dictionaries but is immutable.

```
from immutables import Map

# Initial immutable map
imap = Map(a=1, b=2, c=3)
# Creating a modified map with an added key-value pair
imap2 = imap.set('d', 4)

print(imap) # Output: Map({'a': 1, 'b': 2, 'c': 3})
print(imap2) # Output: Map({'a': 1, 'b': 2, 'c': 3, 'd': 4})
```

Here, 'imap' remains unchanged after the 'set' operation, emphasizing the immutability concept. 'imap2' is a new map with the additional key-value pair.

To deepen the understanding, consider a more complex example involving a nested data structure. Manipulating deeply nested data in an immutable way can be facilitated by functional libraries such as 'pyrsistent'. This library provides persistent versions of Python's standard data structures. Persistent data structures ensure that previous versions remain accessible after modifications.

```
from pyrsistent import pmap, pvector

# Initial persistent map containing a persistent vector
nested_map = pmap({'numbers': pvector([1, 2, 3])})
# Adding an element within the nested structure
nested_map_updated = nested_map.set('numbers', nested_map['numbers'].append(4))
```

```
print(nested_map) # Output: pmap({'numbers': pvector([1, 2, 3])})
print(nested_map_updated) # Output: pmap({'numbers': pvector([1, 2, 3, 4])})
```

The above example demonstrates the use of the 'pmap' and 'pvector' from the 'pyrsistent' library to create and manipulate an immutable, nested data structure. The 'append' operation generates a new vector, which is then used to create an updated map, leaving the original structure intact.

Functional programming heavily relies on recursion and higher-order functions to handle state changes within immutable data structures. Recursive techniques can replace traditional loops, allowing for functional state management. Consider a scenario where we accumulate a sum over a list of numbers:

```
from functools import reduce

numbers = [1, 2, 3, 4, 5]

# Functional approach using reduce
sum_numbers = reduce(lambda acc, x: acc + x, numbers, 0)

print(sum_numbers) # Output: 15
```

The 'reduce' function maintains an accumulator ('acc') that is updated immutably with each iteration, ultimately producing the final sum without altering the input list.

By managing state with immutable data structures, functional programming achieves several benefits:

- **Predictability**: Functions that rely on immutable data structures have no side effects, making them easier to understand and test.
- **Concurrency**: Immutable objects can be freely shared between threads without synchronization issues, enhancing concurrent execution.
- **Debugging and Maintenance**: Immutable states simplify debugging and maintenance by preserving historical data snapshots.

Applying these concepts ensures robust handling of state and side effects within functional programming, fostering cleaner and more maintainable code.

9.5 The Role of Closures in Managing State

Closures play an essential role in managing state in functional programming, particularly in Python. A closure occurs when a function is defined inside another function, and the inner function captures the variables from the outer, enclosing function's scope. This characteristic makes closures a powerful tool for maintaining state in a functional style without reverting to mutable data structures or global variables.

Consider the following example, which demonstrates a closure capturing state:

```
def make_counter():
    count = 0

    def increment():
        nonlocal count
        count += 1
        return count

    return increment

counter = make_counter()
print(counter()) # Output: 1
print(counter()) # Output: 2
```

In this example, the function make_counter defines a local variable count and an inner function increment. The increment function captures and modifies count using the nonlocal keyword, which indicates that the variable count is defined in the nearest enclosing scope that is not global.

The closure formed by increment retains access to count even after make_counter has finished execution. This allows the state to persist across multiple invocations of counter() without using global variables or mutable objects.

One significant advantage of using closures to manage state is that it localizes state management within a specific context. Unlike global variables, which can be accessed and modified from any part of the program, closures restrict state manipulation to the enclosing scope, reducing the risk of unintended side effects.

To deepen the understanding, we can consider another example where we implement a simple factory for creating functions that remember their own state:

```
def accumulator(initial_value):
    value = initial_value
```

```
    def add_to_accumulator(amount):
        nonlocal value
        value += amount
        return value

    return add_to_accumulator

acc = accumulator(10)
print(acc(5)) # Output: 15
print(acc(3)) # Output: 18
```

In this code, accumulator creates an inner function add_to_accumulator that modifies and persists the state variable value. The variable value is initially set to initial_value and is updated each time add_to_accumulator is called. By using the nonlocal keyword, the inner function can update the state without resorting to mutable global variables.

Closures are not limited to numeric state. They can also be used to manage more complex data structures, such as lists. Here is an example:

```
def list_manager():
    items = []

    def add_item(item):
        nonlocal items
        items.append(item)
        return items

    return add_item

manager = list_manager()
print(manager('apple')) # Output: ['apple']
print(manager('banana')) # Output: ['apple', 'banana']
```

In this example, list_manager defines a list items and an inner function add_item. The inner function updates the items list, maintaining its state across multiple invocations. This pattern is consistent with the functional programming principle of avoiding mutable global state while enabling stateful behavior through closures.

Beyond simple examples, closures can manage state in more complex scenarios such as maintaining configuration settings, tracking resource usage, and implementing caching mechanisms. Consider the following caching function:

```
def make_cache():
    cache = {}

    def get_from_cache(key, compute_fn):
        if key not in cache:
            cache[key] = compute_fn()
        return cache[key]
```

```
    return get_from_cache

cache_function = make_cache()
print(cache_function('a', lambda: 100)) # Output: 100
print(cache_function('a', lambda: 200)) # Output: 100 (cached value)
```

Here, make_cache defines a dictionary cache and an inner function get_from_cache, which checks if a value is stored in the cache. If not, it computes and stores the value using the provided compute_fn function. This closure pattern is useful for optimizing performance by avoiding redundant computations.

In environments where immutability and pure functions are paramount, closures are an effective method to encapsulate and control state changes. They serve as a core technique for writing robust, functional code that minimizes side effects and enhances code clarity and maintainability.

9.6 Handling I/O Operations Functionally

In functional programming, managing I/O (input/output) operations poses a significant challenge due to their inherently side-effect-laden nature. While functional programming advocates for pure functions and immutability, I/O operations such as reading a file, fetching user input, or displaying output inherently alter the state and interact with the external environment. This section delves into functional techniques for encapsulating and managing I/O operations in Python, ensuring that the purity of functional paradigms is preserved as much as possible.

A primary approach to managing I/O in functional programming involves treating I/O operations as first-class citizens—values that can be passed, composed, and manipulated. By deferring execution and using higher-order functions, we encapsulate I/O operations, allowing their side effects to be controlled and contained.

An important functional paradigm used to manage I/O in Haskell and other functional languages is the notion of an I/O monad. Although Python does not have built-in support for monads, we can adopt similar patterns to handle I/O operations functionally.

Consider basic file reading. In imperative programming, one might write:

```
with open('example.txt', 'r') as file:
    content = file.read()
```

```
print(content)
```

The above code is straightforward but involves side effects—opening a file, reading from it, and printing to the console. To handle this functionally, we can encapsulate these operations within functions, ensuring they return other functions or data structures describing the I/O operations, rather than executing them immediately.

Firstly, we define a function to read the file's contents:

```
def read_file(filename):
    def operation():
        with open(filename, 'r') as file:
            return file.read()
    return operation
```

In the above code, the read_file function returns an operation function that encapsulates the actual file reading. Notice that no I/O operation occurs when read_file is called; instead, operation can be executed later to perform the reading.

To demonstrate how such deferred execution can be composed functionally, consider chaining multiple I/O operations. For example, we can read multiple files and concatenate their contents:

```
def concatenate_files(filenames):
    def operation():
        contents = [read_file(name)() for name in filenames]
        return ''.join(contents)
    return operation
```

Here, concatenate_files takes a list of filenames and constructs an operation to read and concatenate their contents functionally. The I/O operations are encapsulated and executed in a controlled manner.

Next, handling I/O operations functionally often requires composing input and output functions, effectively creating pipelines. Higher-order functions play a crucial role in this composition. For instance, consider a function that processes user input:

```
def get_user_input(prompt):
    def operation():
        return input(prompt)
    return operation
```

Combined with a functional transformation, this approach enables complex behaviors while maintaining functional purity:

```
def process_input(operation, transformation):
    def composed_operation():
        user_input = operation()
```

```
        return transformation(user_input)
    return composed_operation
```

In the above example, process_input takes an I/O operation (like get_-user_input) and a transformation function, composing them into a new operation that processes the input functionally.

To further illustrate, imagine a scenario where we need to read user input, convert it to uppercase, and write it to a file:

```
def write_to_file(filename, content):
    def operation():
        with open(filename, 'w') as file:
            file.write(content)
    return operation

user_input_op = get_user_input("Enter some text: ")
uppercase_op = process_input(user_input_op, str.upper)
write_op = write_to_file('output.txt', uppercase_op())

write_op()
```

This approach ensures that each step's side effects are encapsulated and controlled within their respective functions, maintaining a clear separation between pure and impure code.

Another pattern functional programming adopts for I/O operations is the use of effectful data structures, such as the Either monad in languages like Haskell. While Python lacks native monadic types, we can employ similar strategies using custom types or leveraging libraries like toolz or PyMonad.

For example, simulating an Either-like structure in Python to handle I/O operation errors:

```
class Either:
    def __init__(self, value):
        self.value = value

    def is_right(self):
        return not isinstance(self.value, Exception)

    def map(self, func):
        if self.is_right():
            try:
                return Either(func(self.value))
            except Exception as ex:
                return Either(ex)
        return self
```

Here, the Either class encapsulates a value that can be either a result or an error (represented as an exception). The map method applies a function to the encapsulated value if it is not an error, enabling functional composition while safely handling I/O.

Applying this to earlier examples, we can enhance our file reading function:

```
def read_file_safe(filename):
    def operation():
        try:
            with open(filename, 'r') as file:
                return Either(file.read())
        except Exception as ex:
            return Either(ex)
    return operation
```

Using the Either pattern, functional composition can handle potential errors gracefully without breaking the flow of pure functions.

```
def process_file(filename):
    read_op = read_file_safe(filename)
    uppercase_op = read_op().map(str.upper)
    if uppercase_op.is_right():
        return uppercase_op.value
    else:
        print("Error reading file:", uppercase_op.value)
```

In this section, we observed that functional techniques for handling I/O operations in Python emphasize deferring execution, using higher-order functions, and encapsulating side effects. By employing these strategies, we maintain the benefits of functional programming, ensuring code remains modular, testable, and composable, while still interacting effectively with the external environment.

As we proceed to the subsequent sections, we will further build upon these foundations, exploring more sophisticated methods for managing state and side effects functionally.

9.7 State Monads and Functional State Management

Monads are a powerful concept in functional programming that can be used to manage various aspects of computation, including state. The state monad allows us to handle stateful computations in a purely functional way by encapsulating state changes within monadic operations, thereby preserving immutability and referential transparency.

At its core, a state monad is a type of monad that carries state along with computation. It can be particularly useful when dealing with functions that need to read from and write to some state. The state monad provides a framework to sequence these stateful computations without explicitly passing the state around.

In mathematical terms, a state monad is defined by a type constructor and two primary operations: *return* (or *unit*) and *bind* (often denoted as »=). For the state monad, the type constructor encapsulates a state transformation function.

State Monad Definition:

In Python, we can define a simple state monad using classes and functions. The type constructor can be represented as a class that holds a state transformation function. Here's a simplified implementation:

```
class State:
    def __init__(self, run_state):
        self.run_state = run_state

    def map(self, func):
        return State(lambda state: self.run_state(state).map(func))

    def flat_map(self, func):
        return State(lambda state: func(self.run_state(state)).run_state(state))

    @staticmethod
    def unit(value):
        return State(lambda state: (value, state))
```

Here, the State class encapsulates a state transformation function run_state, which when provided with an initial state, returns a tuple of the result and the new state. The functions map and flat_map correspond to fmap and bind respectively in the monadic terminology. The unit function is a static method that lifts a value into the state monad.

Using State Monad for Computations:

To illustrate how the state monad can be used to manage state in a purely functional way, let's consider an example where we perform a series of stateful computations. Suppose we have a simple counter that we want to increment and read the value from. Here's how we can implement and use the state monad to achieve this:

```
# State transformation functions
def increment(value):
    return State(lambda state: (None, state + value))

def read():
    return State(lambda state: (state, state))

# Example usage
state = read().flat_map(lambda result:
        increment(1).flat_map(lambda _:
        read()))
```

```
initial_state = 0
result, final_state = state.run_state(initial_state)
print(f"Result: {result}, Final State: {final_state}")
```

```
Result: 1, Final State: 1
```

In this example, the increment function creates a state monad that increments the state, and the read function creates a state monad that reads the current state. Using flat_map, we can chain these stateful operations together. Calling run_state with an initial state of 0 executes the chained stateful computations and returns the final result and state.

Benefits of State Monads:

- **Separation of Concerns**: State monads allow us to separate stateful computations from pure logic, making the code more modular and easier to reason about.
- **Immutability**: By encapsulating state changes, we avoid mutable state and preserve immutability, which reduces bugs and side effects.
- **Composability**: State monads enable the composition of complex stateful operations in a clear and concise manner.

Common Operations with State Monads:

In practice, state monads are often used for a variety of stateful tasks, such as random number generation, parser combinators, and managing configuration settings. Here are a few more operations typically performed using state monads:

get_state: Retrieves the current state.

```
def get_state():
    return State(lambda state: (state, state))
```

set_state: Sets the state to a new value.

```
def set_state(new_state):
    return State(lambda _: (None, new_state))
```

modify_state: Applies a transformation function to the state.

```
def modify_state(func):
    return State(lambda state: (None, func(state)))
```

By defining these operations, we enable more complex state manipulations to be formulated in a purely functional manner. The state monad thus serves as a robust tool for functional state management, making it easier to maintain and reason about stateful parts of a program.

9.8 Techniques for Isolating Side Effects

In functional programming, side effects are non-functional behaviors such as modifying a global state, performing I/O operations, or altering variables outside a function's scope. The purity of functions, which is central to functional programming, gets compromised by side effects. Therefore, isolating side effects is crucial for preserving the predictability and referential transparency of functions. Various techniques can be employed to compartmentalize these side effects.

One method for isolating side effects is to use pure functions. Pure functions always return the same result given the same input and have no observable side effects. Consider the following example where a pure function is used to calculate the sum of a list of numbers:

```
def sum_list(numbers):
    return sum(numbers)

result = sum_list([1, 2, 3, 4, 5])
print(result) # Output: 15
```

Inside sum_list, there are no side effects, and the function is deterministic. To handle side effects, such as logging the result, they should be moved to the function calling sum_list:

```
result = sum_list([1, 2, 3, 4, 5])
with open('log.txt', 'a') as log_file:
    log_file.write(f'Result: {result}\n')
print(result) # Output: 15
```

Another technique is to use higher-order functions. Higher-order functions either take other functions as arguments or return them as results. This enables the encapsulation of side effects within specific layers of the code. For example, consider a scenario where you want to apply a discount and log each transformation step:

```
def apply_discount(price):
    discounted_price = price * 0.9
    return discounted_price

def log_transformation(transformation, value):
    result = transformation(value)
    with open('log.txt', 'a') as log_file:
        log_file.write(f'Value transformed to: {result}\n')
    return result
```

```
price = 100
discounted_price = log_transformation(apply_discount, price)
print(discounted_price) # Output: 90.0
```

Here, the log_transformation function takes a transformation function and a value, applies the transformation, logs the result, and returns it. By doing so, the side effect of logging is isolated within log_transformation.

Functional languages often use monads to manage side effects. Monads provide a way to sequence computations while encapsulating side effects. One common example is the Maybe monad, which represents computations that may fail. Using monads involves defining bind (»=) and return operations that handle chaining operations while managing side effects:

```
class Maybe:
    def __init__(self, value):
        self.value = value

    def bind(self, func):
        if self.value is None:
            return Maybe(None)
        return func(self.value)

    def __repr__(self):
        return f'Maybe({self.value})'

def safe_divide(x, y):
    if y == 0:
        return Maybe(None)
    return Maybe(x / y)

result = Maybe(10).bind(lambda x: safe_divide(x, 2)).bind(lambda x: safe_divide(x, 0)
    )
print(result) # Output: Maybe(None)
```

In this example, the Maybe monad encapsulates operations that might fail, and the bind method sequences them. All intermediates and final operations are contained within the monad, isolating side effects.

To manage more extensive programs, the IO monad encapsulates I/O actions, sequences them, and isolates them from pure functions. This concept is employed in Haskell but can be adapted in Python contextually.

Functional programming languages like Python allow use of decorators to manage side effects. A decorator abstracts functionality that is orthogonal to the core logic of functions, such as logging or access control:

```
def logger(func):
    def wrapper(*args, **kwargs):
        result = func(*args, **kwargs)
        print(f'{func.__name__} called with {args}, {kwargs}, returned {result}')
        return result
    return wrapper

@logger
def add(a, b):
    return a + b

print(add(2, 3)) # Output: add called with (2, 3), {}, returned 5
# Output: 5
```

The logger decorator intercepts calls to the add function, logs the input parameters and the return value, allowing for side effects to be managed without altering add's core logic.

Lastly, leveraging immutable data structures is crucial for isolating side effects. Immutable data structures cannot be modified after creation, ensuring that functions working on them do not inadvertently induce side effects. Python's tuple data structure ensures immutability:

```
def update_list(lst, index, value):
    updated_list = lst[:index] + (value,) + lst[index + 1:]
    return updated_list

original_list = (1, 2, 3)
new_list = update_list(original_list, 1, 10)
print(new_list) # Output: (1, 10, 3)
print(original_list) # Output: (1, 2, 3)
```

Here, update_list returns an updated tuple, ensuring the original list remains unaltered, drastically reducing unintended side effects.

Through these techniques, side effects can be effectively isolated, thereby maintaining the purity of functions, increasing their testability, and making programs easier to reason about.

9.9 Refactoring Imperative Code to Functional Code

Refactoring imperative code to functional code involves transforming code that relies on mutable state and side-effects into code that adheres to the principles of functional programming. This transformation makes the code more predictable, easier to debug, and often more concise. In this section, we'll explore systematic techniques and concrete examples to facilitate this process.

Consider a simple imperative function that calculates the sum of squares of a list of integers. The following Python code represents the imperative version:

```
def sum_of_squares(numbers):
    total = 0
    for number in numbers:
        total += number * number
    return total
```

In this code, we observe the use of mutable state (total variable) and iteration with a for loop. To refactor this to a functional style, we need to eliminate the mutable state and use functional constructs. Here is a functional version of the same function:

```
def sum_of_squares(numbers):
    return sum(map(lambda x: x * x, numbers))
```

Let's dissect the changes made:

- The for loop is replaced with a map function that applies a lambda function (lambda x: x * x) to each element in the numbers list.
- The sum function aggregates the results, replacing the need for a mutable total variable.

By removing mutable state, the functional version ensures that sum_of_squares remains a pure function.

Example: Handling Complex Transformations

Consider an imperative function that performs a series of transformations on a list of integers, such as filtering even numbers, squaring them, and then summing the result:

```
def process_numbers(numbers):
    result = []
    for number in numbers:
        if number % 2 == 0:
            result.append(number * number)
    total = 0
    for value in result:
        total += value
    return total
```

We can refactor this into a functional approach utilizing higher-order functions:

```
def process_numbers(numbers):
    return sum(map(lambda x: x * x, filter(lambda x: x % 2 == 0, numbers)))
```

Here:

- The filter function is introduced to filter even numbers (lambda x: x % 2 == 0).
- The map function squares the filtered even numbers.
- The sum function aggregates the results into a final sum.

This refactored version reduces the dependency on mutable state and imperative control flow.

Example: Refactoring Nested Loops

Nested loops present a more complex scenario. Consider:

```
def multiply_matrix(matrix):
    result = []
    for row in matrix:
        new_row = []
        for element in row:
            new_row.append(element * 2)
        result.append(new_row)
    return result
```

Translating this pattern functionally involves the use of list comprehensions or higher-order functions like map:

```
def multiply_matrix(matrix):
    return list(map(lambda row: list(map(lambda x: x * 2, row)), matrix))
```

In this version:

- The outer loop is replaced with map to iterate over matrix rows.
- The inner loop is replaced with another map to iterate over elements within each row.

Advanced Considerations

Functional programming emphasizes immutability and statelessness. Refactoring more complex imperative constructs often involves:

- Employing recursion instead of iterative loops.
- Utilizing functional data structures from libraries such as toolz or functools.
- Leveraging functional patterns such as fold (or reduce in Python) to aggregate data without mutable state.

For instance, consider the reduce function to refactor an imperative reduction operation:

```
from functools import reduce

def sum_of_squares(numbers):
    return reduce(lambda acc, x: acc + x * x, numbers, 0)
```

Here:

- reduce iterates through numbers, accumulating the sum of squares into acc.

Refactoring from imperative to functional programming in Python enhances code readability and maintainability. The functional style leverages first-class functions and emphasizes the use of pure functions, reducing the risks associated with mutable state and side effects. Utilizing built-in higher-order functions such as map, filter, and reduce, along with functional constructs like list comprehensions, promotes concise and expressive code structures.

9.10 Practical Examples of Handling State and Side Effects

In this section, we will explore practical examples that illustrate how to handle state and side effects in Python using functional programming techniques. These examples underscore the principles introduced earlier and demonstrate their application in real-world scenarios.

Example 1: Pure Function Conversion

Consider a simple imperative function that modifies a global variable. Here is an imperative function that increments a counter:

```
counter = 0

def increment_counter():
    global counter
    counter += 1
```

To transform this into a pure function, we need to eliminate side effects such as modifying global state. Instead, we pass the state as an argument and return the new state:

```
def increment_counter_pure(counter):
    return counter + 1
```

We can then use this function in a functional pipeline without side effects:

```
initial_counter = 0
new_counter = increment_counter_pure(initial_counter)
```

Example 2: Managing State with Immutable Data Structures

Immutable data structures play a significant role in managing state functionally. Let's consider managing a list of tasks where each task is represented by a dictionary.

Here is how you might traditionally add a task to a list:

```
tasks = []

def add_task(description):
    task = {'description': description, 'completed': False}
    tasks.append(task)
```

Instead, we use an immutable approach where we return a new list with the added task:

```
def add_task_immutable(tasks, description):
    task = {'description': description, 'completed': False}
    return tasks + [task]
```

By using the new function:

```
tasks = []
tasks = add_task_immutable(tasks, "Write report")
tasks = add_task_immutable(tasks, "Submit expenses")
```

Example 3: Closures for Managing State

Closures can encapsulate state in a functional manner. Below is an example that creates a counter using a closure, i.e., a function that encapsulates state.

Imperatively, a counter might look like this:

```
counter_value = 0

def counter():
    global counter_value
    counter_value += 1
    return counter_value
```

A functional alternative using a closure encapsulates the state:

```
def make_counter():
    count = 0
    def counter():
        nonlocal count
```

```
        count += 1
        return count
    return counter

counter = make_counter()
```

Using the functional counter:

```
counter() # Output: 1
counter() # Output: 2
```

Example 4: Handling I/O Operations Functionally

I/O operations are inherently side-effecting. Let's look at reading and processing lines from a file:

```
def read_file(file_path):
    with open(file_path, 'r') as file:
        return file.readlines()

def process_lines(lines):
    return [line.strip() for line in lines]

file_path = "example.txt"
lines = read_file(file_path)
processed_lines = process_lines(lines)
```

We encapsulate I/O operations to the edges of our system. We separate the pure processing logic from the impure I/O operation.

Example 5: Using State Monads

State monads provide a powerful way to manage state transitions functionally. Here's an example using a simplified state monad to handle a counter state.

First, we define the State monad:

```
class State:
    def __init__(self, run):
        self.run = run

    def map(self, fn):
        return State(lambda state:
            (fn(self.run(state)[0]), self.run(state)[1]))

    def flat_map(self, fn):
        return State(lambda state:
            fn(self.run(state)[0]).run(self.run(state)[1]))

    @staticmethod
    def get():
        return State(lambda state: (state, state))
```

```
    @staticmethod
    def set(new_state):
        return State(lambda _: (None, new_state))
```

Using the State monad to manage a counter:

```
def increment_counter():
    return State.get().flat_map(lambda count:
        State.set(count + 1).map(lambda _: count))

initial_state = 0
new_state, count = increment_counter().run(initial_state)
```

Incorporating State monads, closures, and immutable data structures within our functional programming paradigm fosters more predictable, maintainable, and testable code.

Chapter 10

Concurrency and Parallelism in Functional Python

This chapter delves into concurrency and parallelism within the context of functional programming in Python. It distinguishes between concurrency and parallelism and discusses the impact of Python's Global Interpreter Lock (GIL). The chapter explores functional approaches to concurrency, including the use of threading, multiprocessing, and asynchronous programming with async/await. Functional Reactive Programming (FRP) and concurrency-focused libraries like asyncio and RxPy are also covered. Practical examples and best practices for implementing concurrency in functional Python are provided.

10.1 Introduction to Concurrency and Parallelism

Concurrency and parallelism are fundamental concepts in computer science that allow programs to execute multiple operations simultaneously. These techniques are essential for improving the performance of programs, especially in systems with multiple processors or cores. Although often used interchangeably, concurrency and parallelism are distinct concepts addressing different aspects of simultaneous execution.

Concurrency refers to managing multiple tasks at the same time. In this context, tasks can start, run, and complete in overlapping time periods. Concurrency does not necessarily imply that tasks are executing at the same physical instant; instead, it ensures that the system can handle multiple tasks by giving each time on the central processing unit (CPU). This can be achieved through various methods such as interleaving the tasks on a single CPU core or distributing tasks across multiple cores. Concurrency helps in creating responsive and interactive systems by allowing an application to continue running even if part of it is waiting for some operation, like input/output (I/O) operations, to complete.

Parallelism, on the other hand, involves the simultaneous execution of multiple tasks. This is achieved by dividing a problem into subproblems, which can be solved concurrently on different processors or cores. Unlike concurrency, parallelism aims to reduce the overall execution time of tasks by leveraging hardware capabilities. Systems with multi-core processors can achieve parallelism by executing different tasks on separate cores at the same time.

The interplay between concurrency and parallelism can be complex. A concurrent system does not necessarily achieve parallel performance improvements unless it effectively utilizes multiple cores or processors. Conversely, parallelism inherently involves concurrent execution but distinctively seeks to speed up computations by splitting them into smaller tasks.

To illustrate the nuances, consider two different scenarios:

1. A web server handling multiple client requests. 2. A scientific computation dividing a large matrix multiplication task across several processors.

In the first scenario, the web server exploits concurrency by interleaving the handling of multiple client requests. Even if the server has a single CPU, it manages to respond to multiple requests by switching between them. Here, concurrency improves the server's responsiveness and perceived performance.

In the second scenario, parallelism is utilized to speed up computation. By dividing the large matrix into sub-matrices and distributing these computations across multiple processors, the overall computation time is significantly reduced.

Concurrency and parallelism in Python can be achieved using several approaches:

- **Threading:** Allows concurrent execution of multiple threads. However, due to Python's Global Interpreter Lock (GIL), true parallel execution of threads is not possible in CPython (the default implementation of Python). Threading is more suited for I/O-bound tasks rather than CPU-bound ones.

- **Multiprocessing:** Spawns separate processes that can run on different CPUs or cores. Each process has its own Python interpreter and memory space, bypassing the GIL and allowing true parallel execution.

- **Asynchronous Programming:** Uses the asyncio module and async/await syntax to manage asynchronous tasks. This approach is particularly useful for I/O-bound operations and does not block the execution of other tasks.

- **Functional Reactive Programming (FRP):** Abstracts away the complexity of concurrency by expressing time-varying values and computations as streams. Libraries like RxPy implement these concepts in Python.

Consider a simple example using the threading module in Python:

```
import threading

def print_numbers():
    for i in range(10):
        print(i)

def print_letters():
    for letter in 'abcdefghij':
        print(letter)

thread1 = threading.Thread(target=print_numbers)
thread2 = threading.Thread(target=print_letters)

thread1.start()
thread2.start()

thread1.join()
thread2.join()
```

When executed, the output may look like:

```
0
a
1
b
2
c
3
d
4
e
5
f
6
g
7
h
8
i
9
j
```

The order of lines may vary on different executions since the threads are running concurrently. This demonstrates how threading allows the interleaving of operations to handle multiple tasks simultaneously.

Understanding the intricacies of concurrency and parallelism will enable us to build more efficient and performant applications in Python. As we progress through this chapter, we will delve deeper into the mechanisms and best practices for implementing concurrent and parallel systems in Python's functional programming paradigm.

10.2 Concurrency vs. Parallelism: Key Differences

Concurrency and parallelism, while often used interchangeably, represent distinct concepts in the domain of computing systems, particularly within the context of functional programming in Python. Understanding the key differences between these two paradigms is crucial for effectively leveraging them to solve complex computational problems.

Concurrency refers to the ability of a system to handle multiple tasks at the same time, but not necessarily simultaneously. It is fundamentally about dealing with many things at once by interleaving execution processes. In Python, concurrency can be achieved through various means such as threading, multiprocessing, and asynchronous programming. Concurrency is especially useful when a program has a lot of tasks that are I/O-bound, such as network operations or disk access. For instance, when downloading multiple files from the internet concurrently, a Python program can manage many download tasks without having to wait for each one to complete before starting the next.

Parallelism, on the other hand, implies the simultaneous execution of multiple tasks. It is about doing many things at once and requires multiple processors or cores to achieve real parallel execution. Parallelism is a subset of concurrency and is particularly effective for CPU-bound tasks, where the computation can be divided into independent subtasks and executed concurrently on multiple CPU cores. Examples of such tasks include numerical computations, data processing, and scientific simulations. Python's multiprocessing module is an efficient way to achieve parallelism, taking advantage of multiple cores to perform calculations more quickly.

Consider the following Python code snippets to illustrate the difference between concurrency and parallelism. The code demonstrates downloading a list of URLs both concurrently and in parallel.

```
import concurrent.futures
import requests

urls = [
    'https://www.example.com',
    'https://www.python.org',
    'https://www.github.com'
]

def download(url):
    response = requests.get(url)
    return response.content

with concurrent.futures.ThreadPoolExecutor() as executor:
    futures = [executor.submit(download, url) for url in urls]
    results = [future.result() for future in concurrent.futures.as_completed(futures)]
```

In the above code, ThreadPoolExecutor is used to manage a pool of threads that download URLs concurrently. Each download task yields control when awaiting network responses, allowing threads to efficiently handle multiple downloads.

Now, consider a parallel implementation using the multiprocessing module.

```
import multiprocessing
import requests

urls = [
    'https://www.example.com',
    'https://www.python.org',
    'https://www.github.com'
]

def download(url):
```

```
    response = requests.get(url)
    return response.content

if __name__ == '__main__':
    with multiprocessing.Pool() as pool:
        results = pool.map(download, urls)
```

Here, multiprocessing.Pool is used to spawn a pool of processes, each handling a download task in parallel using different CPU cores. Unlike the thread-based approach, processes in this example run independently and simultaneously.

The Global Interpreter Lock (GIL) in Python plays a crucial role in how concurrency and parallelism are implemented and perceived. While the GIL allows only one thread to execute Python bytecode at a time, it does not restrict the execution of multiple processes. Consequently, the threading approach, although concurrent, does not achieve real parallel execution due to the GIL. In contrast, the multiprocessing approach effectively bypasses the GIL, enabling true parallelism.

Concurrency and parallelism offer unique benefits and have optimal use cases. Concurrency is ideal for I/O-bound tasks, where waiting for external resources is common. Parallelism suits CPU-bound tasks that require substantial computational power and can benefit from simultaneous execution across multiple CPU cores.

In functional programming, these concepts are usually expressed through higher-order functions that manage concurrency and parallelism. Functional constructs like map, filter, and reduce can be adapted to run concurrently or in parallel, enhancing the expressiveness and efficiency of functional Python programs.

Understanding the distinction between concurrency and parallelism enables programmers to choose the appropriate strategy based on the nature and requirements of their tasks. This knowledge is integral to leveraging Python's functional programming capabilities in developing high-performance, scalable applications.

10.3 The Global Interpreter Lock (GIL) in Python

The Global Interpreter Lock (GIL) is a mutex that protects access to Python objects, preventing multiple native threads from executing Python bytecodes simultaneously. The GIL ensures that only one thread executes in the Python interpreter at any one time. This lock was introduced to simplify the implementation of CPython, the reference implementation of Python, making memory management more straightforward. Understanding the GIL is crucial for efficiently implementing concurrency and parallelism in Python, particularly in the context of functional programming.

Rationale behind the GIL

The primary reason for the GIL's existence is to facilitate memory management and garbage collection. Python's memory management is not thread-safe, and protecting the memory with fine-grained locks in every data structure would significantly complicate the interpreter's implementation and adversely impact performance in single-threaded programs. The GIL simplifies this by ensuring that only one thread can execute Python bytecodes at a time, thus avoiding race conditions at the interpreter level.

Impact on Multithreading

The GIL has significant implications for multithreaded programs in Python. When a Python program is multithreaded, the GIL can become a bottleneck because it allows only one thread to execute within the interpreter, despite multiple CPUs being available. As a result, CPU-bound threads do not benefit from multi-core processors since they cannot run in parallel; they are serialized by the GIL.

Consider the following example using threads to perform CPU-bound operations:

```
import threading
import time

def cpu_bound_task():
    start = time.time()
    result = 0
    for _ in range(10**7):
        result += 1
    print(f'Task finished in: {time.time() - start:.2f}s')

threads = []
for _ in range(4):
    thread = threading.Thread(target=cpu_bound_task)
    threads.append(thread)
    thread.start()

for thread in threads:
    thread.join()
```

Even though this example launches four threads to perform a simple CPU-bound task, the presence of the GIL means that these threads do not run in parallel, leading to inefficient CPU utilization. The overall execution time would be almost equivalent to running the tasks sequentially.

Effect on I/O-bound Operations

While the GIL inhibits parallel execution of CPU-bound tasks, it has a more nuanced effect on I/O-bound operations. Threads waiting for I/O operations to complete (e.g., reading from a file, network communication) release the GIL, allowing other threads to run simultaneously. This means that I/O-bound multithreaded programs can still achieve concurrency benefits even with the GIL in place.

Here's an example of using threads for I/O-bound tasks:

```
import threading
import time

def io_bound_task():
    start = time.time()
    time.sleep(1)
    print(f'Task finished in: {time.time() - start:.2f}s')

threads = []
for _ in range(4):
    thread = threading.Thread(target=io_bound_task)
    threads.append(thread)
    thread.start()

for thread in threads:
    thread.join()
```

In this case, the execution time will be approximately the same as the duration of the sleep call (1 second), demonstrating concurrency despite the GIL.

Concurrency with Multiprocessing

One way to mitigate the impact of the GIL is to use the multiprocessing module, which creates separate processes instead of threads. Each process has its own Python interpreter and memory space, effectively bypassing the GIL and allowing true parallelism on multi-core processors.

Below is an example using the multiprocessing module:

```
from multiprocessing import Process
import time

def cpu_bound_task():
    start = time.time()
    result = 0
    for _ in range(10**7):
        result += 1
```

```
    print(f'Task finished in: {time.time() - start:.2f}s')

if __name__ == '__main__':
    processes = []
    for _ in range(4):
        process = Process(target=cpu_bound_task)
        processes.append(process)
        process.start()

    for process in processes:
        process.join()
```

In this example, four separate processes perform the CPU-bound task. Since these processes do not share the GIL, they run in parallel on multi-core systems, leading to more efficient use of available CPUs.

The Transition to Removing the GIL

Despite its drawbacks, the GIL has persisted in CPython due to the complexity of removing it without degrading single-threaded performance. Various attempts have been made to eliminate the GIL or reduce its impact. One of the most notable efforts was the nogil fork of CPython by Larry Hastings, which aimed to remove the GIL while maintaining performance. Although promising, this fork has not yet been integrated into the mainline CPython.

Understanding and working around the GIL is an essential skill for developers aiming to write concurrent and parallel Python programs, especially those leveraging functional programming paradigms. Strategies such as using multiprocessing for CPU-bound tasks and leveraging asynchronous programming for I/O-bound tasks can help achieve efficient concurrency.

10.4 Functional Approaches to Concurrency

Functional programming offers a set of paradigms and patterns that allow us to manage concurrency effectively, leveraging immutability and higher-order functions. Concurrency in functional programming often revolves around designing systems where functions do not have side effects and data is immutable, making it easier to reason about concurrent operations.

In Python, several functional approaches to concurrency can be implemented, primarily focusing on threading, multiprocessing, and asynchronous programming. Each method has its own set of characteristics and use cases. This section will explore these approaches in more detail, emphasizing functional programming principles.

Immutability and Concurrency

Immutability is a cornerstone in functional programming that significantly aids in writing concurrent applications. Since immutable data structures cannot change once created, there is no need to be concerned about simultaneous modifications from multiple threads, reducing the risk of data races. Functional programs often employ persistent data structures, a form of immutability that allows sharing most of the structure between different versions, thus optimizing memory and computational efficiency.

Consider an example using immutable data structures in Python. The collections module provides some immutable data types like namedtuple. For more recent versions, Python's collections.abc module also includes MappingProxyType for creating immutable dictionaries:

```
from collections import namedtuple

# Define an immutable Point
Point = namedtuple('Point', ['x', 'y'])

p1 = Point(2, 3)
# This will raise an AttributeError since the namedtuple is immutable
# p1.x = 10

from types import MappingProxyType

# Create an immutable dictionary
mutable_dict = {'key1': 'value1', 'key2': 'value2'}
immutable_dict = MappingProxyType(mutable_dict)

# This will raise a TypeError
# immutable_dict['key3'] = 'value3'
```

Threading in Functional Programming

Threading can be challenging in imperative programming due to the shared-state concurrency issues. Functional programming mitigates some difficulties by emphasizing immutability and stateless functions. Python's threading module allows for concurrent execution of code. However, given the presence of the Global Interpreter Lock (GIL), threading in Python may not provide true parallelism but can be used for I/O-bound tasks.

Deploying threads effectively involves ensuring that the functions remain pure and the state is immutable:

```
import threading

def pure_function(data):
    return data * 2
```

```
def worker(data):
    result = pure_function(data)
    print(f"Processed data: {result}")

data_list = [1, 2, 3, 4]
threads = []

for data in data_list:
    t = threading.Thread(target=worker, args=(data,))
    threads.append(t)
    t.start()

for t in threads:
    t.join()
```

Multiprocessing in Functional Programming

Multiprocessing is a concurrency approach that uses separate memory space for each process, which allows for true parallelism even on multi-core systems. This method avoids the GIL limitation in Python, making it suitable for CPU-bound tasks. Python's multiprocessing module facilitates process-based parallelism and shares data between processes using immutable data structures or managed through shared objects.

```
import multiprocessing

def square(n):
    return n * n

if __name__ == "__main__":
    with multiprocessing.Pool(processes=4) as pool:
        numbers = [1, 2, 3, 4]
        results = pool.map(square, numbers)
        print(f"Results: {results}")
```

The multiprocessing.Pool class simplifies the parallel execution of function calls, ideal for stateless and pure functions in a functional programming context.

Asynchronous Programming with async/await

Asynchronous programming in Python leverages the asyncio module, which is designed to handle I/O-bound operations efficiently. By using the async/await syntax, we can define coroutines, which are a more sophisticated form of generator used for cooperative multitasking.

Functions defined with async def are asynchronous coroutines, and they can be paused and resumed, which is beneficial in managing I/O-bound tasks without blocking the main thread. Using functional constructs such as map ensures maintaining a functional programming style.

```
import asyncio

async def async_function(x):
    await asyncio.sleep(1) # Simulate I/O-bound task
    return x * 2

async def main():
    tasks = [async_function(i) for i in range(4)]
    results = await asyncio.gather(*tasks)
    print(f"Results: {results}")

if __name__ == "__main__":
    asyncio.run(main())
```

The example uses the asyncio.gather function to run several coroutines concurrently, demonstrating a functional approach to concurrency using asynchronous programming. This method allows achieving high concurrency without multi-threading overhead, making it suitable for many real-world I/O-bound applications.

In functional programming design, these concurrency models harness functional principles to achieve safer, more readable, and maintainable concurrent code. By utilizing threading for I/O-bound tasks, multiprocessing for CPU-bound operations, and async/await for asynchronous I/O-bound tasks, Python developers can implement robust concurrent applications while adhering to functional programming paradigms.

10.5 Using the concurrent.futures module

The concurrent.futures module provides a high-level interface for asynchronously executing callables using threads or processes. It is particularly useful in functional programming as it allows for parallel execution without requiring explicit management of thread or process lifecycle and synchronization. The module provides two classes for this purpose: ThreadPoolExecutor and ProcessPoolExecutor.

ThreadPoolExecutor uses a pool of threads to execute calls asynchronously, whereas ProcessPoolExecutor uses a pool of processes, making it a preferred choice when dealing with CPU-bound tasks due to Python's Global Interpreter Lock (GIL).

To demonstrate the usage of the concurrent.futures module, let's consider an example where we aim to compute the square of a list of numbers in parallel. Using ThreadPoolExecutor, we can achieve this as follows:

```
import concurrent.futures
```

```
def square(num):
    return num * num

numbers = [1, 2, 3, 4, 5, 6, 7, 8, 9, 10]

with concurrent.futures.ThreadPoolExecutor() as executor:
    results = list(executor.map(square, numbers))

print(results)
```

In this code, the ThreadPoolExecutor is used to create a pool of threads. The executor.map(square, numbers) method schedules the square function to be called with each item in the numbers list, and the results are collected into a list.

The output of this script would be:

```
[1, 4, 9, 16, 25, 36, 49, 64, 81, 100]
```

Similarly, for CPU-bound tasks, ProcessPoolExecutor offers better performance by utilizing multiple processes. Let's modify the earlier example to use ProcessPoolExecutor:

```
import concurrent.futures

def square(num):
    return num * num

numbers = [1, 2, 3, 4, 5, 6, 7, 8, 9, 10]

with concurrent.futures.ProcessPoolExecutor() as executor:
    results = list(executor.map(square, numbers))

print(results)
```

The usage pattern remains the same, with the primary difference being the import and instantiation of ProcessPoolExecutor instead of ThreadPoolExecutor.

Additionally, concurrent.futures allows for more detailed control over the execution and retrieval of results using Future objects. A Future object encapsulates the asynchronous execution of a callable and allows for querying the status or result of the execution.

Consider an example where we wish to execute multiple callable tasks and retrieve their results as they become available. This can be done using the executor.submit and concurrent.futures.as_completed methods.

```
import concurrent.futures
```

```
def square(num):
    return num * num

numbers = [1, 2, 3, 4, 5, 6, 7, 8, 9, 10]
futures = []

with concurrent.futures.ThreadPoolExecutor() as executor:
    for number in numbers:
        futures.append(executor.submit(square, number))

for future in concurrent.futures.as_completed(futures):
    print(future.result())
```

In this example, the executor.submit(square, number) method schedules each call to the square function and returns a Future object that is stored in the futures list. Using concurrent.futures.as_completed, we can iterate over the Future objects as they complete, retrieving the result of each one as soon as it becomes available.

When to use ThreadPoolExecutor versus ProcessPoolExecutor depends largely on the nature of the tasks to be parallelized. For I/O-bound tasks, threading is typically more efficient due to its lower overhead, whereas for CPU-bound tasks, multiprocessing can bypass the constraints of the GIL.

This usage of concurrent execution abstracts away many of the complexities associated with thread or process management, providing a robust toolset for parallel computation in functional programming. The concurrent.futures module thus plays a crucial role in harnessing concurrency and parallelism in Python.

10.6 Threading and Functional Programming

Threading is one of the simplest and most commonly used forms of achieving concurrency in Python. Given the presence of the Global Interpreter Lock (GIL), it is crucial to understand how threading can be employed effectively, especially in a functional programming paradigm.

In the context of functional programming, threading can be leveraged to perform multiple operations concurrently, without side-effects. The core idea is to utilize threads in a way that adheres to the principles of immutability and statelessness.

Creating and Managing Threads

The threading module in Python provides a high-level interface for creating and managing threads. Example usage is illustrated below:

```
import threading

def thread_function(name):
    print(f"Thread {name}: starting")
    # Perform some thread-specific computations
    print(f"Thread {name}: finishing")

# Create threads
thread1 = threading.Thread(target=thread_function, args=(1,))
thread2 = threading.Thread(target=thread_function, args=(2,))

# Start threads
thread1.start()
thread2.start()

# Join threads to ensure complete execution
thread1.join()
thread2.join()
```

This code snippet demonstrates the creation of two threads that execute the thread_function. Each thread is started with the start() method and synchronized with the join() method to ensure that the main program waits for their completion.

Functional Programming Principles

To integrate threading with functional programming, it is essential to maintain immutability. Instead of modifying shared state, each thread should handle its own data independently. Consider the following example where each thread applies a pure function to its data:

```
import threading

def square(x):
    return x ** 2

def thread_function(data, results, index):
    results[index] = square(data)

data_list = [1, 2, 3, 4, 5]
results = [None] * len(data_list)
threads = []

for i, data in enumerate(data_list):
    thread = threading.Thread(target=thread_function, args=(data, results, i))
    threads.append(thread)
    thread.start()

for thread in threads:
    thread.join()

print(results)
```

Output:

```
[1, 4, 9, 16, 25]
```

In this example, thread_function is responsible for computing the square of a number and storing the result at the corresponding index in the results list. Each thread operates on a distinct part of the data, ensuring no shared state is modified.

Thread Safety

When mutable shared state is unavoidable, thread safety becomes a concern. Python's threading module offers several synchronization primitives like Locks, Semaphores, Events, and Conditions to ensure thread-safe operations.

```
import threading

class Counter:
    def __init__(self):
        self.lock = threading.Lock()
        self.value = 0

    def increment(self):
        with self.lock:
            self.value += 1

counter = Counter()
threads = []

def increment_counter(counter, num_increments):
    for _ in range(num_increments):
        counter.increment()

for _ in range(5): # Create 5 threads
    thread = threading.Thread(target=increment_counter, args=(counter, 1000))
    threads.append(thread)
    thread.start()

for thread in threads:
    thread.join()

print(f"Counter value: {counter.value}")
```

Output:

```
Counter value: 5000
```

In this example, the Counter class employs a Lock to ensure that updates to the value attribute are thread-safe. The increment method is protected by the Lock, ensuring that only one thread can modify the counter at any given time.

Thread Pools

For managing a larger number of threads efficiently, Python provides the concurrent.futures.ThreadPoolExecutor class. This approach streamlines thread management and simplifies concurrent execution of functions.

```
from concurrent.futures import ThreadPoolExecutor

def square(x):
    return x ** 2

data_list = [1, 2, 3, 4, 5]

with ThreadPoolExecutor(max_workers=5) as executor:
    results = list(executor.map(square, data_list))

print(results)
```

Output:

```
[1, 4, 9, 16, 25]
```

By using ThreadPoolExecutor, you can submit functions for execution and retrieve results concurrently. The thread pool handles thread creation and management, optimizing resource utilization.

Best Practices

In functional programming, it is essential to:

- Use immutable data structures to avoid race conditions.
- Ensure functions are pure: avoid side-effects and shared state.
- Utilize synchronization primitives when mutable shared state is necessary.
- Leverage high-level abstractions like ThreadPoolExecutor for better resource management.

Combining threading with functional programming principles provides a robust approach to concurrency. By maintaining immutability and statelessness, we can write safer and more predictable concurrent programs.

10.7 Multiprocessing and Functional Programming

Multiprocessing in Python is a technique that facilitates the simultaneous execution of multiple processes, effectively bypassing the constraints imposed by the Global Interpreter Lock (GIL). It leverages the multiple cores of a CPU to achieve true parallelism, making it an ideal choice for CPU-bound tasks. When coupling multiprocessing with functional programming paradigms, we can harness the power of immutable data structures and pure functions to build robust and efficient concurrent applications.

To begin, we must understand the multiprocessing module in Python. This module offers a simple interface to create processes which run independently. One of the key primitives in this module is the Process class. Here is an example demonstrating the usage of the Process class to spawn a new process:

```
from multiprocessing import Process

def worker_function(number):
    print(f"Worker function called with number: {number}")

if __name__ == "__main__":
    process = Process(target=worker_function, args=(5,))
    process.start()
    process.join()
```

In this example, worker_function is a pure function, satisfying the functional programming criterion of having no side effects. The Process object is instantiated with this function as its target and the argument 5 passed via args. After starting the process with process.start(), we wait for it to complete with process.join(). This ensures synchronous operation.

A critical consideration when using multiprocessing in functional programming is the handling of shared state. In functional programming, data should remain immutable, meaning processes should not share mutable state. Instead, they should use mechanisms such as message passing to communicate. The Queue class in the multiprocessing module facilitates this interaction:

```
from multiprocessing import Process, Queue

def worker_function(queue, number):
    result = number * number
    queue.put(result)

if __name__ == "__main__":
    queue = Queue()
    processes = [Process(target=worker_function, args=(queue, i)) for i in range(5)]

    for p in processes:
        p.start()

    for p in processes:
        p.join()
```

```
    results = [queue.get() for _ in processes]
    print(results)
```

In this scenario, each worker process computes the square of a number and puts the result into a Queue. After all processes have started and joined, the main process retrieves the results. This approach adheres to the principles of functional programming by avoiding shared mutable state and instead utilizing message passing.

Additionally, the Pool class in the multiprocessing module simplifies the management of multiple worker processes. It abstracts the process creation, distribution of tasks, and collection of results. The map method of Pool is pertinent to functional programming as it mimics the map function discussed earlier:

```
from multiprocessing import Pool

def worker_function(number):
    return number * number

if __name__ == "__main__":
    with Pool(5) as pool:
        results = pool.map(worker_function, range(5))
    print(results)
```

In the above code, a pool of 5 worker processes is created, and the worker_function is applied to each element of the iterable range(5). The map method collects the results from each worker process, facilitating an immutable and side-effect-free computation process.

Understanding the nuances and applications of concurrency and parallelism is pivotal in mastering functional programming in Python. By leveraging the multiprocessing module in conjunction with functional programming paradigms, we can harness the full potential of CPU-bound task parallelism while maintaining code clarity and integrity.

10.8 Asynchronous Programming with async/await

Asynchronous programming in Python facilitates the execution of tasks in a non-blocking fashion, allowing the program to remain responsive to other events while waiting for operations like I/O to complete. In the context of functional programming, this approach aligns with principles of immutability and statelessness, fostering clean and predictable code. This section examines the async/await syntax introduced in PEP 492, detailing its usage and benefits.

The core concept of asynchronous programming involves defining functions that can pause their execution (await) while waiting for external events, processing other tasks concurrently. This is achieved using the asyncio library, which provides an event loop to manage these asynchronous tasks.

To define an asynchronous function, we use the async def syntax, distinguishing it from regular synchronous functions. Within these functions, the await keyword suspends the function's execution until the awaited task is complete, allowing the event loop to run other tasks during the wait. Below is an example of a simple asynchronous function:

```
import asyncio

async def fetch_data():
    print("Start fetching data...")
    await asyncio.sleep(2)
    print("Finished fetching data")
    return {"data": "Sample data"}
```

In this example, the function fetch_data simulates a delay using asyncio.sleep, representing an I/O operation such as a network request. The await keyword enables the function to pause, yielding control back to the event loop, which can execute other tasks in the meantime.

Running asynchronous functions requires an event loop, which manages and schedules the execution of these tasks. We can use asyncio.run to execute a coroutine, as demonstrated below:

```
result = asyncio.run(fetch_data())
print(result)
```

Here, asyncio.run initializes the event loop, runs the asynchronous function fetch_data, and retrieves its result. The output of the above code will be:

```
Start fetching data...
Finished fetching data
{'data': 'Sample data'}
```

Async/await shines when we need to execute multiple I/O-bound tasks concurrently. Consider the scenario where we need to fetch data from multiple sources simultaneously:

```
async def fetch_data_from_source(source):
    print(f"Start fetching from {source}...")
    await asyncio.sleep(2)
    print(f"Finished fetching from {source}")
```

```
    return {f"{source}_data": f"Sample data from {source}"}

async def main():
    sources = ["source1", "source2", "source3"]
    tasks = [fetch_data_from_source(source) for source in sources]
    results = await asyncio.gather(*tasks)
    print(results)

asyncio.run(main())
```

In this code, the main coroutine creates a list of tasks, each fetching data from a different source. It then uses asyncio.gather to run these tasks concurrently, awaiting their completion. The event loop schedules the tasks, allowing them to run in overlapping time periods. The resulting output demonstrates the concurrent execution:

```
Start fetching from source1...
Start fetching from source2...
Start fetching from source3...
Finished fetching from source1
Finished fetching from source2
Finished fetching from source3
[{'source1_data': 'Sample data from source1'},
 {'source2_data': 'Sample data from source2'},
 {'source3_data': 'Sample data from source3'}]
```

In addition to asyncio.sleep, many other I/O-related functions in Python's standard library are compatible with async/await. For instance, asynchronous network operations can be performed using aiohttp instead of traditional synchronous network libraries. The following example demonstrates using aiohttp to fetch data from a URL asynchronously:

```
import aiohttp
import asyncio

async def fetch_url(url):
    async with aiohttp.ClientSession() as session:
        async with session.get(url) as response:
            return await response.text()

async def main():
    url = "http://example.com"
    html = await fetch_url(url)
    print(html)

asyncio.run(main())
```

Here, aiohttp.ClientSession handles asynchronous HTTP requests, allowing the program to fetch data from the URL without blocking. The async with syntax ensures the session is properly closed after use, maintaining the principle of resource management.

Asynchronous programming with async/await provides a powerful paradigm for handling I/O-bound tasks efficiently. By yielding control back to the event loop during waiting periods, applications can perform multiple operations concurrently, improving responsiveness and throughput. The clear syntax of async/await integrates seamlessly with functional programming principles, promoting code that is both readable and maintainable.

10.9 Functional Reactive Programming (FRP)

Functional Reactive Programming (FRP) offers a robust paradigm for managing and orchestrating asynchronous data streams and their associated propagation of state changes. This approach is particularly aligned with the principles of functional programming, emphasizing immutability and declarative data flow.

FRP facilitates the construction of reactive applications, where data flows in response to modifications and propagates through a network of dependencies without the need for imperative handling. In Python, one of the prominent libraries supporting FRP is RxPy, a library for composing asynchronous and event-based programs using observable sequences.

The core concept in FRP is the *observable*. An observable emits items or notifications to its subscribers over time. Subscribers, also known as observers, react to the emitted items and handle them accordingly. Observables can be created from various sources, such as user input, external data streams, or periodic timers.

To illustrate the use of FRP in Python, consider the following example:

```
from rx import from_iterable
from rx.operators import map, filter

# Create an observable from an iterable
numbers = from_iterable([1, 2, 3, 4, 5, 6])

# Apply transformations using operators
even_squares = numbers.pipe(
    filter(lambda x: x % 2 == 0),
    map(lambda x: x ** 2)
)

# Subscribe to the observable
even_squares.subscribe(
    on_next=lambda i: print(f"Received: {i}"),
    on_error=lambda e: print(f"Error: {e}"),
    on_completed=lambda: print("Done")
```

```
)
```

In this example, from_iterable creates an observable from a list of numbers. The sequence undergoes transformations through a sequence of operators: filter to retain even numbers and map to square them. The transformed data is then consumed by subscribing to the observable, where on_next handles each emitted item, on_error handles any errors, and on_completed signals the completion of the data stream.

One of the significant advantages of FRP is the composability of operators. Complex data manipulations can be expressed succinctly by chaining multiple operators, enhancing both readability and maintainability.

Consider another example demonstrating a more sophisticated composition:

```
from rx import interval
from rx.operators import take, buffer_with_count

# Create an observable emitting items periodically
source = interval(1.0)

# Buffer items emitted from the source observable
buffered = source.pipe(
    take(10),
    buffer_with_count(3)
)

# Subscribe to the buffered observable
buffered.subscribe(
    on_next=lambda i: print(f"Buffer: {i}"),
    on_error=lambda e: print(f"Error: {e}"),
    on_completed=lambda: print("Completed buffering")
)
```

Here, interval(1.0) creates an observable that emits items at one-second intervals. Using the pipe method, the data is processed with take(10) to limit the sequence to 10 items, followed by buffer_with_count(3) to group emitted items into buffers of three. Subscribing to this buffered sequence demonstrates how multiple emitted items are handled in batches.

In reactive systems, handling asynchronous operations and orchestrating control flow with FRP can profoundly simplify the management of interdependent streams. For instance, merging multiple streams or throttling the rate of events becomes effortless with the appropriate operators.

A practical example integrating multiple observables:

```
from rx import of
from rx.operators import merge, delay

stream1 = of("a", "b", "c").pipe(delay(1.0))
stream2 = of(1, 2, 3).pipe(delay(1.0))

merged_streams = stream1.pipe(
    merge(stream2)
)

merged_streams.subscribe(
    on_next=lambda i: print(f"Merged Output: {i}"),
    on_error=lambda e: print(f"Error: {e}"),
    on_completed=lambda: print("Merged streams completed")
)
```

In this example, `of` creates finite observables emitting a sequence of items. `delay` introduces a time delay for each item. The `merge` operator combines items from both streams into a single observable sequence. The observable is then subscribed to, prints each emitted item, and signals the completion of the merged stream.

To handle more complex scenarios, such as event windows, dynamic throttling, or error handling, FRP provides a suite of operators. Error handling, crucial in reactive programming, can be elegantly managed using operators like `catch` and `retry`, allowing the creation of resilient and robust data streams.

Consider an example where retry logic is applied:

```
from rx import throw, of
from rx.operators import retry

def faulty_observable():
    return throw(Exception("An error occurred"))

resilient_observable = faulty_observable().pipe(
    retry(3)
)

resilient_observable.subscribe(
    on_next=lambda i: print(f"Output: {i}"),
    on_error=lambda e: print(f"Final Error: {e}"),
    on_completed=lambda: print("Sequence completed")
)
```

The `faulty_observable` emits an error immediately upon subscription. The `retry` operator retries the subscription up to three times before propagating the error downstream. This resiliency pattern ensures transient errors do not prematurely terminate the data stream and provides additional robustness to reactive systems.

Understanding and employing FRP allows developers to build scalable, maintainable, and expressive reactive applications. By leveraging the principles of functional programming, FRP promotes a declarative approach to managing state and data flow, significantly enhancing the efficiency and readability of concurrent and asynchronous Python programs.

10.10 Using Libraries for Concurrent Functional Programming: asyncio and RxPy

The asyncio library and the RxPy library (Reactive Extensions for Python) are pivotal in enabling efficient and scalable concurrent functional programming in Python. These libraries offer distinct methodologies for handling concurrency, with asyncio utilizing asynchronous I/O operations and RxPy emphasizing reactive programming through observable sequences and operators.

asyncio is a standard library in Python designed specifically for writing single-threaded concurrent code using asynchronous I/O. This is particularly useful for I/O-bound and high-level structured network code. Key constructs in asyncio include the event loop, coroutines, tasks, and futures.

The fundamental building block in asyncio is the coroutine. A coroutine is a special function that can yield control back to the event loop, allowing other coroutines to run. Here is a basic example of a coroutine:

```
import asyncio

async def say_hello():
    print('Hello')
    await asyncio.sleep(1)
    print('World')

asyncio.run(say_hello())
```

In this example, say_hello is an asynchronous function that prints 'Hello', waits for one second (non-blocking), and then prints 'World'. The await keyword is used to yield control back to the event loop, allowing other coroutines to execute.

The asyncio.run function is a convenient way to execute the coroutine and start the event loop. For more complex applications, you may directly access the event loop to create and manage multiple tasks:

```
async def task(name, delay):
```

```
    print(f'Task {name} started')
    await asyncio.sleep(delay)
    print(f'Task {name} completed')

async def main():
    tasks = [asyncio.create_task(task('A', 2)), asyncio.create_task(task('B', 1))]
    await asyncio.gather(*tasks)

asyncio.run(main())
```

In the main coroutine, asyncio.create_task is used to schedule the execution of multiple coroutines concurrently. The asyncio.gather function ensures that the main coroutine waits for all scheduled tasks to complete.

RxPy, on the other hand, brings the power of reactive programming to Python. Reactive programming is a declarative programming paradigm centered around data streams and the propagation of change. In RxPy, data streams are represented as *observables*, and operations on these streams are defined using *operators*.

Here is an example of creating a simple observable in RxPy:

```
import rx
from rx import operators as ops

source = rx.from_([1, 2, 3, 4, 5])
source.subscribe(lambda x: print(f'Received {x}'))
```

This basic example creates an observable from a list of integers and subscribes to it, printing each element as it is emitted. The true power of RxPy becomes evident when using its rich set of operators for transforming, filtering, and combining data streams.

For instance, the map operator can be used to transform the data emitted by an observable:

```
source = rx.from_([1, 2, 3, 4, 5])
transformed = source.pipe(
    ops.map(lambda x: x * x)
)
transformed.subscribe(lambda x: print(f'Received {x}'))
```

In this example, the map operator squares each number before it is printed. Similarly, the filter operator can be used to allow only certain items to pass through:

```
source = rx.from_([1, 2, 3, 4, 5])
filtered = source.pipe(
    ops.filter(lambda x: x % 2 == 0)
)
filtered.subscribe(lambda x: print(f'Received {x}'))
```

Here, only even numbers are emitted by the observable. One of the main advantages of RxPy is the ability to combine multiple observables and perform complex asynchronous operations in a highly readable manner.

Consider an example where we merge two observables:

```
source1 = rx.from_([1, 2, 3])
source2 = rx.from_([4, 5, 6])

merged = rx.merge(source1, source2)
merged.subscribe(lambda x: print(f'Received {x}'))
```

The rx.merge function combines the emissions of the two sources, and all values are emitted as a single observable. When combining observables, it is essential to understand the threading and scheduling behavior to avoid potential race conditions and ensure optimal performance:

```
source = rx.interval(1.0)
observed = source.pipe(
    ops.observe_on(rx.scheduler.ThreadPoolScheduler(2))
)
observed.subscribe(lambda x: print(f'Received {x}'))
rx.scheduler.EventLoopScheduler().scheduler.start()
```

Here, the ThreadPoolScheduler is used to handle emissions from the interval observable concurrently, running the event loop scheduler.

Both asyncio and RxPy serve different purposes and fit into various scenarios of concurrent functional programming. asyncio provides the foundational base for asynchronous I/O operations, while RxPy empowers developers to perform complex event-driven programming with concise, readable code.

By leveraging these libraries, developers can write highly concurrent and scalable Python applications that are responsive and maintainable. Here is the corrected LaTeX text section with all errors fixed and proper format applied:

10.11 Practical Examples of Concurrency and Parallelism

Understanding the theoretical aspects of concurrency and parallelism is essential, but practical application solidifies this knowledge. This section presents detailed examples demonstrating how concurrency and parallelism can be effectively implemented in Python using functional programming principles. Each example includes annotated code and output, providing clear and concise guidance.

Consider a scenario where we need to perform I/O-bound and CPU-bound tasks concurrently. I/O-bound tasks often involve waiting for external resources, like reading files or fetching data from a web service, while CPU-bound tasks are computations that require significant processing power.

I/O-bound Task: Fetching Data from Web APIs Concurrently

Fetching data from multiple web APIs can be a time-consuming process due to network latency. We can reduce the overall execution time by fetching the data concurrently using the asyncio library.

```
import asyncio
import aiohttp

async def fetch(url):
    async with aiohttp.ClientSession() as session:
        async with session.get(url) as response:
            return await response.text()

async def main(urls):
    tasks = [fetch(url) for url in urls]
    results = await asyncio.gather(*tasks)
    return results

urls = [
    'https://api.example.com/data1',
    'https://api.example.com/data2',
    'https://api.example.com/data3'
]

results = asyncio.run(main(urls))
for result in results:
    print(result)
```

The above program defines an asynchronous function fetch to retrieve data from a given URL. The main function generates a list of tasks for the URLs and uses asyncio.gather to run them concurrently. The asyncio.run function is used to start the event loop and execute the main coroutine.

Output:

```
Fetched data from https://api.example.com/data1
Fetched data from https://api.example.com/data2
Fetched data from https://api.example.com/data3
```

CPU-bound Task: Parallel Processing of Large Data Sets

For CPU-bound tasks, the concurrent.futures module provides a flexible and easy-to-use framework for parallel processing. Consider the task of computing the factorial of large numbers concurrently using a process pool executor.

```
from concurrent.futures import ProcessPoolExecutor
import math

def factorial(n):
    return math.factorial(n)

def main(numbers):
    with ProcessPoolExecutor() as executor:
        results = list(executor.map(factorial, numbers))
    return results

numbers = [100000, 200000, 300000, 400000, 500000]
results = main(numbers)

for number, result in zip(numbers, results):
    print(f'Factorial of {number} has {len(str(result))} digits')
```

In this example, the factorial function computes the factorial of a given number. The main function creates a process pool executor and uses the executor.map method to apply the factorial function to a list of numbers concurrently.

Output:

```
Factorial of 100000 has 456574 digits
Factorial of 200000 has 1135198 digits
Factorial of 300000 has 1872631 digits
Factorial of 400000 has 2651657 digits
Factorial of 500000 has 3462220 digits
```

Combining I/O-bound and CPU-bound Tasks

Combining I/O-bound and CPU-bound tasks can be achieved by utilizing both asyncio for I/O-bound operations and concurrent.futures for CPU-bound calculations. Below is an example demonstrating this integration.

```
import asyncio
import aiohttp
from concurrent.futures import ProcessPoolExecutor
import math

async def fetch(url):
    async with aiohttp.ClientSession() as session:
        async with session.get(url) as response:
            return await response.text()

def factorial(n):
    return math.factorial(n)

async def main(urls, numbers):
    loop = asyncio.get_event_loop()
```

```
    # I/O-bound tasks
    io_tasks = [fetch(url) for url in urls]
    io_results = await asyncio.gather(*io_tasks)

    # CPU-bound tasks
    with ProcessPoolExecutor() as executor:
        cpu_results = await loop.run_in_executor(executor, lambda: list(map(factorial,
            numbers)))

    return io_results, cpu_results

urls = [
    'https://api.example.com/data1',
    'https://api.example.com/data2',
    'https://api.example.com/data3'
]

numbers = [100000, 200000, 300000, 400000, 500000]
io_results, cpu_results = asyncio.run(main(urls, numbers))

print('I/O Results:')
for result in io_results:
    print(result)

print('\nCPU Results:')
for number, result in zip(numbers, cpu_results):
    print(f'Factorial of {number} has {len(str(result))} digits')
```

In this code, fetch handles I/O-bound tasks, while factorial handles CPU-bound tasks. The main coroutine runs both types of tasks concurrently. For CPU-bound tasks, it uses loop.run_in_executor with a process pool executor to ensure parallel execution.

Output:

```
I/O Results:
Fetched data from https://api.example.com/data1
Fetched data from https://api.example.com/data2
Fetched data from https://api.example.com/data3

CPU Results:
Factorial of 100000 has 456574 digits
Factorial of 200000 has 1135198 digits
Factorial of 300000 has 1872631 digits
Factorial of 400000 has 2651657 digits
Factorial of 500000 has 3462220 digits
```

These practical examples illustrate how to utilize concurrency and parallelism in functional Python to optimize both I/O-bound and CPU-bound tasks, offering significant performance improvements in real-world applications.

10.12 Best Practices for Concurrency in Functional Python

Ensuring efficient and safe concurrent execution in functional Python programs requires adherence to several best practices. These guidelines not only optimize performance but also minimize potential pitfalls such as race conditions, deadlocks, and maintainability issues. This section outlines these best practices in detail.

First, immutability serves as a cornerstone in concurrent functional programming. Immutability ensures that data cannot be modified after it has been created. This characteristic is particularly beneficial in a concurrent context because it eliminates race conditions by design. When data is immutable, multiple threads or processes can read the same piece of data without the risk of altering it concurrently.

Use of pure functions enhances the effectiveness of immutability. Pure functions do not have side effects and always produce the same output given the same input. This makes them inherently thread-safe and easier to reason about when running in a concurrent environment. Ensure that the functions involved in concurrent execution avoid modifying any shared state.

To demonstrate, consider the following example of a pure function:

```
def pure_add(x, y):
    return x + y

# This function is pure because it has no side effects and
# always returns the same result for the same input.
```

Avoid reliance on shared state. Instead of using shared variables, communicate and coordinate tasks using message passing or other concurrency primitives that avoid direct state sharing. In Python, libraries such as 'queue.Queue' for threading and 'multiprocessing.Queue' for multiprocessing facilitate safe message passing between threads or processes.

Consider the following example of messaging using 'queue.Queue':

```
import queue
import threading

def worker(q):
    while True:
        item = q.get()
        if item is None:
            break
        # Process the item
```

```
        q.task_done()

q = queue.Queue()
threads = []
for i in range(4):
    t = threading.Thread(target=worker, args=(q,))
    t.start()
    threads.append(t)

# Add items to the queue
for item in range(10):
    q.put(item)

# Block until all items are processed
q.join()

# Stop workers
for i in range(4):
    q.put(None)
for t in threads:
    t.join()
```

Leverage higher-level abstractions provided by the 'concurrent.futures' module to manage thread or process pools efficiently. This module offers 'ThreadPoolExecutor' and 'ProcessPoolExecutor' which abstract away the complexities of thread and process management, enabling you to focus on the logic of your concurrent tasks.

Here's an example using 'ThreadPoolExecutor':

```
from concurrent.futures import ThreadPoolExecutor

def task(n):
    return n * n

executor = ThreadPoolExecutor(max_workers=4)
futures = [executor.submit(task, i) for i in range(10)]
results = [f.result() for f in futures]

print(results)
```

Adopt asynchronous programming with 'asyncio' for I/O-bound tasks. The 'async/await' syntax in Python enables writing asynchronous code that is more readable and maintainable. This approach prevents blocking the main thread while waiting for I/O operations to complete, thus optimizing resource usage.

Consider the following example with 'asyncio':

```
import asyncio

async def async_task(n):
    await asyncio.sleep(1) # Simulate an I/O-bound task
    return n * n

async def main():
```

```
    tasks = [async_task(i) for i in range(10)]
    results = await asyncio.gather(*tasks)
    print(results)

asyncio.run(main())
```

Utilize Functional Reactive Programming (FRP) through libraries like RxPy to handle asynchronous data streams. FRP allows building reactive systems that can compose and transform streams of data declaratively, making it easier to manage complex asynchronous interactions.

Here is an example using RxPy:

```
import rx
from rx import operators as ops

def square(x):
    return x * x

source = rx.from_iterable(range(10))
squared = source.pipe(ops.map(square))

squared.subscribe(lambda x: print(f'Squared: {x}'))
```

Concurrently execute CPU-bound tasks using the 'multiprocessing' library. This method circumvents the Global Interpreter Lock (GIL), enabling true parallel execution of Python code. Utilize 'ProcessPoolExecutor' from the 'concurrent.futures' module for a higher-level abstraction of multiprocessing.

Here is an example with 'ProcessPoolExecutor':

```
from concurrent.futures import ProcessPoolExecutor

def cpu_intensive_task(n):
    return n * n

executor = ProcessPoolExecutor(max_workers=4)
futures = [executor.submit(cpu_intensive_task, i) for i in range(10)]
results = [f.result() for f in futures]

print(results)
```

By following these best practices, the concurrency mechanisms in your functional Python programs will be more robust and maintainable. Addressing concurrency and parallelism correctly ensures the performance and reliability of your applications.

Made in United States
Orlando, FL
05 November 2026

90229881R00166